Interpreting Islam

Politics and Culture

A Theory, Culture & Society series

Politics and Culture analyses the complex relationships between civil society, identities and contemporary states. Individual books will draw on the major theoretical paradigms in politics, international relations, history and philosophy within which citizenship, rights and social justice can be understood. The series will focus attention on the implications of globalization, the information revolution and postmodernism for the study of politics and society. It will relate these advanced theoretical issues to conventional approaches to welfare, participation and democracy.

Also in this series

Nation Formation
Towards a Theory of Abstract Community
Paul James

Virtual Politics
Identity and Community in Cyberspace
edited by David Holmes

Gender and Nation
Nira Yuval-Davis

Feminism and Citizenship
Rian Voet

Culture and Citizenship
edited by Nick Stevenson

Interpreting Islam

Edited by
Hastings Donnan

SAGE Publications
London • Thousand Oaks • New Delhi

First published 2002

SAGE Publications Ltd
6 Bonhill Street
London EC2A 4PU

SAGE Publications Inc
2455 Teller Road
Thousand Oaks, California 91320

SAGE Publications India Pvt Ltd
32, M-Block Market
Greater Kailash - I
New Delhi 110 048

British Library Cataloguing in Publication data

A catalogue record for this book is available from the British Library

ISBN 0 7619 5421 X
ISBN 0 7619 5422 8

Library of Congress control number available

Typeset by SIVA Math Setters, Chennai, India
Printed and bound in Great Britain by Athenaeum Press, Gateshead

CONTENTS

LIST OF CONTRIBUTORS

Ilyas Ba-Yunus was born in Karachi, and undertook postgraduate study at the universities of Minnesota and Oklahoma State. He has written about Muslim demography in North America and has published *Islamic Sociology: An Introduction* (co-authored with Farid Ahmed, Hodder and Stoughton, 1985), *Major Contributions: 100 Years of American Sociology* (Norton, 1989) and *Ideological Dimensions of Islam: Making Sense out of History* (forthcoming). Dr Ba-Yunus is a professor of sociology at State University of New York at Cortland, and is presently conducting research on Muslims in North America.

Jonathan Benthall is an Honorary Research Fellow in the Department of Anthropology, University College London, and Chair of the Board, International NGO Training and Research Centre, Oxford. Until 2000 he was Director of the Royal Anthropological Institute and Editor of *Anthropology Today*. His publications include *Disasters, Relief and the Media* (I.B. Tauris, 1993) and some recent articles on organized charity in the Arab–Islamic world.

Hastings Donnan is Professor of Social Anthropology and Head of the School of Anthropological Studies at Queen's University Belfast. He has carried out field research in the Himalayan foothills of northern Pakistan focusing initially on arranged marriages and subsequently on Muslim pilgrimage. He has also conducted research on Muslims in Ireland. He is the author of *Marriage among Muslims* (E.J. Brill, 1988), co-author of *Borders: Frontiers of Identity, Nation and State* (with T.M. Wilson, Berg, 1999), and co-editor of a number of books including, most recently, *Islam, Globalization and Postmodernity* (with A.S. Ahmed, Routledge, 1994), *Family and Gender in Pakistan* (with F. Selier, Hindustan Publishing Co., 1997), *Culture and Policy in Northern Ireland* (with G. McFarlane, Institute of Irish Studies, 1997) and *Border Identities: Nation and State at International Frontiers* (with T.M. Wilson, Cambridge University Press, 1998).

Susan L. Douglass is Principal Researcher and Writer for the Council on Islamic Education, Fountain Valley, California. Her publications include a seven-part series of elementary teaching units on Muslim history (International Institute of Islamic Thought and Kendall/Hunt, 1994–6), *Strategies and Structures for Presenting World History, with Islam and Muslim History as a Case Study* (Amana Publications, 1994), and teaching resources such as *Beyond a Thousand and One Nights: A Sampler of Literature from Muslim Civilization* (Council on Islamic Education, 2000), *Images of the Orient: Nineteenth-Century European Travelers to Muslim Lands* (National Center for History in the Schools, 1998) and (co-authored with Karima D. Alavi) *The Emergence of Renaissance: Cultural Interactions between Europeans and Muslims* (Council on Islamic Education, 1999). *Teaching About Religion in National and State Social Studies Standards* was jointly published by the Council on Islamic Education and the Freedom Forum First Amendment Center in 2000.

Ross E. Dunn is Professor of History at San Diego State University and Director of World History Projects for the National Center for History in the Schools, UCLA. His books include *Resistance in the Desert: Moroccan Responses to French Imperialism, 1881–1912* (University of Wisconsin Press, 1977) and *The Adventures of Ibn Battuta, a Muslim Traveler of the 14th Century* (University of California Press, 1990).

Between 1993 and 1996 he served as Coordinating Editor of the National Standards for World History. Following the public controversy over those standards, he co-authored with Gary B. Nash and Charlotte Crabtree, *History on Trial: Culture Wars and the Teaching of the Past* (Vintage Books, 2000). He recently edited *The New World History: A Teacher's Companion* (Bedford/St. Martin's, 2000), a collection of essays on the problems of conceptualizing and teaching world history.

Charles Lindholm is University Professor of Anthropology at Boston University. He did his original fieldwork with the Swat Pukhtun of northern Pakistan and has written a number of publications dealing with them, including his ethnographic work *Generosity and Jealousy* (Columbia University Press, 1982). He has also published a more general book entitled *The Islamic Middle East: An Historical Anthropology* (Blackwell, 1996). His other academic interests include the culture of the United States and psychological anthropology, with a special focus on idealization. His most recent book is *Culture and Identity* (McGraw-Hill, 2000).

Beverley Milton-Edwards is a Reader in the School of Politics and Assistant Director of the Centre for the Study of Ethnic Conflict at Queen's University Belfast. She is the author of *Islamic Politics in Palestine* (I.B. Tauris, 1996), *Contemporary Politics in the Middle East* (Polity Press, 2000) and has recently co-authored books on *Jordan: A Hashemite Legacy* (with P. Hinchcliffe, Harwood Academic, 2001) and *Conflicts in the Middle East since 1945* (with P. Hinchcliffe, Routledge, 2001). She has also published a variety of articles on political Islam, democracy and policing in deeply divided societies.

Xavier de Planhol is Professor Emeritus at the University of Paris–Sorbonne (where he holds the chaire de géographie de l'Afrique blanche et du Moyen-Orient) and a member of the Academia Europaea. He has carried out field research in Turkey, Iran, Afghanistan, Libya and Algeria. Among his many books and other publications on Islam are *The World of Islam* (Cornell University Press, 1959), *Les fondements géographiques de l'histoire de l'Islam* (Flammarion, 1968), *Les nations du Prophète: Manuel géographique de politique musulmane* (Fayard, 1993), *Minorités en Islam: Géographie politique et sociale* (Flammarion, 1997) and *L'Islam et la mer: La mosquée et le matelot* (Perrin, 2000). He has also published widely on deserts, as well as the book (with Paul Claval, Cambridge University Press, 1994) *An Historical Geography of France*. His work has been translated into many different languages, including English, German and Spanish.

Malise Ruthven is the author of *Islam in the World* (Penguin/Oxford University Press, 1984/2000), *Islam: A Very Short Introduction* (Oxford University Press, 1997/2000), *The Divine Supermarket: Shopping for God in America* (Chatto/Morrow, 1990) and several other books. A former editor and scriptwriter with the BBC Arabic Service and World Service in London, he has worked in BBC newsrooms and has made or collaborated in several radio and TV documentaries. He has taught Islamic studies and comparative religion at universities in Scotland and the United States. His most recent academic appointments have been as Visiting Professor at the Colorado College, Colorado Springs and at the University of California, San Diego.

Martin Stokes graduated from the Institute of Anthropology at Oxford University in 1989, taught ethnomusicology and anthropology at Queen's University of Belfast from 1989 to 1997, and is currently Associate Professor in Music at the University of Chicago. He is the author of *The Arabesk Debate: Music and Musicians in Modern Turkey* (Clarendon, 1992) and the editor of various collections, including *Ethnicity, Identity and Music: The Musical Construction of Place* (Berg, 1994). He has done fieldwork in Turkey and, more recently, in Egypt.

Bryan S. Turner has held professorial positions in England, Holland and Australia. He was Dean of the Faculty of Arts, Deakin University, Australia from 1993 to 1998 before joining the Faculty of Social and Political Sciences at the University of Cambridge in 1998, where he is currently Professor of Sociology and head of the department. He is the founding editor of the journal *Citizenship Studies* and co-founder with John O'Neill of the *Journal of Classical Sociology*. Professor Turner has been closely associated with the debate about Orientalism since the publication of *Weber and Islam* (Routledge and Kegan Paul, 1974). His current research interests include human rights, cosmopolitanism and religion.

ACKNOWLEDGEMENTS

When originally conceived, this book was to be co-edited by Akbar S. Ahmed, then a full-time academic and film-maker and a Fellow of Selwyn College Cambridge. The demands of Professor Ahmed's subsequent appointment in London as High Commissioner for Pakistan, however, regrettably prevented him from seeing the book through to completion. I nevertheless remain extremely grateful to him for our many long discussions concerning the book's content and intellectual direction. Justin Dyer did a superb job on the copy-editing, for which the contributors and I are most grateful.

Hastings Donnan

1

INTERPRETING INTERPRETATIONS OF ISLAM

Hastings Donnan and Martin Stokes

Disciplinarity and Islam

Islam is known in a bewildering diversity of ways in an increasingly interconnected world. What one knows about Islam, one knows, inevitably and inescapably, with reference to the ways in which other people come to know about Islam. How one goes about constructing an argument, or articulating a point, about the Muslim world increasingly relies on a knowledge of how other people might use the same facts to construct another kind of argument, or articulate another kind of point. Islamist arguments thus increasingly demand familiarity with the terminologies and procedures of secularist arguments. The reverse is every bit as true, as many have noted with regard to secularism in Turkey (Gellner 1981: 60). Selves rely on and involve Others with an increasing self-consciousness, in today's Muslim world and elsewhere. This does not imply, of course, the inevitable emergence of broad areas of agreement and consensus in the management of difference – the liberal dream. If anything, an awareness of intellectual diversity seems to have increased the vociferousness of those who claim particularity, and the imperative of managing difference on their terms only. This book constitutes, we believe, a different kind of response to the diversity of contemporary knowledge about Islam. Its implicit argument, throughout, is that patterns can be observed in the bewildering and seemingly anarchic diversity of disciplinary approaches to Islam, and that we, Muslims and non-Muslims alike, might learn much by reflecting on them.

What has generated academic diversity in the field(s) of Islamic studies? Differences between national scholarly traditions loom large. French Orientalist scholarship was marked by its entanglement with a distinct locale (North Africa), and to a certain extent remains so. The close connection between colony and former colonial domain is marked both by the presence of large Arab communities in French cities, and by the continuing political force of francophonie in Morocco, Algeria and Tunisia. Violent decolonization struggles are far from distant memories; the anti-colonial struggle continues to reverberate. It does so across lines separating, for many in France and North Africa, not only colonizer from colonized, but also civilization from civilization. The sheer proximity and intensity of historical and geographic entanglement, it seems, has demanded the most dramatic and all-encompassing terms of distinction. Throughout most of the twentieth century, much Anglo-Saxon scholarship was marked, in contrast, by an apprehension of Islam as localized and diverse 'culture' rather than unitary 'civilization'. The culture concept has been implicated in a very different kind of colonial and post-colonial experience: a more distant historical relationship in comparison to France, different techniques for structuring and managing the differences between colonizers and colonized, and more fractured struggles for independence in India, Palestine and Cyprus. Subsequently, the culture concept adapted itself well to the mediation of relationships with 'minorities' in the Anglo-Saxon nation-states (and those in their sway) in the post-colonial period. Anthropology, whether in its social (British) or cultural (American) manifestation, has produced some of the most intellectually persuasive accounts of the Muslim world by non-Muslims, depicting an Islam localized and embedded in plural cultural worlds. Though the different colonial histories implied by the culture concept and the notion of civilization explain a certain amount about the different trajectories of French and Anglo-Saxon writing on Islam, however, there has been much slippage between the two terms as well. The western world still needs its others, and these have become hard to find after the collapse of the Soviet Empire. Islam, understood now more as 'civilization' than 'culture', has filled the gap conveniently (see Samuel Huntington 1993), as is well known. Diverse colonial and post-colonial histories thus pattern distinct national trajectories in thinking about the Muslim world.

The market for news and non-academic publications has also had a significant impact on the diversification of knowledge about Islam. Popular knowledge about Islam in the West does not exist in a totally separate, hermetically sealed cultural space. In many cases, university academics participate actively in the proliferation of popular literatures on Islam. The motives and imperatives at work here are varied: demands for publication on the part of university administrators; vanity and fantasies of intellectual omnipotence on the part of authors; a sincere commitment to public education and reaching beyond the university campus; the varied demands of the culture of the public intellectual (or responses to its lack, or demise); the pressures of academic publishers seeking cross-over readerships – all play a part. Academic writers respond to, as well as contribute to, popular knowledge about Islam. Anybody involved in teaching, writing and thinking about Islam in the non-Muslim world comes across popular literatures or other traditions of representing Islam on a more or less daily basis. Converts require a 'how to' literature, videos and instructional tapes. Tourism requires its myths of exotic others, with sights and sounds that can make a trip necessary and worthwhile. The popular western press habitually reminds its readers of the premodern horror of life in Muslim society, 'the position of women' still the main issue (women's magazines provide an interesting case study). Radio and television, both locally and nationally, make space for western society's 'minorities' with special programming for the month of Ramadan, explained sensitively before, during or after the main feature for the benefit of non-Muslims who might still be up at that hour. Odd corners of 'everyday' public space pick up on and play with Orientalist tropes: science fiction villains have quasi-Arabic or Turkish names, and act like the Oriental despot of nineteenth-century sociological imagination. Doom-laden scenarios in television documentaries use background music with clearly 'Islamic' references and samples. A day spent wandering around in any Western European or North American city, or simply spent watching television, will bring anyone interested in Islam face to face with an extraordinary diversity of knowledges and modes of representation, shading a news item or piece of popular reportage, an ideological turn in a conversation, a domestic soundscape, a detail of visual or architectural décor. These imprint academic practice in diverse ways. More importantly, they inform academic authors of the kinds of knowledge about the Muslim world that they might take for granted amongst their non-academic readership. They provide some sense of habitual ways of thinking about Islam that might be manipulated or turned to authorial advantage, or indicate habits of thinking that must be confronted and overturned. Popular and specialist knowledge about Islam do not exist in hermetically sealed spaces, but increasingly bear on one another in productive and varied ways.

This volume is mainly concerned with matters of academic disciplinarity. These have been decisive in academic traditions of writing about Islam. The study of Islam in the western academy has characteristically been divided between departments of humanities and departments of social sciences. The lines are blurred, but there are important differences, which are relevant even when the object or issue being approached remains the same. Hermeneutic traditions in the humanities have resulted in historical and cultural ways of knowing Islam, from bodies of law, to miniature painting, to theories of government, to styles of religiosity. Specificity and local patterns of meaning are important to grasp in the hermeneutic tradition whether or not these are subordinated to some master teleology, some over-arching generality (though the relationship between general and specific is a matter of explicit concern in most interpretative traditions). Description and prescription, subjects and objects are dialectically entangled. Interpretation has a performative aspect, bringing critical thinking to bear on the present and hoped-for futures. What matters, for example, about an account of Islamic jurisprudence in a provincial Yemeni town as observed by an American anthropologist in the late twentieth century is not simply that 'the way things were' in a particular place at a particular point in time is now preserved in print for all eternity, but that readers elsewhere might learn ways of demystifying and transforming their common-sense assumptions about writing and law. The local, in this respect, speaks for itself (appropriately translated) and establishes its own context.

Within the social sciences, writing about Islam has been more explicitly concerned with forms of generalization and prediction; this constitutes the theoretical context against which 'the local' is read. As has often been stressed (see, for example, Turner, Chapter 2, this volume), Islam has, at least since Marx and Weber, been figured in terms of absences, against which the story of European distinction has habitually been read. Modernization theory in the social sciences dominated the view of Islam for much of the later twentieth century, and still continues to do so in some circles. Daniel Lerner's classic study *The Passing of Traditional Society: Modernizing the Middle East* (1958) enshrined the view that

Islam and modernity were incompatible, and that the task of social science was to quantify the movement between the two in order to be able to point to the success stories (Turkey) and the failures (Iran): the policy implications have always been obvious, at least from an American perspective. The lines separating humanities and social science research have, in recent years, been productively blurred. Epistemological concerns in the social sciences have found their way into humanities departments; questions of interpretation have, conversely, borne more and more strongly on the practice of social science.

The notion of disciplinarity (which is to say, the critical reflection on disciplinary practice) implies the notion of interdisciplinarity, or at least some kind of trans-disciplinary space from which the observer can reflect calmly and abstractly on the shortcomings of (narrowly conceived) disciplinary practice. It is worth reflecting on this briefly, since all of the contributors to this volume imply the value of an interdisciplinary approach to Islam, and imply interdisciplinarity in their critiques of their own disciplinary practice. The gaze from interdisciplinary space involves a certain critical pessimism quite in keeping with the dominant intellectual ethos of the last twenty years, even though this is often dressed up in the language of intellectual entrepreneurialism and opportunity. It suggests that institutions may constrain as well as generate knowledge. It suggests that we may have something to learn about the circuitry of power within the discipline by reflecting on what disciplines select for attention and what they repress. It is harder, though, to say what the implications of this should be. Do we step out of disciplinary space into a trans-disciplinary space? Or do we shuttle between disciplines, reading them against one another dialectically to produce fresh insights? Is there a self that, unconstrained by the particular regimes of truth a particular discipline organizes, can come to reasonable conclusions about a discipline's shortcomings? Can the strengths of several be combined in order to initiate more progressive and productive lines of inquiry?

There are plenty of reasons to be critical of what one might call the naïve perspective on interdisciplinarity, or at least to qualify its liberal implications. It nurtures a vision of 'true' knowledge freed from institutional shackles and disciplinary tradition, a vision that unfortunately chimes with right-wing critics of academic obscurity, faddishness and 'political correctness'. More directly, perhaps, it promotes a fantasy of the 'free-range' academic: shaken from the cosy security of his or her disciplinary perch, the interdisciplinary professor can be relied upon to do a reasonable and unprotesting job in whichever department university downsizing blows him or her into next. It also obscures the processes by which certain intellectual traditions come to occupy a central place in interdisciplinary thinking. In these contexts, 'interdisciplinary' activity can mean little more than a poorly represented discipline in a particular institutional setting adopting a theoretical vocabulary from a stronger one. This perpetuates the illusion that the weaker discipline is engaged in a mutually beneficial conversation with the powerful one, whilst, clearly, nothing of the sort is happening. Rather, interdisciplinarity might be seen to involve a 'nesting' model of theoretical capability: the less powerful disciplinary apparatus nests inside one more powerful, and that in turn can nest inside another, and so on. It also involves some deeply rooted intellectual habits, in which certain disciplines have been particularly privileged. In continental Europe, sociology has effectively been the master discipline. In the Anglo-Saxon world, lacking a strongly independent sociological tradition, literary criticism, at least since Leavis (and arguably since Coleridge), has fulfilled this function. Anthropology has sat uncomfortably between the two, both in Europe and in North America, though it derives much of its energy from this situation. Sociology, anthropology and literary criticism compete with one another to attract those who have become unstuck from their disciplinary moorings.

We might usefully consider how and why some books appear to occupy a central space in interdisciplinary reflection on Islam. Said's study of Orientalism (1978) has undoubtedly been of extraordinary importance in questioning not only how we think about Islam, but also how we think about interdisciplinarity. It is worth pointing out that this is not the only work that is read and discussed widely across the main disciplines concerned with the study of Islam today. One would also have to include the work of Akbar S. Ahmed, Aziz al-Azmeh, Dale Eickelman, John Esposito, Ernest Gellner, Michael Gilsenan, Bernard Lewis, Fatima Mernissi, Brinkley Messick, James Piscatori, Maxime Rodinson, Bryan S. Turner, and Sami Zubaida, to name only a few writers representing very different intellectual traditions. What, then, are the specific qualities of Said's work that have made it so crucial to interdisciplinary conversation? First, and this should not be underestimated, the writing has a humane intelligence to it without which it simply would not sustain prolonged scholarly interest. Second, the impact of Said's work has been pronounced in the Anglo-Saxon world, tied as it is to the colonial and neo-colonial dynamics of the Israeli-Palestinian struggle. For a variety of reasons, anglophone scholarship is globally predominant today, which is not to ignore the significance of work written in other European or Asian languages, but simply to state that work written in English and published by an English or American academic publisher reaches the larger global readership. Third, Said's work, along with that of Homi Bhabha and Gayatri Spivak, represents the consolidation of activist post-colonial critique in North America's most prestigious academic institutions. The voice from the margins is now, in a sense, firmly located in the centre, and radicalism can now speak with all of the authority that the centre can muster. This is a relatively new moment in Anglo-Saxon academia (though, again, not in France: recall Sartre on the Algerian crisis), and the energies that sustain this scholarship and attract people to it can easily be understood. Fourth, it represents the continuing role of literary criticism as the dominant disciplinary framework in the world of Anglo-Saxon scholarship; though anthropologists and sociologists claim as their own the basic insight that knowledge is a social construction serving complex political ends, they often do so now in a style that owes more to Said, Bhabha and Spivak than it does to Evans-Pritchard or to Merton. Said's work has thus been of particular importance in shaping interdisciplinary conversation in the study of Islam, as many of the contributors to this volume indicate. The complex politics of interdisciplinarity, however, should not be forgotten, since they do at least as much as the politics of disciplinarity to shape the ways in which we come to understand and interpret Islam as scholars today.

Interpreting Islam

Calling this collection of essays *Interpreting Islam* clearly begs a number of questions, such as who is doing the interpreting, for what audience, and for what purpose? Even to ask how we are to understand Islam raises questions about the ways in which 'we' can have a range of shifting rhetorical referents that are not always explicit, and for each category of which interpreting Islam may involve a different process and a different outcome: fellow readers of this book, those who share an academic discipline, other scholars in general, other westerners, other Muslims, and so on. For each of these, there may be different ways of knowing, different ways of interpreting, and no grand over-arching or universalizing scheme. *Orientalism* exposed the intellectual and interpretative certainties of an earlier age for what they were: not the disinterested, objective studies that scholars supposed, but a kind of political discourse that both grew out of and helped to constitute global relations of power. As a result, we are all conscious now that the pursuit of knowledge has political implications, as a form of domination, control and even subjugation. Knowledge and power are inextricably linked. And although different academic disciplines have responded to Said's critique in different ways, accommodating his insights to greater or lesser extent, most are now necessarily more self-conscious than before of the nature of their voice, their audience and the contexts from which they write.

Said's work poses something of a conundrum for scholars, one that raises ethical and moral dilemmas, as well as presenting an intellectual and epistemological challenge to those who seek to understand alien cultures. For Said, all work that takes as its starting point a dichotomy between 'Occident' and 'Orient', and that essentializes the Oriental mind, 'Islam' or the 'Arabs', is characteristic of a style of thought that he calls 'Orientalist'. This Orientalist perspective has systematically misrepresented the East in ways that legitimate the West's understanding of itself as a civilizing, rationalizing and modernizing force, and that contribute to global inequalities of power at the same time as they arise from them. Orientalist images of the East are shown to be the outcome of the Orientalists' own ideological and cultural prejudices, with imperial administrators and academics alike equally enmeshed in this web of politically and culturally mediated imaginings. The knowledge that results is thus imbued with the power to dominate. And since all observers are inevitably culturally and politically positioned, it would seem that all representations are forever destined to be misrepresentations: they arise from, and serve, some other cause beyond the observer's apparently well-meaning wish to supply a disinterested account. This, then, is the challenge with which Said confronts his readers. 'How does one *represent* other cultures?' (1978: 325, emphasis in original). How does one escape or step outside the political, cultural and biographical factors that shape how we see the world? It would seem impossible to talk about others without misrepresenting them at some level.

Said has his supporters and his detractors, both in large numbers, this critical attention being in itself an obvious measure of the importance and reach of his argument (see, for instance, summaries in Halliday 1993; Yeğenoğlu 1998: 14–26).

Some of Said's detractors, notably Ernest Gellner and Bernard Lewis, have engaged in furious polemic with him. Gellner (1993) sprang to the defence of Enlightenment reason and modular man in the face of what he understood as an attack on the autonomy of thought. Lewis (1993) sprang to the defence of Orientalism as benign cultural curiosity, emerging, according to him, much earlier than the moment of colonial expansion with which Said identifies it. It is probably true to say that the polemic generated by Said's book has done less to advance thinking about the issues it raised than its more modulated reception within the fields of post-colonial theory, cultural studies and literary criticism. Here, discussion tended to focus on some significant contradictions in Said's work as a whole: between a Foucauldian determinism concerning intellectual production, and a refusal fully to understand his own capacity for critical awareness as itself socially determined; between an insistence on understanding the western canon in terms of the colonial processes it represses, and his evident feeling that texts (particularly 'great texts') speak for themselves; between the call for action on the part of the public intellectual, and his recognition that the epistemological grounds for political action are always flawed. These tensions in his work have undoubtedly promoted a great deal of constructive reflection, as many of his critics acknowledge (see, for example, Moore-Gilbert 1997). Turner's chapter in this volume is firmly situated in this genre of critique. As Turner reminds us, Said exaggerated the degree of coherence within western discourse on the Orient. He concentrated heavily on literary works on Islam, as opposed to the historical and social scientific literature on the subject, and failed to acknowledge crucial shifts in the institutional circuitry of Orientalism over the course of the twentieth century (from 'strong' and nation-state-centred to 'weak' and cosmopolitan). Orientalism, Turner argues, needs to be seen as part of an ensemble of 'othering' processes (for example, an 'Occidentalism' that looked to the Celtic Fringe) that attended the birth of modern nation-states, and not in isolation, as Said implied. The Orientalism hypothesis, finally, fails to grasp what Turner describes as 'good Orientalism', fictions circulating during the formation of the modern nation-state that articulated crucial notions of civic consciousness and practice. If Said has been justifiably criticized for not offering a way out of the dilemmas he identifies (Lindholm 1995: 808), those such as Turner, engaging with his work from within the traditions of scholarship he represents, have done much to move the argument forward (see also Turner 1994: 31, 45).

Scholars thus still grapple with the issues of interpretation and representation that Said's *Orientalism* so compellingly raised, issues now perhaps made even more complex by a world of accelerating communications technology, transnational migration and cultural displacement, one in which grand narratives and over-arching theories have been largely rejected. None of the options that have emerged in response to the postmodern critique seems that attractive or persuasive: advocacy of dialogical exchange with those being studied, a call to gather under a neo-positivist banner, and a let's-note-the-problems-but-get-on-with-it-anyway approach are all examples of such options, which, while addressing aspects of the critique, often simply end up generating a different set of difficulties. In this volume we suggest that it is possible to get some critical leverage on such issues by further reflecting on the process of interpretation itself; by drawing attention to how scholars with diverse intellectual and personal biographies and from different disciplinary traditions have written about Islam. Since Islam is made known to us in their writings through these disciplinary and biographic filters, it is critical that we grasp the nature of what these filters emphasize and sift from view. Why are some topics selected for study and not others? To what extent might gender refract interpretation? What images of Islam predominate within and across disciplines? How might this skew our interpretation of Islam? These are some of the questions addressed by our contributors.

We do not set out to provide a compendium or to be encyclopaedic, something that space alone prohibits. Consequently, not every discipline is represented, nor every national tradition of study. Nor have we been able to include every possible (or even very many) permutation(s) of biographical/personal and disciplinary combination. Though different disciplines may be viewed differently by variously positioned practitioners within them, we can offer little more than a flavour of such perspectival spread. Instead, the essays gathered here are intended to generate questions about, and to be illustrative of, the kinds of processes likely to be found whatever the disciplinary approach or circumstances of the author. They remind us of the disciplinary and methodological diversity that characterizes the 'field' of 'Islamic studies', and thus of the many ways in which 'our' knowledge and interpretations of Islam are partial, contestable and forever threatening to fragment. A reflexive grasp of what is involved here might at least enable us to interpret the interpretations that result. This is especially important in a field where the right to interpret as well as the interpretations themselves are disputed.

Some contested interpretations

One aspect of Islam that provides an especially good example of how interpretations are contested is 'fundamentalism'. Amongst the West's gathering anxieties about post-war shifts in geopolitical trends, the press of events towards the end of the 1970s, and subsequently, ensured that 'Islamic fundamentalism' bubbled to the top of the pot. This notion has been hotly debated throughout the academy and in much popular reporting ever since. It is easy to see why. The images with which Islamic fundamentalism came to be associated in the popular western imagination, stimulated to a large extent by media coverage, as we consider below, were impossible to ignore: bearded, kalashnikov-carrying clerics, urban carnage and scimitars dripping with blood. Saatchi and Saatchi could not have done better had their brief been to strike fear into every western heart and instil a sense of vulnerability. A projected medieval and naturalized barbarity had been fused with contemporary politics. The message was clear: they're coming to get you. At the same time, however, Islam clearly and self-evidently involved much more than an apparent will to destroy the West, and much more than a radical political perspective. Even those labelled 'fundamentalist' were not everywhere of the same order. How, then, are these selective and prominent images of threat that attach to fundamentalism to be understood? What do they tell us about Islam and the state of Islamic scholarship in the West?

Milton-Edwards tackles the vexed issue of interpreting 'radical Islam' in Chapter 3. Although at first glance it may seem slightly contradictory to suggest that what looks like the most conservative form of Islam – a back to basics 'fundamentalism' – is in fact the most 'radical', these terms are now often used synonymously, even if, taken as a pair, they frequently mean rather different things to those who use them. Milton-Edwards distinguishes two main analytical camps among those who write about radical Islam: the '(neo-)Orientalists' and the 'apologists', both of these being terms of abuse in use by one camp of the other (rather than being self-descriptions). She explores how radical Islam has come to be written rather differently by each of these camps, which, at least in the field of politics and Islamic studies that Milton-Edwards describes, confront each other across an interpretative chasm with an intensity and passion matched only by that of some of those they set out to study. The (neo-)Orientalist perspective, according to Milton-Edwards, associates Islamic politics exclusively with violence, authoritarianism, terrorism, fundamentalism, clerical domination and hostility to modern, 'western', secular democratic government, a constellation of negatives that the 'radical' in 'radical Islam' then signifies and evokes. This interpretation of Islam is somewhat monolithic, drawing, for instance, on studies of the Iranian revolution to show that 'Islam' is inherently revolutionary (while ignoring critical differences between Sunni and Shi'a) and, by placing so much emphasis on politics, even squeezing out its ethical and religious significance. Islam thereby becomes equated not just with radical politics, but with a radical politics associated only with violence and mayhem. Radical, in this view, becomes all that Islam is about. By contrast, the 'apologists', with whom Milton-Edwards has more sympathy, advocate a view of radical Islam that, she says, seeks to understand the violence while recognizing at the same time that many Muslims also engage in more passive forms of protest and resistance. Rather than ascribing a radical character to Islam itself, these critics of the (neo-)Orientalist position stress the need for political scientists to recognize the many instances of radical Islam that have nothing to do with terrorism, and to set these – and their violent counterparts – in their wider political and socio-economic contexts, something that the other social sciences have so far perhaps been better at. Not only has there not yet been any real *rapprochement* between these two antagonistic positions, but the vituperative exchange between them seems set to continue and even intensify. Part of the problem, of course, is that underlying the rival interpretations of each camp is to some extent the (often unexamined) personal politics of their adherents. Milton-Edwards' suggestion that to understand radical Islam we should draw upon a hitherto underused feminist epistemology, and that we should pay more attention to a new generation of Muslim intellectuals attempting to rethink the issues from 'within', may be just the reframing that is needed, provided, of course, that such new approaches remain reflexively aware that they too are driven, in part, by personal politics.

This debate within the discipline of politics about how to interpret radical Islam has percolated through into popular understandings of the religion, not only because high-profile projects – such as the American Academy of Arts and Sciences' 'Fundamentalism Project' – bring the arguments to public attention, but also because the views of political scientists are probably more likely than those of researchers in other disciplines to be sought for television news and current affairs programmes, where, unsurprisingly, the kinds of interpretation and image mentioned above regularly appear stripped of all subtlety in even starker, sound-bite size. Though it is a cliché to note the media's pre-eminent role in shaping how we see the world, it is of course no less true because of it. Understanding the processes by which the media have shaped and shape our views of Islam, as well as the recursive interpretative loop between media and academy, whereby analyses and debate in one influence and are influenced by analyses and debate in the other, is essential if we are to gain some critical purchase on a major source of our interpretations.

Ruthven (Chapter 4) begins his account of Islam in the media by noting the striking contrast between the glare of publicity that surrounded the death of Princess Diana and the comparative obscurity and lack of interest in Dodi al-Fayed, the man who died at her side. The disparity is hardly surprising, but it leaves Ruthven wondering about what kinds of question might have been opened up had the couple survived and their relationship flourished. We will never know of course, but it is an interesting speculation, for here was the mother of the heir to the throne mixing with a man from a world that the British tabloid press in particular was given to describing in images of medieval barbarity and backwardness. Deleting Dodi from the reports of Diana's death is just one instance of the many ways in which media accounts of Islam are highly selective. In *Covering Islam* Said (1981) has shown how the western media have obscured Islam by reporting only those aspects of it that are consistent with the pursuit of western economic, political and cultural aims. The broader picture of Muslim faith and practice is played down, and differences among Muslims flattened out. The result is, as Ruthven illustrates, a view of Islam dominated by images of extremism, especially in relation to gender and violence, a demonization that others have noted and that, in Britain, has been the subject of a specially commissioned inquiry (cf. Ahmed 1992; Runnymede Trust 1997). What has not always been so clear, however, is how Muslims themselves interpret and contest these selective projections of their lives and religion.

In an increasingly globalized media, Muslims themselves are obviously consumers, audience to western images of Islam, many of which they roundly and rightly condemn. But how might they best respond? Drawing on the work of Baudrillard, Hall, Eco and Thompson, among others, Ruthven suggests that we should approach media-transmitted images as a kind of quasi-interaction in which, though a common stock of cultural knowledge among the audience is often presupposed by those who transmit, the audience interpret and 'decode' according to their situation, leading to wide variability and even unpredictability of interpretation. Ruthven considers a series of examples of how television can have a polarizing effect on the subject of Islam, among which he includes a BBC report on the Ayodhya riots of 1992. This report shows quite clearly how audio-visual images can be interpreted very differently by western and Muslim audiences, even when in the hands of the most experienced and sympathetic of journalists. Ruthven argues that in this report the voice-over is critical to the interpretation of the visual images transmitted. Turn off the sound, or assume that the audience cannot understand English, and viewer interpretations are likely to diverge. The inability to hear or understand the commentary, which tells how Hindu leaders condemned the anti-Muslim violence at Ayodhya and explains why the Indian police did not intervene, leaves only scenes of destruction as Hindu demonstrators over-run the Babri mosque at the centre of the conflict while the police stand idly by. To such a viewer, Ruthven suggests, it could only seem that the Indian government was out to get the mosque. Cases like this indicate just how complicated it can be to identify and to respond to Muslim misrepresentation in the media, even though we may recognize it is there. Perhaps the best possible response to perceived media bias towards them, Ruthven concludes, is for Muslims to generate their own alternatives.

The graphic sensationalism of so many of the skewed media portraits of Islam – with their unrelenting but gripping emphasis on violence and extremism – makes them difficult to ignore. Even Ruthven, whose experience of working for the BBC World Service gives him a particular insight into the ambivalent demands of programming, confesses that the need for good copy sometimes persuaded him to employ the articulate and media-friendly militant at the risk of reproducing images of Islam that he regarded as biased. Scholars who wish to present a more rounded picture of the religion and its adherents may find themselves similarly constrained by publishers whose commercial interests dictate the striking or gory image. Authors may learn that the cover proposed for their book implicates them in the very view they are trying to supplant or dislodge. Worse still, scholars themselves may be tempted to enliven an otherwise dull and dusty text with gratuitous scenes of violence and sensuality taken from the Muslim world, or surround it with a romanticized and exoticized serenity as epitomized by the ubiquitous image of the sun rising (or is it setting?) beyond the rounded domes and pencil-like minarets of the mosque. For such writers, claims to irony may offer no defence. Immensely difficult, then, is the task of the textbook writer charged with outlining the broad sweep of Islam and interpreting it for the student, the subject of Douglass and Dunn's chapter.

Douglass and Dunn (Chapter 5) tell us that twenty-five years ago in the US the popular media's interpretation of Islam was the main source of information about the religion for young Americans. Ironically, it was as these media representations grew ever more negative throughout the 1970s that work began to develop the new educational materials through which American schoolchildren are now taught interpretations of Islam. Douglass and Dunn critically reflect on the content and representations of Islam in eleven such texts in context of the wide-ranging debates over curriculum reform that were the impetus for their emergence. One of the most important factors in reaching a consensus in the debate about the desirability of promoting understanding of different religions in the schoolroom was the development of criteria to distinguish between teaching religion and teaching about religion, a general debate to which American Muslims themselves directly contributed. With the ground rules thus established, texts on 'world history' began to appear in which Islam was an element. Although Islam is now a fashionable topic in American classrooms, largely due to the high profile of Muslim countries in the news and to the growth of the Muslim population in the US itself, only a handful of publishers produce these school texts and they have been reluctant to go beyond what they believe will be acceptable to state textbook adoption boards.

These school texts on world history with their sections on Islam not only provide the student with factual information about the religion and the faithful, but they also offer the conceptual framework within which to place Muslim history in relation to everything else. As Douglass and Dunn make clear, depending on the order of the chapters, students may learn to interpret Islam as antiquarian and exotic, or as an integral and continuing dimension of human history and community. Chapter order is paramount in determining the textbook interpretations, some of which are highly contestable because they retard student understanding of the chronology of how world history unfolded or obscure the connections that existed among people in different parts of the globe. In three of the eleven texts, for instance, the 'Ottoman Empire is sent into decline before students read about the early modern Iberian expansion or the development of bureaucratic states and religious wars in sixteenth-century Europe'.

The tendency of these school texts to treat each of the religions they discuss, including Islam, as independent cultural entities – typically offering outlines of their origins, key beliefs and practices – reinforces the rather monolithic interpretation of Islam prevalent in the popular media: as homogeneous, essentialized and ahistorical. Traditions shared with other religions are played down – most notably the Abrahamic tradition shared with Judaism and Christianity – a glossing over that Douglass and Dunn argue is one way in which the texts sustain an interpretation of these three faiths as neatly discrete, an interpretation widely challenged by Muslim critics. Some basic facts are ignored, others selectively emphasized. Moreover, Muslims all but disappear from view in these texts after the sixteenth century, except for walk-on parts in the twentieth century in variations of the 'sick-man-of-Europe' role. In short, Douglass and Dunn suggest that these texts interpret Islam not as Muslims would understand it, but in terms thought acceptable to textbook adoption committees. Only a more human-centred approach to world history, Douglass and Dunn conclude, as well as advice from Muslim reviewers, will counteract such interpretations, which too often recall the kind of misrepresentations that we have noted can characterize the media.

As with Ruthven, therefore, Douglass and Dunn suggest that one way in which to tackle bias or misrepresentation of Islam in the media or school texts is to have Muslims generate their own alternatives, or, less radically, to have Muslims at least enter into conversation with those currently responsible for these forms of cultural production. This would seem like common sense, though, of course, as these authors are aware, it is not just as easy as that, since such alternative interpretations will be just as positioned, albeit in different ways, as any other. So far we have been considering some examples of how interpretations of Islam are contested, but let us now turn to examine the different perspectives and insights into Islam that have been generated by those differently positioned by discipline and personal and biographical background.

Some contending interpreters

The basis of the authority that underpins different interpretations of Islam is not always something that is closely examined or revealed. What can make a particular account, explanation or interpretation compelling/authoritative – or more authoritative than other competing interpretations – is not just the agreed criteria of scholarship such as internal coherence, elegance and parsimony of explanation, important as these are, but the disciplinary and personal credentials of the individual offering the interpretation, credentials to which we may be differentially predisposed. In the marketplace of academic interpretation, some scholars, or some kinds of scholar, are better able to sell their wares than others, and if we are to understand why this is so, we need to understand some of the processes that operate there.

We have already mentioned how several of our contributors advocate greater Muslim participation in the production of materials that interpret their religion and its adherents for people in the West. Clearly an element of brokerage or cultural translation is at issue here. There is a feeling that the 'insider', in this case a Muslim, can provide new depths of understanding and a different perspective, one that may act as a balance, allowing us to 'triangulate' on the subject of study, and so improve the interpretations on offer. There may even be a feeling that Muslim involvement in the production of interpretations about Islam lends them greater credibility, at least among other Muslims (though one could also argue the opposite). These claims are thought to be no less true of academic writing than of media and textbook interpretations.

In an analysis that recalls Akbar Ahmed's argument in *Discovering Islam* (1988), the Muslim sociologist Ilyas Ba-Yunus (Chapter 6) advocates a holistic approach in order to avoid what he refers to as the 'confusing array of perceptions' that arise from the varied cultural, political and disciplinary biases of scholars who write about Islam. He roots this holistic approach in a combination of Parsonian functionalism and the Qur'anic notion of *deen* in an effort to determine what a 'living Islamic society' might look like if such existed today. In this regard, his chapter might be seen as an extension of his earlier advocacy of an 'Islamic sociology', which sought to incorporate into western social science the values and intellectual traditions of Islam in order better to understand the forces operating in Muslim society and history (Ba-Yunus and Ahmed 1985; on the related attempt to formulate an 'Islamic anthropology', see Ahmed 1986). As Ba-Yunus outlines, the *deen* of the Qur'an provides for a full set of institutions essential to human society – for economic, domestic, political and religious life – and in so doing offers, he suggests, at least when practised in its totality, a median course between a range of extremes such as asceticism and materialism, selfishness and altruism, democracy and authoritarianism. Contemporary realities in Muslim societies, and elsewhere, frequently depart radically from this model, as Ba-Yunus notes, so that the model's value lies less in accounting for these realities than in allowing us to measure the extent of this departure. It also, Ba-Yunus suggests, offers an 'insider's' insight into the worldview of contemporary Islamic movements that otherwise would be relatively inaccessible to a western readership.

Such calls for 'insider' accounts certainly find a positive reception in a discipline like anthropology, with its emphasis on 'the native's point of view', and it is not surprising to find here that there have been a number of prominent attempts at insider–outsider authorial collaborations. Probably the best known of these is Fischer and Abedi's *Debating Muslims: Cultural Dialogue in Postmodernity and Tradition* (1990), whose very title epitomizes what is at issue here. Although a rich repository for the intrepid reader, the book explicitly offers no less than three routes through it, a potentially shifting sand of interpretative ambivalence as far as some critics have been concerned, and a positive advantage in the eyes of others. The danger of drawing upon such different voices may be the temptation to try to reconcile them, rather than leaving them to speak for themselves. Each can offer different things, with the insider bringing insight into the 'intimate cultural reverberations of a symbol or motif' to the outsider's 'entitlement to integrate parochial perspectives into a global context' (Bedford 1994: 84). According to Bedford (1994: 84), this was Fischer and Abedi's failing: that they sought to go beyond this and to 'contrive to exploit their dissimilar speaking positions to forge a unity of utterance which is all the more misleading the more authoritative it appears'. It is impossible in places for the reader to disentangle one voice from the other, yet the negotiations and compromises that must inevitably underlie such passages in *Debating Muslims* are rarely made clear. The resulting 'omniscience', laments Bedford, is far from reassuring, and where such different voices are presented we should strive to reveal, as the better model, the 'dialogue' involved. But equally there will be those who balk at Bedford's suggested intellectual division of labour. Why should insiders be confined to providing local knowledge, while the outside observer runs off with the global and comparative models? At one's most pessimistic and most cynical, attempts at dialogical interpretation could seem merely to replicate in microcosm the very structures of power one had hoped they might transcend.

Perhaps one of the reasons that anthropology has seemed peculiarly receptive to insiders studying their own cultures is because these 'indigenous ethnographers' appear to epitomize how the discipline has historically validated its knowledge: through the ability to claim that 'I was there'. Anthropologists are expected to accumulate experiential 'inside' knowledge of the worlds they study through long-term participative residential research, something that in some sense 'insiders' clearly already possess. Such eye-witness accounting has long been the ultimate legitimation of ethnographic endeavour and, in part, is what has helped to distinguish anthropological work on Islam from that of other researchers, particularly those who concentrate on texts. It also partly explains why anthropology came relatively late to the study of Islam, as Lindholm shows in Chapter 7.

Extended residential fieldwork obviously entails an interest in the everyday preoccupations of those one is living alongside. In the tribal, segmentary societies of the Middle East that were so often the focus of attention for anthropologists of

Lindholm's generation and earlier, this usually meant politics. It rarely meant religion. Where Islam surfaced at all in ethnographic accounts, it was generally to note the mediatory role played by Sufi saints in conflicts between warring factions. Reflecting the apparent lack of interest in religion among their rural hosts, Islam was for many anthropologists in the 1960s and 1970s a taken-for-granted assumption and background noise that they did little to probe or record. Other factors too deflected or discouraged anthropological interest in Islam. Anthropological accounts of religion generally revelled in imaginative decodings of cosmology, myth and symbol, a type of analysis that Islam's apparently uncomplicated and straightforward codes of behaviour and belief did not readily invite. Islam hardly ever found its way into the discipline's introductory textbooks (see Ba-Yunus, Chapter 6), in contrast to the pages and pages devoted there to unravelling the symbolism of a religion that might have only a handful of adherents. Lindholm offers many such examples of this neglect of Islam, including, compellingly, his own.

For anthropologists of this period, then, gripped by the dynamics of rural, tribal politics, the Middle Eastern towns and the Muslim scholars who lived there might never have existed. Islamic texts and Muslim historiography simply seemed an elitist irrelevance to a discipline principally concerned with downtrodden and largely illiterate tribesmen. The result was a division of labour in which, Lindholm argues, 'anthropologists avoided cities, and rarely read texts' while Orientalist historians were uninterested 'in tribal societies or even in living people'. Although this was an unproductive and shortsighted partition of tasks between parties that had potentially so much to learn from each other, fieldwork and textual scholarship quickly became institutionalized as divergent academic pursuits, and it was to be many years, Lindholm notes, before anthropology incorporated the study of Muslim texts and history as an integral and complementary part of its practice.

Anthropology was thus something of a late starter in the field of Islamic studies, which was dominated for years by disciplines that could muster more by way of textual clout (cf. Gilsenan 1990: 230). If someone wanted to learn about Islam, he or she was more likely to turn to the work of a historian or philosopher than to that of an anthropologist. Anthropologists consequently had to learn their trade in a context where the research agenda was set by other kinds of expert. Text-based interpretations of Islam generally held greater sway than those based on ethnography. It is only in the last decade or so that anthropologists have begun to make a name for themselves and their subject in the study of Islam, and to overcome the previously widespread conviction that Islam's true nature could only be understood through texts and not fieldwork, which some were inclined to dismiss as the collection of folk superstitions. And only now, too, is the value of traditional anthropological fieldwork being recognized for its ability to locate in time and space 'the Islam' of the Muslims it describes, tempering any temptation to think, in a world obsessed by Islamic revivalism, that all Muslims are preoccupied by debating doctrine and pursuing apostates. While textual scholars and fieldworkers still challenge one another's views, there are signs that interpretations of Islam now increasingly draw on a convergence of their expertise: with knowledge of texts informing fieldwork and fieldwork informing our reading of the texts.

Interpreting the margins

The final three chapters shed light on disciplinary formations in scholarship on the Muslim world by attending to areas that have attracted relatively little critical attention: sea-faring, music and charity. Characteristically western scholarship has grasped these areas in terms of failure, as Xavier de Planhol's provocatively titled chapter suggests. The notion of failure is, of course, a persistent Orientalist trope, in which Islam is deemed responsible for lacks and absences, which in turn leave the Muslim world chronically ill equipped for modernity. Of course, the failure lies not with Islam but with scholarship, which has often posed its questions and selected its terms of analysis in such a way that the answer ('failure') is inevitable. All of the final chapters suggest ways in which these absences can be turned into productive and revealing social and historical presences.

Planhol's chapter concludes by reminding us just how much of modern western history has revolved around advances in seafaring. By the fifteenth century, when a global economy was beginning to emerge and the exploitation of the Americas was well underway, Muslim powers had apparently fallen behind in the race for maritime supremacy, and this was to have crucial consequences. As Planhol starkly asserts, had this not been the case, 'the fate of the world could well have been different'. The evidence is certainly compelling, but more complex than one might at first expect. Sifting through a variety of documentary sources to illuminate the interplay of geography, politics and economics, Planhol reveals complex social and cultural formations connected with the sea and seafaring in classical Islamic society. Across the Mediterranean, the Muslim powers relied on Christian minorities for naval prowess. Fishing and piracy were also largely in the hands of Christians, renegades or recent converts (such as the Berbers). The partial exception to this picture was the Indian Ocean, though here, Planhol argues, Muslim domination of maritime trade took place in the absence of sustained resistance. What were the reasons for this? Planhol argues that it was not simply a case of falling behind technical developments being pursued in the Christian West. The practical consequences of an asymmetry in the field of naval power were negligible, even though heavier and slower boats were clearly a factor in the defeat of the Ottoman navy by the Habsburgs at the decisive battle of Lepanto (in 1571). There was, Planhol points out, 'no intrinsic ineptitude, no individual incompatibility', as the careers of such exemplary Ottoman seafarers as Barbarossa Hayreddin Paşa demonstrate. The answer, as Planhol meticulously documents, was a cultural disposition, which resulted not only in a certain social stigma attached to sea-faring in medieval and early modern Muslim society, but also in an active indifference on the part of its rulers. What was at issue here was a conflict of cultural values, which closely identified seafaring with pastoral nomadism in the minds of the civic-minded urban elites of the Arabian Peninsula in the early years of Islam. Just as the conflict between sedentary, urban Islam and the Islam of the nomadic tribes shaped early medieval Islam in crucial ways, as Ibn Khaldun noted, so the conflict between 'Islam and the sea', as Planhol puts it, was to have decisive and far-reaching consequences.

Inevitably, as Rosaldo (1988: 79) has pointed out, certain topics of study are overlooked because they do not conform to standard disciplinary expectations about what is theoretically interesting or worthwhile. Such absences not only leave gaps in our knowledge, but may also hint at the ideological assumptions that underlie existing interpretations. One such absence has been the study of organized charity, which, as Milton-Edwards hints (Chapter 3, this volume), is not something that has generally figured large in either popular or academic imaginings of Islam. In fact, when Benthall (Chapter 9) began his research on Muslim charity he could find practically nothing at all written about any of the twenty-eight Red Crescent national societies. This is surprising, since the obligation to be charitable has, of course, such high visibility as one of Islam's 'five pillars'. While mentioned briefly in practically every book that has ever been published on Islam, charity is paradoxically probably one of the religion's least written about and most poorly analysed elements, its very self-evidentness perhaps being partly what keeps it from view. Benthall's interest in researching Muslim charity developed out of his earlier involvement in the management and study of a range of western non-governmental organizations (NGOs). Focusing particularly on Jordan and the Middle East, Benthall explores the relationship between these western NGOs and their Islamic equivalents, showing how the latter have adapted and 'localized' some of the practices of the former to produce a voluntary sector characterized by many different types of organization, from quasi-state bodies to popular movements for radical change. This process has unfolded in a context with a long history of Islamic charitable trusts informed by extensive and doctrinally elaborate Qur'anic teachings on the giving of alms that are only dimly and incompletely known to the West. It is only comparatively recently, Benthall suggests, that western NGOs have begun to recognize and appreciate the role played by such local, non-western charitable welfare provision. For a long time the Judaeo-Christian West saw organized charity as its own unique domain, an assumption that, with more than a trace of Orientalism, constructed the non-West in general and Islam in particular as the objects of charity rather than its agent. Such an assumption would certainly help to explain why Muslim charity is generally missing from western scholarly accounts of Islam, as another 'failure' that can take its place beside the Muslim failure at sea.

Stokes' final chapter discusses the variety of disciplinary formations that bear on the study of music in the Muslim world. Hadithic condemnation has in various ways and at various times relegated music and musicians to a marginal position in Muslim society, in stark contrast to the situation that has pertained in Europe, at least since the middle of the nineteenth century. It is not surprising that musicologists who have looked at the Muslim world have found it to be full of all manner of lacks and absences, and understood these in terms of a monolithic and, by implication, culturally repressive Islam. The Orientalist reflexes of an earlier musicology have been absorbed and reproduced in Europe by the popular market. 'Islamic' samples by the popular cultural avant garde invest the trope of cultural repression with a sado-masochistic eroticism, most strikingly represented in Jocelyn Pook's soundtrack to Stanley Kubrick's film *Eyes Wide Shut* (in which the sound of Qawwali accompanies the orgy at the masked ball). Ethnomusicologists have had to work hard to challenge these kinds of unwitting reflex ascriptions and identifications, not least by pointing out that what is routinely heard as 'Islamic' in a Middle Eastern context may have nothing to do with Islam, or Muslims, at all. Stokes' chapter evaluates historical and ethnographic traditions of thinking in ethnomusicology, and some of the consequences of the division between the two. As Lindholm (Chapter 7, this volume) also suggests of anthropology, the rift between historical and ethnographic study has been debilitating. But in both cases, as Stokes demonstrates, the critical ethnomusicological tradition has done much to disentangle the study of Middle Eastern musics from the Orientalist idea of a musical culture dominated by a historically inert Islam.

Stokes' consideration of the separation between historical and ethnographic perspectives in ethnomusicology returns us to the space of interdisciplinarity with which we began, and which implicitly provides a platform for many of our contributors to survey their disciplinary practice. While the disciplines they review in the essays that follow are diverse, the processes that shape these disciplinary knowledges are shown to share some similarity of form. Only by reflecting on these processes, we believe, will we begin to understand what is involved in interpreting Islam.

References

Ahmed, A.S. 1986. Toward Islamic anthropology. *The American Journal of Islamic Social Sciences* 3 (2): 181–230.

Ahmed, A.S. 1988. *Discovering Islam: Making Sense of Muslim History and Society*. London: Routledge and Kegan Paul.

Ahmed, A.S. 1992. *Postmodernism and Islam: Predicament and Promise*. London: Routledge.

Ba-Yunus, I. and Ahmed, F. 1985. *Islamic Sociology: An Introduction*. Cambridge, The Islamic Academy: Hodder and Stoughton.

Bedford, I. 1994. Debating Muslims: A review article. *Canberra Anthropology* 17 (1): 70–87.

Fischer, M.J. and Abedi, M. 1990. *Debating Muslims: Cultural Dialogue in Postmodernity and Tradition*. Madison: University of Wisconsin Press.

Gellner, E. 1981. *Muslim Society*. Cambridge: Cambridge University Press.

Gellner, E. 1993. The mightier pen? *Times Literary Supplement*, 19 February.

Gilsenan, M. 1990. Very like a camel: The appearance of an anthropologist's Middle East. In R. Fardon (ed.), *Localizing Strategies: Regional Traditions of Ethnographic Writing*. Edinburgh: Scottish Academic Press; Washington, DC: Smithsonian Institution Press.

Halliday, F. 1993. Orientalism and its critics. *British Journal of Middle Eastern Studies* 20 (2): 145–63.

Huntington, S. 1993. The clash of civilizations? *Foreign Affairs*, Summer: 22–49.

Lerner, D. 1958. *The Passing of Traditional Society: Modernizing the Middle East*. New York: Free Press.

Lewis, B. 1993. *Islam and the West*. Oxford: Oxford University Press.

Lindholm, C. 1995. The new Middle Eastern ethnography. *Journal of the Royal Anthropological Institute* 1 (4): 805–20.

Moore-Gilbert, B. 1997. *Postcolonial Theory: Contexts, Practices, Politics*. London: Verso.

Rosaldo, R. 1988. Ideology, place and people without culture. *Cultural Anthropology* 3: 77–87.

Runnymede Trust 1997. *Islamophobia – A Challenge For Us All.* London: Runnymede Trust.
Said, E.W. 1978. *Orientalism.* Harmondsworth: Penguin.
Said, E.W. 1981. *Covering Islam: How the Media and the Experts Determine How We See the Rest of the World.* London: Routledge and Kegan Paul.
Turner, B.S. 1994. *Orientalism, Postmodernism and Globalism.* London: Routledge.
Yeğenoğlu, M. 1998. *Colonial Fantasies: Towards a Feminist Reading of Orientalism.* Cambridge: Cambridge University Press.

2

ORIENTALISM, OR THE POLITICS OF THE TEXT

Bryan S. Turner

Introduction: Orient and Otherness

Perhaps the recent preoccupation with texts, textuality and intertextuality is testimony to the contemporary assumption that any adequate understanding of knowledge must take into account the field of power that constitutes and makes possible such knowledge. We have to understand the self-referencing of texts as an interplay of power, and thus all hermeneutics is an effect of power relations and power struggles. This principle of power/knowledge is clearly borne out in the history of the analysis of the Orient. While the modern debate about western views of the Orient was re-established by Edward Said's *Orientalism* in 1978, the controversy about the character of 'other religions' can be traced back through the encounter between Christian theology and its antagonists. However, Said's controversial paradigm established the notion of 'Orientalism' as a distinctive and pervasive ideology of the Orient as Otherness. This critique has established the foundation for an extensive inquiry into the problematic relationships between political power, sexual desire and intellectual dominance (McClintock 1995; Young 1995).

Said's thesis and its criticisms are well known and I shall merely summarize their major components (see Turner 1994). First, 'the Orient' is constructed in western ideology as a permanent and enduring object of knowledge in opposition to the Occident as its negative and alternative pole. Second, Orientalism creates a stationary East through the essentialization of the divergent cultural phenomena of Oriental societies into a unitary, integrated and coherent object of the scrutiny of western literary and scientific discourse. The Orient is reiterated and interpellated over time and space by these ideological forces; the Orient is thus called up and to account as a subject of western scholarship. While the Occident develops through history in terms of a series of modernizing and violent revolutions, the stationary Orient exists outside of history. Karl Marx in the so-called 'Asiatic mode of production' contended that India and China had no real history, that is, no historical revolutions that brought about significant change in the basis of the social order through the introduction of private property (Turner 1978). Third, the Orient is, in Said's perspective, studied through Michel Foucault's analysis of the necessary combination of power/knowledge, and the lineage of Oriental concepts is mapped out by the historical formation of power between Occident and Orient, namely through the history of imperialism and colonial expansion. For Foucault, the conventional separation of power and knowledge in liberal theory obscures the fact that the Orient is an effect of imperial powers, and cannot be known independently of that power/knowledge combination.

The Foucauldian argument is that discursive formations are constructed around both positive and negative contrasts or dichotomies. These polarities constitute knowledge of an object (Foucault 1972). As a result, Orientalism produces a balance sheet or an audit of negativities between West and East in which the Orient is defined by a series of lacunae: historical stasis, the missing middle class, the erosion or denial of active citizenship, the absence of autonomous cities, the lack of ascetic disciplines and the limitations of instrumental rationality as the critical culture of natural science, industrial capitalism and rational government. In the social sciences, this negative accounting sheet found its classical expression in both Karl Marx's Asiatic mode of production and Max Weber's analysis of patrimonialism (Turner 1996). The absolutist tradition of Oriental polities placed decisive limitations on the capacity for such systems to adapt and evolve. Weber sought the cultural origins of capitalism in asceticism, means–ends rationalism and secularism in *The Protestant Ethic and the Spirit of Capitalism* (Weber 1930). The Orient lacked the dynamic impact of autonomous cities, rational law, work discipline and rational administration. Weber's sociology, then, was organized around a comparative project that involved the analysis of the economic ethics of religious traditions and their impact on the social capacity for transformation.

In the geography of the imagination, the Orient is that part of the political map by which the West has historically and negatively 'oriented' itself. The Orient has been the negative Other that defines the edges and boundaries of the civilized world, and thus marshals the transgressive possibilities of culture. The Occident was part of the ethical cartography of the West that celebrated the Puritan interior of moral responsibility and probity. The noun 'Orient', which defines a geographical arena, is also a verb 'to orient', that is, Orientalism offers a political and psychological positioning that constitutes social identities in a condition of antagonism. Orientalism as a textual practice divided the world into friends and strangers whose endless struggles define 'the political'.

It is this geographic Otherness that defines our subjective inwardness; our being is articulated in a terrain of negativities that are oppositional and, according to Said, permanent and ineluctable. In *Culture and Imperialism*, Said (1993) claims that the modern identity of the West has been defined by its colonies, but these colonies are not merely physical places in a political geography; they also organize the boundaries and borders of our consciousness by defining our attitudes towards, for example, sexuality and race. Within the paradigm of Weber's Protestant Ethic, the aboriginal is defined as somebody who is not only poor and traditional but licentious and lazy. Colonial policy and ideology produced a wide range of national types based on the myth of the lazy native (Alatas 1977). For example, in the evolution of Orientalism, the plays of Shakespeare present a valuable insight into the characterology of such Oriental figures. *The Tempest*, probably written in 1611, was based on naval records describing shipwrecks from the period. Caliban, who is probably modelled on early encounters with the indigenous peoples of the West Indies and North America, is treacherous and dangerous, contrasting as a negative mirror image of Miranda, who is perfect, naïve and beautiful. Caliban's sexual desire for 'Admir'd Miranda' forms part of the moral struggle of the play under the careful scrutiny of the island's patriarch. It is Prospero's rational interventions that master both storms and characters (Tillyard 1958). In this respect it is the foundation of the literary analysis of modern colonialism, because the magical island offered Shakespeare an ideal context for representing the struggles between European reason and its colonial subjects as a confrontation between magic and anarchy, on the one hand, and reason and statecraft, on the other. It was Prospero's neglect of statesmanship that resulted in his original downfall, and his careful management of the sexuality of his island subjects that eventually restores peace and good order to the land.

These components briefly describe the principal features of Said's argument in *Orientalism*. I can now indicate some of the major criticisms of Said (see also Turner 1994). First, he exaggerates the degree of coherence in the western academic discourse on Islam and he also neglects the range of heterogeneous views that characterized different disciplines within the Orientalist sciences. It is difficult to classify neatly and unambiguously Gustave von Grunebaum, Louis Massignon, Wilfred Cantwell Smith, Maxime Rodinson, Montgomery Watt and Marshall G.S. Hodgson in Said's paradigm as occupying the same location within the Orientalist field. In any case, Said concentrates primarily on literary figures and not on historians and social scientists. Second, many radical writers have often used either 'Asia' or 'Islam' as a device to attack or to question western culture.

Both Nietzsche and Foucault, who are obviously crucial in Said's own theoretical evolution, looked towards Islam as a means of critically attacking aspects of western culture of which they disapproved. Nietzsche's attitude may itself be Orientalist, but nevertheless he praised Islam in *The Anti-Christ* as a strong heroic or manly religion, in contrast to Christianity, which he treated as a form of sickness and weakness. Islam is 'noble' because it 'owed its origins to manly instincts, because it said Yes to life' (Nietzsche 1968: 183). He argued that 'In Christianity neither morality nor religion come into contact with reality at any point' (Nietzsche 1968: 125). All of its main theological concepts are imaginary. By contrast, Nietzsche praised Buddhism for its realism, its philosophical objectivity and rationalism; Buddhism had already dispensed with the concept of God long before Christianity appeared on the historical horizon. Nietzsche's studies in comparative religions are ironic comments on the problems of religious truth in an epoch of relativism and perspectivism. His comparative critique of religion as sickness provided a foundational ethic for the analysis of the moral value of modern cultures. In Weber's sociology, this critique was redirected towards an analysis of the religious bases of utilitarian economics (Stauth and Turner 1988). In a similar fashion, Foucault in his journalistic writing on Iran in *Corriere della Sera* treated the Iranian revolution as a significant 'spiritual revolution'. The Iranian revolution provided Foucault with an occasion to express his emotional commitment to the idea of a spiritual revolution as a way of life, which contrasted with the mundane and routine reality of the everyday world. The religious revolution was a triumph of values over the profane world of materialist activity.

Finally, if Orientalism expresses a particular combination of power and knowledge, then it must vary and change over time and between different national configurations and traditions. Because Said concentrated primarily on French Orientalism, he neglected important variations between, for example, English or German branches of Orientalism. Furthermore, while there is good reason to believe that classical Orientalism created 'Islam' as a changeless essence, Oriental discourse itself changes over time. In this chapter I distinguish between classical Orientalism, which was dominant in academic circles until the 1930s, and weaker, less strident and more uncertain forms of Orientalism since 1945. It is important to recognize that there have been significant changes in Orientalism since the second half of the twentieth century that reflect changes in state relations with globalization, the changing status of intellectuals in modern society, and political changes following the collapse of communism. In short, globalization has brought about a sense of confusion in the world map that has produced a degree of (dis)orientation in contemporary scholarship.

Because Said's analysis was driven to a large measure by his commitment to the Palestinian movement in general and by the contradictory status of the Palestinian intellectual in the United States in particular, his attention was oriented outwards to the question of imperialism and post-colonialism. As a consequence, there is a neglect in his work of the parallel internal dynamic to Orientalism that we may call 'Occidentalism' (Carrier 1995). While Orientalism created a series of stereotypes towards outsiders and strangers who inhabited the new colonies of emerging capitalism, it also set up a collection of negative pictures of subordinate or marginal populations through a process of internal colonialism. In Britain in particular, the so-called 'Celtic Fringe' represented a challenge to the Englishness of the Anglican Establishment in the formation of the nation-state (Hechter 1975). The Irish were a suppressed 'black' interior that had to be managed and controlled in order to protect England as 'a green and pleasant land' (Lebow 1976).

If Caliban represents one formative figure in the evolution of European colonial literature, Shylock presents another. *The Merchant of Venice*, which was probably written in 1596, has some parallels with Marlowe's *The Jew of Malta*, and expresses the anti-Semitism of Elizabethan England. There is a general anti-Semitism in Europe, in which antagonism to Jews has often accompanied hostility to Muslims. Generally speaking, the critique of Orientalism has not noticed the ironic connection between two forms of racism, namely against Arabs and against Jews. In his Introduction to *Orientalism*, Said (1978: 27–8) writes that in

> addition, and by an almost inescapable logic, I have found myself writing the history of a strange, secret sharer of Western anti-Semitism. That anti-Semitism and, as I have discussed it in its Islamic branch, Orientalism resemble each other very closely is a historical, cultural, and political truth that needs only to be mentioned to an Arab Palestinian for its irony to be perfectly understood.

In a reply to his critics, Said also noted the parallels between what he calls 'Islamophobia' and anti-Semitism. There are thus two discourses of Orientalism for Semites, one relating to Islam and the other to Judaism. In my own *Religion and Social Theory* (Turner 1983: 29), I argued that within Orientalism, there are two related discourses for Semites, namely 'the Islamic discourse of gaps and the Judaic discourse of contradictions'. By this observation, I meant that while Islam had been defined by its absences (of rationality, cities, asceticism, and so forth), Judaism had been defined by the contradictory nature of its religious injunctions, where, for example, its dietary laws transferred the quest for personal salvation into a set of ritualistic prescriptions that inhibited the full expression of its monotheistic rationalism according to Weber's analysis in *Ancient Judaism* (1952). For Weber, the rationality of Jewish monotheistic prophecy was undermined by a ritualistic dietary scheme. The West oriented its identity between two poles – the lazy, sensual Arab and the untrustworthy Jew. Weber criticized the Islamic paradise as merely a sensual reward for warriors; Jewish communities have suffered from the label of a 'pariah status group', because their social and geographical migrations were seen to be politically dangerous.

I will argue shortly that Jews disturbed the consciousness of the Christian West because they were cosmopolitan and strange. The notion of the 'wandering Jew' pinpoints the idea that their commitment to the national polity could not be taken for granted. Hitler's hatred of Viennese Jews arose from his experience of a seathing mass of unfriendly and strange faces (Oxaal 1990). While Jews were strange, they were also guilty of religious treachery. Now rejection of these two stereotypes was crucial if Christianity as the foundation of western values was to maintain its difference from other Abrahamic faiths. Precisely because Judaism and Islam shared so much in common (monotheism, prophetic and charismatic revelation, the religion of the Book, and a radical eschatology), they had to be separated culturally by a discourse of ethnic and moral difference. Jewish separate identity raised significant questions about the character of civilization processes in Europe (Russell 1996: 83).

We can now summarize this introduction by showing that Orientalism can be described in terms of two dimensions. First, there is internal and external Orientalism in which attention is focused inwards on national subcommunities or outwards towards an externalized Otherness. Second, there is a dimension that is divided into positive and negative evaluations. By combining these two dimensions, we can produce a four-cell property space that generates a useful typology of the politics of Oriental interpretations.

Classical Orientalism involved a negative/external framework of critical rejection of the Other as alien and dangerous. The stereotypes of the 'lazy Arab' and the 'wandering Jew' perfectly express this interpretative option. In the opposite direction, positive/internal Occidentalism identified some communities within the nation-state as a positive expression of identity and consciousness. For example, in Victorian England there was a romantic view of Scottishness in which the heroic Scotsman could safely enter the English consciousness. Queen Victoria did much to legitimize this image of the brave Scottish soldier as the cornerstone of British colonial power. This position contrasts with internal/negative

Occidentalism, which treated the Irish as a dangerous, but ultimately pathetic, adversary within the evolving English polity. Finally, there is positive/external Orientalism, which converted the native peoples of North America into 'the Noble Savage'. This typology helps us to understand that Orientalism also produced Occidentalism, and that racial stereotypes can be both positive and negative. For Islam, there was a positive view of the manly ethic of Arabic nomadism that was embraced by writers like T.E. Lawrence. There was a strong movement of Orientalism that assumed a positive view of the East as a land of promise, sensuality and difference that contrasted with the pale grey reality of bourgeois Europe. This mood was closely associated with the aristocratic tradition of the Grand Tour (Tregaskis 1979) and with the sensuality of Gerard de Nerval's *Voyage en Orient* (1980).

Imaginary states and classical Orientalism

The creation of nation-states in Europe from the seventeenth century necessarily involved the creation of nationalistic 'imagined communities' (Anderson 1983), which asserted and partly created homogeneous populations that were held together, against the pressures of class and community, by nationalistic ideologies. If we identify the Treaty of Westphalia in 1648 as the origin of the modern world system of nation-states, then state formation throughout Europe involved the creation of nationalist identities on the basis of a double colonization, both internal and external. Here again 'the wandering Jew' provided the pretext in many European states for 'ethnic cleansing' in order to create a homogeneous population, but in a less violent form one can find various political and social pressures to create civil societies on the basis of common languages, a shared religious culture and a single ethnic identity.

What produced this process of cultural standardization? One argument is that the rise of the system of nation-states coincided with the rise of national forms of competitive capitalism. It was the capitalist mode of production that undermined the conventional patterns of rural communities based on traditional forms of agrarianism. Industrial capitalism saw the emergence, through urbanization and the demographic revolutions of the late eighteenth and the early nineteenth century, of a large urban proletariat that was a potential threat to the new order of nation-states. Nationalism was created by nation-states either as a substitute for, or in combination with, religion as the social glue of an urban society that was organized around conflicting class structures.

The political and cultural processes of nation formation involved various forms of internal colonialism whereby minority or subordinate cultures and traditions were destroyed or excluded. However, these violent forms of exclusion were also accompanied by what one might regard as more positive modes of inclusion and incorporation, namely the building of modern patterns of social citizenship (James 1996). In an influential argument, Michael Mann (1988) has argued that the history of social citizenship and the welfare state was a history of 'ruling class strategies' to include and co-opt the working class into capitalist society through the construction of reformist policies of social security. Citizenship confers not only economic and political rights, but also socio-cultural identities, loyalties and commitments. It thus establishes exclusionary boundaries and borders that define insiders and outsiders. Therefore the nature and extent of the processes of incorporation into citizenship by various combinations of descent and residence are highly instructive comparative indicators of national identity; for example, migration policies that determine the opportunities of naturalization by residence are strong indications of the openness of social communities. Migration policy is thus a clear and definite statement of the state's claim to sovereignty over both people and territory. One of the primary functions of (rich) nation-states is to keep (poor) foreigners out. Although this exclusionary thrust is primarily based on economic and military interests, it is also deeply cultural and symbolic. To quote Norton (1993: 55–6): 'In choosing what they will reject, nations determine what they signify and what they will become. The recognition that polities are defined in difference should teach them to choose their enemies with care. Their enmities define them. They determine the direction of development, the distribution of resources.'

The imagined communities that were constituted by the growth of literacy and nationalist strategies formed the social basis of the new nation-states arising out of the Treaty of Westphalia. I have argued that these imagined communities then constituted themselves by a double enmity – outwards as Orientalism and inwards as Occidentalism. The enemies of these states were constructed around racist parameters and were seen to be communities that existed at the borders of society. The wandering Jew represented a dangerous cosmopolitanism, and therefore the loyalties of Jews were seen to be suspect. Gypsies had the same qualities, because their quasi-nomadic existence and 'Oriental' origins set them apart. Muslim Arabs occupied another borderland, one that separated reason and asceticism from luxury and lasciviousness. The paintings of Jean Léon Gérôme, whose painting of the youthful snake charmer adorns the cover of Said's *Orientalism*, are a perfect illustration of the genre of French Orientalism, which depicted the East as a place of magical sexuality and sensuality. Again Shakespeare's figure of the 'Moor' in Othello captures the sense of sexual danger to the stability of Christian society.

My argument in this chapter is thus that Orientalism in its strong, classical form is a necessary product of rising nationalism that created the solidaristic basis of the western polity from the middle of the seventeenth century. Jews and Muslims were special targets of this discourse because their relationship to Christianity was paradoxically too close. A robust form of identification with the state was required because the economic market in capitalism has a corrosive effect on religion and community, the traditional binding forces of pre-capitalist societies. In Great Britain, for example, the distinctive regions were partly eroded by the growth of literacy and by the dominance of English culture over its Celtic margins; one could also argue that through the Victorian period monarchy grew as a crucial political linkage of the United Kingdom. I want to suggest that we can think of this type of nationalist consolidation along two dimensions of loyalty and solidarity. Following an anthropological notion, I shall distinguish between thick and thin solidarity. In Émile Durkheim's sociological commentaries on

Australian aboriginal communities there is a clear notion of strong, thick, effervescent solidarity that characterized tribalism. Traditional religious ceremonies generate a thick solidarity, characterized by its emotional intensity, complexity and duration. Modern patterns of eating with the McDonaldization of social relations are thin and sporadic. Following an expression of Marshall McLuhan (1964), I identify hot and cool loyalties. Hot attachments are intensive and passionate, whereas cool loyalty follows the sociological notion of role distance. By combining these dimensions, we can produce a matrix to understand social commitments and solidarities. Nineteenth-century nationalism when combined with racism resulted in hot/thick identities that defined the citizen in terms of a clear boundary or border between insiders and outsiders. Classical Orientalism was a product of strong identification in terms of citizens who enjoyed thick solidarity in a nationalist civil society and who were expected to display hot loyalties in adherence to and the service of the state. Orientalism and Occidentalism in their strong forms followed the emergence of hot/thick nationalism as the appropriate culture of the nation-state. In this chapter, this matrix provides a general orientation to the politics of text, but I do not attempt to analyse every possible cell.

The end of classical Orientalism?

A series of events have transformed classical Orientalism into a more ironic and reflexive view of cultural difference. First, political globalization and the erosion of the constitutional sovereignity of the nation-states have disrupted the old Westphalian pattern of separate and autonomous states. Economic globalization has created rapid and voluminous flows of labour, goods and services. Of course, it is important not to exaggerate these global processes. With the increasing dominance of transnational corporations, there are newly emergent patterns of politics and cultural structures between states. Alongside these changes in the international system, there has been a period of decolonization that started shortly after the Second World War. Classical Orientalism was the expression of a dominant mood of imperialism. Decolonization is associated with a weaker and more hesitant pattern of Orientalist assumptions. However, it is important to recognize that despite the growth of a borderless world, there are still strong patterns of economic hegemony. In this context, overt political imperialism has been replaced by more covert and indirect structures of economic colonialism (Miyoshi 1996).

Second, with the collapse of organized communism and the end of the Cold War in 1989, there has been an identification of Islam as the principal threat to the West. The Gulf War resulted in a further demonization of the Arab as the main antagonist in the international system (Halliday 1997). Increasing conflict in Israel between right-wing religious groups and Hizbollah Shi'ite forces has reinforced the negative view of Arab fanaticism. Television coverage of Israeli civilians blown to bits by suicide bomb attacks has resurrected the image of the secretive, irrational Arab. Islam is, of course, also perceived as an internal

European threat. The Rushdie Affair (Asad 1993) had many dimensions, but one centred on the feeling that Iran's radical Shi'ite leadership could strike at any location in Europe and North America; Islam had become a major threat to civil liberties and individual freedoms in Europe.

Third, Said's theory of what one might call 'one-way Orientalism' neglected the fact of Japanese economic imperialism. For many Asians, economic imperialism means Japanese imperialism. With the growth of the Asian Tiger Economies until the late 1990s, the notion of the lazy native could not be easily sustained. In addition, Said's thesis understates the strength of racial images that have been generated against western intrusion. Orientalism is always relational and dialogic. The issue of 'the yellow cab women' and general dislike of white foreigners or *Gaijin* give a clear expression of Japanese ambiguity towards contact with the outside world (Kelsky 1996). 'Yellow cab women', in the sexual imaginary of racial stereotypes against male outsiders, are defined as rich, sexually aggressive women who travel to exotic locations in search of sexual conquests. They challenge the image of the chaste Japanese woman in *Madame Butterfly.* These 'yellow' women can, like the yellow taxi cab, be ridden at any time. In this discourse *Gaijin* (white men) are often compared with cruel Japanese men. Japan can be taken as an illustration of what we might call 'reverse Orientalism'. International racial stereotypes force us to consider a dialogue of Oriental positions that are mutually negative. One specific example was the accusation that the Asian currency crisis of late 1997 was caused by international Jewry, a charge that raised obvious comparisons with Hitler's attack on Jewish economic interests in the 1930s; an accusation made notably by Malaysia's Prime Minister Mahatmir bin Mohamad, who stormed into the IMF annual meeting in Hong Kong in September 1997 denouncing George Soros and 'Jewish speculators' (Coyle 2000: 20).

Fourth, Said's original theory did not consider the responses to these colonial changes, namely the growth of fundamentalism in many of the 'world religions' as a defensive protest against incorporation and dilution into western consumerism and western life-styles. With the failure of communism, Islamic fundamentalism becomes one of the few remaining political options in the Third World as a protest against secularization and consumerism. One could also see the movement for the Islamization of science in the same light, namely as an attempt to check secularization and incorporation into a western model of scientific knowledge (Stenberg 1996). Islamic fundamentalism challenges the universalistic claims of western natural and social sciences, and offers an alternative model of understanding and significance (Tibi 1995). Other cultural movements have also questioned the dominance of western literature and arts, resulting in a widespread debate on decolonization, subaltern studies and hybridity. These social and cultural movements can all be seen as an erosion of the authority and legitimacy of the English literary canon as the principal criterion of value.

Finally, these socio-economic changes have also brought into question the role of the public intellectual in the West. I follow Zygmunt Bauman's argument in *Legislators and Interpreters* (1987) that in postmodern societies the state no longer assumes responsibility for the protection and promotion of high culture and instead relies upon the market to determine what constitutes cultural taste and distinction. Intellectuals no longer have the authority of the state and the elite institutions behind them when they come to pronounce on culture. As a result, they have stopped being cultural legislators and are now merely cultural interpreters. Intellectuals have become increasingly uncoupled from the state. With the rise of nationalism, intellectuals had been important in defining national cultures – hence, for example, the importance of ethnographic studies in defining and shaping core values and standards. The commercialization of culture, the growth of mass culture, the integration of high and low culture in postmodernity, and the transformation of universities by economic rationalism has undermined the traditional role of the public intellectual. The great popularity of cultural studies and the decline of traditional departments of English literature in many British and Commonwealth universities are indicative of these changes in the modern university. Intellectuals no longer have the authority and state support that characterized the intellectuals of the late nineteenth century in the heyday of classical Orientalism.

We can also understand this decline of the public intellectual as an example of postmodernization in a culture that is increasingly dominated by information technology. If we define postmodernism as scepticism towards grand narratives (Lyotard 1984), then in the contemporary world intellectuals are unwilling or unable to defend grand narratives, since academic intellectuals no longer have the authority to pronounce on such matters. This uncertainty about what Richard Rorty (1989) calls our 'final vocabularies' means that self-confidence to pronounce on other people's cultures is generally uncharacteristic of contemporary intellectuals. Anthropological relativism and postmodern uncertainty are dominant moods of the academy, at least in the humanities and the social sciences. Hence strong classical Orientalism has been disoriented, leaving behind weak, fragmented and contradictory versions of it. There are obviously exceptions to this scepticism towards grand narratives in writers like Francis Fukuyama's triumphalist liberalism (1992), but generally the mood of academics appears to me more inclined to uncertainty, self-doubt or guilt. Reflexive modernity is less certain of universal truths and more inclined to recognize local and particularistic visions of contingent and incomplete realities.

Conclusion: Postmodernism and cosmopolitan irony

Rorty (1989) has argued that postmodernism involves or requires irony, that is, a sense of distance from our beliefs (our final vocabularies), because as postmodern liberals we will be uncertain as to their ultimate validity. This irony is another way of expressing the idea that intellectuals will remain sceptical about grand narratives.

Why is this? I think it is partly that intellectuals have become disconnected from the nation-state or the national culture, and they therefore operate within an academic marketplace that is global and largely borderless. They are increasingly cosmopolitan in their outlook and orientation, precisely because they are disconnected from specific cultures and local political systems. Their local authority may indeed be challenged by the global network made possible by electronic delivery systems. Even if these university intellectuals do not have the funds to travel to international conferences, they are linked through the web to a discourse that is global rather than local. From a national or nationalistic point of view, they are cosmopolitan in their networks and their commitment to the local society is typically thin/cool rather than hot/thick. The thick solidarities and the hot loyalties of previous social systems, which were based on national culture, have been replaced by cosmopolitan distance and indifference.

These cosmopolitan intellectuals are the new symbolic analysts, who are probably more likely to work for the think-tank of a global corporation than for a public university. Their pattern of commitment could be said to be Rortian in its disloyalty, irony and scepticism. They are the individuals who are driving the debate about borderless worlds within which one will not need to orient to any particular pole. If they evince any trace of Orientalism, it will be thin/cool preferences for multiculturalism. Such cosmopolitan intellectuals may well be accused of cultural prostitution, in a context where the marketization of knowledge means a transfer of loyalty and identity to a more ironically indifferent pattern of the global village. The traditional game of the Orientalist text appears to have come to an end.

References

Alatas, S.H. 1977. *The Myth of the Lazy Native.* London: Frank Cass.

Anderson, B. 1983. *Imagined Communities: Reflections on the Origin and Spread of Nationalism.* London: Verso.

Asad, T. 1993. *Genealogies of Religion: Discipline and Reasons of Power in Christianity and Islam.* Baltimore and London: Johns Hopkins University Press.

Bauman, Z. 1987. *Legislators and Interpreters: On Modernity, Post-modernity and Intellectuals.* Cambridge: Polity.

Carrier, J.G. (ed.) 1995. *Occidentalism: Images of the West.* Oxford: Clarendon Press.

Coyle, D. 2000. *Governing the World Economy.* Cambridge: Polity.

Foucault, M. 1972. *The Archaeology of Knowledge.* London: Tavistock.

Fukuyama, F. 1992. *The End of History and the Last Man.* New York: Free Press.

Halliday, F. 1997. Neither treason nor conspiracy: reflections on media coverage of the Gulf War 1990–1991. *Citizenship Studies* 1 (2): 157–72.

Hechter, M. 1975. *Internal Colonialism: The Celtic Fringe in British National Development 1536–1966.* London: Routledge and Kegan Paul.

James, P. 1996. *Nation Formation: Towards a Theory of Abstract Community.* London: Sage.

Kelsky, K. 1996. Flirting with the foreign: interracial sex in Japan's 'international' age. In R. Wilson and W. Dissanayake (eds), *Global/Local: Cultural Production and the Transnational Imaginary.* Durham, NC, and London: Duke University Press.

Lebow, R. 1976. *White Britain, Black Ireland: The Influence of Stereotypes on Colonial Policy.* Philadelphia: Institute for the Study of Human Issues.

Lyotard, J.-F. 1984. *The Postmodern Condition: A Report on Knowledge.* Manchester: Manchester University Press.

McClintock, A. 1995. *Imperial Leather: Race, Gender and Sexuality in the Colonial Contest.* London and New York: Routledge.

McLuhan, M. 1964. *Understanding Media: The Extensions of Man.* Toronto: McGraw Hill.

Mann, M. 1988. *States, War and Capitalism: Studies in Political Sociology.* Oxford: Basil Blackwell.

Miyoshi, M. 1996. A borderless world? From colonialism to transnationalism and the decline of the nation-state. In R. Wilson and W. Dissanayake (eds), *Global/Local: Cultural Production and the Transnational Imaginary.* Durham, NC, and London: Duke University Press.

Nerval, G. de 1980. *Voyage en Orient* (2 vols). Paris: Flammarion.

Nietzsche, F. 1968. *Twilight of the Idols: The Anti-Christ.* Harmondsworth: Penguin.

Norton, A. 1993. *Reflections on Political Identity.* Baltimore: Johns Hopkins University Press.

Oxaal, I. 1990. Die Juden im Wien des jungen Hitler: Historische und soziologische Aspekte. In G. Boltz, I. Oxaal and M. Pollak (eds), *Eine zerstoerte Kultur: Juedisches Leben und Anti-semitismus in Wien seit dem 19. Jahrhundert.* Buchloe: Druck und Verlag Obermayer.

Rorty, R. 1989. *Contingency, Irony and Solidarity.* Cambridge: Cambridge University Press.

Russell, S. 1996. *Jewish Identity and Civilizing Processes.* London: Macmillan.

Said, E.W. 1978. *Orientalism.* Harmondsworth: Penguin.

Said, E.W. 1993. *Culture and Imperialism.* New York: Alfred A. Knopf.

Stauth, G. and Turner, B.S. 1988. *Nietzsche's Dance: Resentment, Reciprocity and Resistance in Social Life.* Oxford: Blackwell.

Stenberg, L. 1996. *The Islamization of Science: Four Muslim Positions Developing an Islamic Modernity.* Lund: Novapress.

Tibi, B. 1995. Culture and knowledge: the politics of Islamization of knowledge as a postmodern project? The fundamentalist claim to de-westernization. *Theory Culture & Society* 12 (1): 1–24.

Tillyard, E.M.W. 1958. *Shakespeare's Last Plays.* London: Chatto and Windus.

Tregaskis, H. 1979. *Beyond the Grand Tour.* London: Ascent Books.

Turner, B.S. 1978. *Marx and the End of Orientalism.* London: Allen and Unwin.

Turner, B.S. 1983. *Religion and Social Theory.* London: Heinemann.

Turner, B.S. 1994. *Orientalism, Postmodernism and Globalism.* London: Routledge.

Turner, B.S. 1996. *For Weber: Essays on the Sociology of Fate.* London: Sage.

Weber, M. 1930. *The Protestant Ethic and the Spirit of Capitalism.* London: George Allen and Unwin.

Weber, M. 1952. *Ancient Judaism.* Glencoe, IL: Free Press.

Young, R.J.C. 1995. *Colonial Desire: Hybridity in Theory, Culture and Race.* London and New York: Routledge.

3

RESEARCHING THE RADICAL

The quest for a new perspective

Beverley Milton-Edwards

> The focus on radicalism and the equation of Islam with an extremism that threatens to confront the West has become commonplace. Too often we are exposed in the media and the literature to a sensationalised, monolithic approach which reinforces facile generalisations and stereotypes rather than challenging our understanding of the 'who' and the 'why' of history, the specific causes or reasons behind the headlines. (Esposito 1992: 173)

This chapter, on researching and writing on radical Islam, will focus on a number of debates that currently characterize the discipline of politics and Islamic studies in general. At the heart of these debates is a central question that asks of us: 'What terms and values do we utilize in our research and writing on radical Islam?' The nature of these debates is fierce, impassioned and reflects on the personal politics, perceived or otherwise, of those who research radical Islam in either its theoretical, theological, state or organizational form. I wish to engage in four tasks. First, I examine the current fascination with radical Islam and ascertain its origins. Second, I wish to state some of the most important arguments associated with researching the subject, including the current divisions within politics and Islamic studies among western academics, namely that between conservative Orientalists/neo-Orientalists and apologists. Third, I will explore the new discourse of religious terrorism as an example of researching radical Islam, and will consider postmodernist debates about the 'other', the way in which radical Islam has been signified through terrorism studies, and the impact of this largely neo-Orientalist approach. Finally, I hope to suggest a new approach to researching radical Islam that takes account of hitherto ignored feminist epistemology and includes a critique of the current patriarchal nature of scholarship on radical Islam. My primary focus will be the Middle East, on which I feel best qualified to speak and where the majority of academic work on radical Islam to date has been conducted. It is not my intention to seek confrontation (even though the genre of radical Islam is premised on such notions). I do, however, question the domination of particular approaches and views that I believe actually contribute more to confusion than to understanding regarding radical Islam in the way that scholars write about it.

Putting the radical into Islam

A common view of Islam and its current political manifestations as frequently portrayed in the western media and much conservative-Orientalist academic writing can be summed up in the following way: Islamic politics is generally perceived as radical, associated with violence, terrorism and attempts to bring about the revolutionary overthrow of modern secular government. As one author asserts, 'in Islam's war against the West and the struggle to build Islamic states at home, the end justifies the means ... radical political Islam placed atop these societies in the Middle East has created a combustible mixture. ... They are, and are likely to remain, anti-western, anti-American and anti-Israeli' (Miller 1993: 33). An Islamic state, meanwhile, represents theocratic, conservative, radical, anti-democratic and violent politics. Islam, from this perspective of politics, is commonly associated with a threat to the international order as we know it, and Muslims are presented as engaged in a *jihad* against the West. Bernard Lewis (1990: 53), the patriarch of conservative Orientalism, champions this perspective, declaring that 'the Muslim world is again seized by an intense – and violent – resentment of the West. Suddenly America has become the archenemy, the incarnation of evil, the diabolic opponent of all that is good, and specifically, for Muslims, of Islam'. This view of Islam is not new. Indeed, Islam has traditionally been viewed by western scholars of a variety of disciplines in this way. What is perceived as a deep connection between radicalism, religion and an associated violence sets Islam apart from other religious traditions.

As such, the view that Islam was established through the 'sword', that the Prophet Muhammad was a radical military and political leader as well as a man of holy vision, has sunk deep into the collective cultural consciousness of the West. V.S. Naipaul, writing in *Among the Believers: An Islamic Journey* (1981: 16), encapsulates this view:

> Islam, going by what I saw of it from the outside, was less metaphysical and more direct than Hinduism. In this religion of fear and reward, oddly compounded with war and worldly grief. ... The glories of this religion were in the remote past; it had generated nothing like a Renaissance. Muslim countries, where not colonised, were despotisms and nearly all, before oil, were poor.

In addition, the Crusader past remains with us today to shape and tailor the West's view of Islam, the stereotype exaggerated by time and the twists of history and vice versa. All this leads us to a view of Islam reflected in western popular culture – from books, films, television, photo images and newspaper reports to a perspective supported by a corpus of academic research from the conservative-Orientalist school that is associated with themes of militancy, radicalism, violence, revolution, the world of war (*dar al harb*) and the world of peace (*dar al Islam*), only the West's world of war is Islam and its world of peace revolves around some global order dominated by democratic and benign western powers. This leads one to question the role of those who research and write specifically about radical Islam, in both its abstract and concrete forms, in either perpetuating or advancing such perspectives or attempting a more careful reading of that which is radical Islam.

In the last two decades, however, it has also been argued, by authors such as Fred Halliday, that Islam itself and, more specifically, fundamentalist Muslims have played a part in the current western fixation with the radical rather than other representations of the religion. It is asserted that Muslim leaders from Algiers to Harlem have urged their followers to return to the 'straight path' and practise their religion as it was intended. It is the fundamentalists who encourage the notion of the Muslim billions empowered by a return to the 'faith'; a faith commonly perceived as militant and radical is viewed as a real threat by many westerners, who see such aspirations as a declaration of war from Islam. The conservative Orientalists also argue that it is Islam that has invented the western threat. As such, it is asserted that Islam itself has done much to exaggerate the fear or threat posed by its own revival. Within the Islamic world itself the accusations levied by the West cannot simply be refuted. As Halliday (1996: 110) reminds us, Islamists have done much to create and perpetuate mutual suspicion and hostility between, to paraphrase Anderson (1983), two 'imagined communities': the neo-Crusader West and the Muslim fundamentalist East. The revival of faith, however, in the Muslim context, is not perceived as the same as the revival of faith in the Christian context, where evangelical movements are not perceived as a threat to any regional or international order. As Roy (1994: 203) argues, 'It has been a long time since Christianity was Islam's other. Even if there is a religious revival among Christians and Jews, it is in no way parallel to that of the fundamentalists.' The revival of Islam is a new menace, is radical, fundamentalist (even neo-fundamentalist) and associated with acts of extremism and terrorism that pose a threat, strategic and political, to the global order. In this context, any act of global terror or violence is initially perceived as Islamically inspired; Islam is held guilty until proven innocent. This monolithic vision of Islam has persisted and become pervasive, and the culture industry in print, spoken word and film supports, portrays and further exaggerates this view.

The view of Islam as radical Islam works in an insidious manner, from Disney's *Aladdin*, to Hollywood's *Executive Decision* or *The Siege*, and persistent television images of masked Muslim terrorists brandishing the Qur'an in the right hand and a kalashnikov in the left. Indeed, it is generally agreed in the world of publishing and the media that the images of Muslim violence pictured on the covers of books sell, while passive images of Muslims at prayer or helping the needy do not. Televisual images are saturated with unadulterated radicalism and the associated violence: bombs on the Paris subway; letter-bombs in London; kidnappings in Lebanon; war in Afghanistan; revolution in Iran; beheadings in Saudi Arabia; the terror attack on the World Trade Center; the terror training camps in Sudan and Iran and Islamic terrorists in Damascus; suicide bombers on buses in Tel Aviv; special documentaries and news features about terror connections from Kabul to Kettering, Baghdad to Baltimore, Libya to Lyon; 'Jihad USA' – the Muslim threat is everywhere. The threat is associated with the radical nature of Islam itself. This threat becomes the West's chief connection with Islam. The West engages in psychological linkages that unconsciously associate the facile – palm trees, sand and deserts – with its fears – Islam, terrorists, guns and *jihad.* The conflicts that beset the West's own societies, the threats of violence that characterize our own contemporary context, pale in significance to Islam. Even the war in Northern Ireland (with all its class, religious and ethnic permutations) is nothing compared to Islam; as a Belfast taxi driver once pointed out to me, 'Now, it may be bad here but you wouldn't catch me hanging out with them Hamas boys. They could teach Ian Paisley a thing or two about religion.' Strange words from a man who until the cease-fires of 1994 and 1997 daily faced the threat of death from paramilitary violence in his own society. Yet his fear of Islam was greater.

This fear is based on an image of Islam as radical and violent. It is the perception rather than the reality that matters. It would, therefore, be nothing new to state that, for example, during the Cold War the perception of the Soviet menace widespread in the West ultimately bore little resemblance to the strategic reality. Similarly with Islam. Our perceptions have been shaped by the research of a variety of academic disciplines on radical Islam and the attention such work has been given in the popular representation of Islam through the media in the current age. Over two decades ago Edward Said (1978: 298), in his thinly veiled attack on such writing, pointed out that the impact of such work has been to present Islam as 'a series of reductions and eliminations by which Islam could be represented as a closed system of exclusions'. This reduction of Islam, Said argued, places violence and, more specifically, acts of terrorism high on the Muslim agenda, particularly in the contemporary era when Muslims struggle with the forces of modernization and development. However, many writers over the past two decades or so have disagreed with this approach and have argued that fundamentalist, radical Islam is 'much ado about something' (Kramer 1993: 39). The construction by the authors whom Said identifies as 'Orientalist' is sold as real empirical and acceptable evidence that the principal preoccupation of the Islamic faith is radicalism and bloodthirsty violence, and that Muslims 'thrive on repression' (Kramer 1993: 41). The Muslim, as Said argues, is represented as a negative 'other' by the tradition of Orientalism that has characterized western scholarship of the Middle East.

In this field of scholarship the Muslim, to reflect Laclau's (1996) approach, is portrayed as a political signifier that is filled, by the Orientalists, with a series of presumptions that lead inevitably to its negative signification. Thus, the Muslim or Islam can only be represented and understood properly in the negative, contributing further to a Saidian 'other' in a classic Orientalist sense. Islam is portrayed as radical and a curse that is only significant in its malign and negative intent if contrasted against the Judaeo-Christian West. Radical Islam (and associated violence and terror) only acquires its meaning because it is different from Christian traditions of pacifism and just war. In the development of writing on radical Islam many of the authors of this approach have often resorted to the construction and experience of social antagonism as part of the discourse. The 'other' is represented in the construction of a frontier and an identity that prohibit the development of a full and positive identity for Muslims. Reality is antagonism, both internally within Muslim society and outside it where fundamentalists wage a war against the West.

Unfortunately, Said's contribution to debunking the Orientalist dominance of researching radical Islam did not play an important part in emerging scholarship of Islam and politics in the early 1980s. Thus, much of the research and writing that appeared on the revolution in Iran continued to characterize political Islam as a wholly radical and violent phenomenon. In addition, the Iranian example, despite its Shi'a Persian characteristics, was held up as a reflection of the status of Islam throughout the region. Research on Islam and politics from this point largely became dominated by the attempt to write about the radical menace. Thus, despite Said's arguments, researching radical Islam, analysing the radical threat, seeking it out in movements throughout the Middle East remained the chief preoccupation of a variety of writers and fieldworkers from both the academic world and the media. Islam itself, rather than particular organizations or groups, was ascribed a radical character. Hence, work like Emmanuel Sivan's *Radical Islam, Medieval Theology and Modern Politics* (1985) promoted a thesis that Islam's failure to confront modernity and secularism (something that Muslims themselves recognize) had given rise to ordeal and discord (*mihna wa fitna*), compelling the faithful into 'pitched battle' against the evil of their own societies. Writers like Sivan (1985: xi) believe that radical Islam is the 'cutting edge of the Islamic resurgence' and, therefore, represents the 'revival movement as a whole'.

The 'radical' prefix in Islam, according to this perspective, is supposed to denote a variety of characteristics, including law-breaking, violence, militancy, fundamentalism, conservatism, hostility to the West, terrorism, authoritarianism, clerical rule and revolution. Since the 1980s, radical Islamic movements have now been 'discovered' and described in every country of the Middle East and beyond. The threat that these groups allegedly pose is both to internal political systems and, increasingly, to the global order. As such, one presumes, these groups can be distinguished from other Islamic movements that have reformist, moderate and non-revolutionary aims. Or can they?

As we have seen above, other writers, like Sivan (1985), argue that the radical element is representative in some way of the 'resurgence' phenomenon. A problem, therefore, with the current 'radical' prefix and the meanings associated with it is that almost every manifestation of political Islam in the contemporary era may variously be described as 'radical'. This radical character and ascription to a variety of organizations, movements and state policies only heightens the degree of anxiety and fear aroused in the West. Academic research on radical Islam has been primarily political in nature due to the predominant association between religion and politics ascribed to the phenomenon itself. Nevertheless, more recently signs of an interdisciplinary approach to the subject have emerged and largely support the research and discourse on radical Islam that the conservative Orientalists have themselves described as apologist. The apologists have played their part in opening up the field of research on radical Islam. Yet politics remains prominent, its contribution to researching radical Islam has been controversial, and has played a major part in shaping popular understanding of Islam. To an extent, the postmodern wave that has struck at other aspects of the discipline of politics is currently largely under-utilized by the political scientists researching radical Islam, many of whom prefer the traditional methods of explaining Islamic politics even in the modern secularist post-Enlightenment age.

One field of scholarship where an attempt was made to counter the conservative-Orientalist hegemony emerged from some Muslim and Arab scholars of the religion. These scholars of radical Islam have attempted to rethink the theoretical and ideological framework in which many western scholars are located. Many, working from a secular leftist perspective, have challenged the assumptions behind much western scholarship and research on the subject. Orientalism, for example, has always had its Muslim and Arab critics, including Said (1978) and al-Azun (1981). The Muslim/Arab critique of western scholarship on radical Islam is distinguished by two strands. The first is inherently linked to the aforementioned Orientalist critique increasingly prominent in works on radical Islam by scholars such as Ayubi (1991), Haddad et al. (1991), al-Azmeh (1993), and Hussein et al. (1984). Moreover, some western scholars, labelled by the conservative-Orientalists and neo-Orientalists as apologists, have contributed to the attempt to rethink research on radical Islam. Eickelman and Piscatori (1996), for example, attempt to repackage Islam's reputation for violence and radicalism. They argue that the politics of Muslims can be defined in terms of a more generic prefix of 'protest'. The politics of Muslim protest acknowledges that violence may, sometimes, play a role, but it also points to other forms of action, which include passive or silent protest as a form of Muslim political activity.

The second strand of the Muslim/Arab critique of western scholarship is located within the field of political Islam itself, among a new generation of Islamic thinkers who have sought new approaches to current western perceptions and assumptions about the religion. These scholars have variously been labelled Islamic or Muslim 'liberals', 'moderates', 'modernists' and 'modernizers'. Their works indirectly challenge the monolithic assumptions behind many conservative-Orientalist and neo-Orientalist debates on the phenomenon of radical Islam and its impact on the religion as a political force *per se.* In Egypt, for example, Islamic liberal authors and intellectuals such as Nasser Hamid Abu Zayd, Fu'ad Zakariyya, Muhammed Ahmad Khalafalla and Muhammed Said al-Ashmawi have posited new questions within contemporary Islam that challenge the perceived hegemony of the fundamentalists. They have thus contributed to internal debates within Islamic circles and the Muslim world in which the assumed linkages between Islam and politics, protest and radicalism, change and violence are questioned. As Ayubi (1991: 212) points out, 'The Islamic liberals, and the liberal Muslims, have started to answer the challenge of the fundamentalists, and many of them are conducting this debate in Islamic terms, which must add substantially to the credibility of their argument.' Nevertheless, such scholarship has not directly altered the methodology of researching radical Islam, nor have the ideas of these intellectuals resulted in a broad-based support from the Muslim mass. The combination of the two approaches, however, does at least signpost positive developments in this particular field of scholarship.

Out of Iran

Many of the first books on Islam and politics that emerged in the early 1980s remained largely untouched by, or refuted the debates arising from, Said's *Orientalism.* Written primarily to account for the Shi'a Iranian revolution in 1979 and the Shi'a manifestation of Hizbollah following the Israeli invasion of Lebanon in 1982, the texts on radical Islam by Orientalist authors such as Daniel Pipes (1983) and Martin Kramer (1980) informed the reader about the manifestation of Islam at a particular historical juncture. In addition, the Shi'a nature of the Iranian and Lebanese experiences was largely represented as Political Islam *per se*, as Shireen Hunter (1995: 319) reminds us:

> During the first years [of the 1980s], most Western scholars tended to view the Islamist trend as a mainly Shi'a and Persian phenomenon. ... According to this school of thought, certain characteristics of the Shi'a faith, along with the structure of the Shi'a clerical establishment, made Shi'ites more susceptible to extremist Islamist tendencies.

Not only did such versions fail to account accurately for a region-wide resurgence of Islam that embraced many more Sunni than Shi'a Muslims, but they also underestimated the political and socio-economic context within which the resurgence was taking place. The goal of such writers in researching radical Islam at this stage was to sound the alarm, and alert the West and the USA in particular to the threat within Islam, a threat that was violent and divinely inspired. For the conservative Orientalists, the signifying 'radical' was written into Islam and identified as the principal symbol or motif of the religion. The reader was encouraged to believe that the radical prefix explained the entire religion. The religion itself, from prayer to fasting, *zakat* to *jihad*, *ijtihad* to Sufism, was subordinated to the preoccupation with the radical feature of the faith. The faith, its history, norms, rules, sacred texts and traditions were often left unexplained, and the radical element was offered as the essential of the religion, its inner core, its heart. Such research sometimes also revealed something that Halliday (1996: 162) identifies as 'anti-Muslimism'. This anti-Muslimism was revealed in much of the early research on radical Islam and was predicated on the assumption that it was the Muslims themselves, as radical, hostile and violent, who 'deserved or provoked' resentment.

These initial representations of radical Islam paid scant attention to the deep doctrinal, spiritual and religious differences between Sunni and Shi'a Islam. The complex patterns within Islam were ignored in favour of an approach that stressed the simple representation of the faith; something that many Muslims themselves had even been encouraged to believe was the way in which to represent the religion. After all, within Islam, the essence is supposed to guide the follower: there is one God, there are five pillars, including a simple oath of faith to be adhered to. Clear belief and unity of faith is the way forward. These tendencies allowed the conservative-Orientalist authors of radical Islam the space to represent the faith in the same manner. Moreover, much of the research that did contextualize the resurgence of Islam within wider socio-economic factors was generated outside the discipline of politics in the realm of ethnography, sociology and anthropology.

By the end of the 1980s, research on Islamic fundamentalism and radical Islam (terms often used synonymously) was perceived and represented in much of the literature as a region-wide product of the Iranian revolution and Ayatollah Khomeini's theocratic republic. As it was understood, radical Islam and its fundamentalist dimension were anti-modern trends that championed a return to barbarism. Although writers like Aziz al-Azmeh (1993: 23) argue that 'Islamist revanchism in the Arab world is not a "return" to a primitivist utopia', this is how Islam currently appears to 'present itself'. Such perspectives are reinforced through the funding of major studies like the American Academy of Arts and Sciences 'Fundamentalism Project', which, while seeking to understand better the 'fundamentalist' impulse as a global phenomenon, also goes some way to supporting the view that radical Islam (Islamic fundamentalism) is 'essentially antidemocratic, anti-accommodationist, and anti-pluralist and that it violates, as a matter of principle, the standards of human rights defended ... by Western democracies' (Marty and Appleby 1993: 5). The representation of Muslims as fundamentalist (and a particular type of fundamentalist) was apparent in the research of Orientalists and neo-Orientalists who declared Islamic fundamentalists were 'as violent and dogmatic as any in the world. These [are] people who mix nostalgia with grievance to produce a millenarian vision ... a vision so powerful that its pursuit justified any means'; their 'radical programme ... has little precedent' (Kramer 1993: 35–36). The fundamentalist label on radical Islam was presented as a threat of global proportions.

In the discipline of politics much of the research on radical Islam that emerged in the early 1980s thus represented the conservative-Orientalist approach, which either ignored or sidelined manifestations of political Islam that were not immediately predicated on violence, terrorism, revolution and barbarity. By the mid- to late 1980s, however, western academics such as Esposito and Piscatori, along with non-western authors, were presenting research that made a case for a multifaceted resurgence of Islam in which radical Islam was but one element. But only in the early 1990s did scholarship on radical Islam identify the less-than-radical strand of thought that had emerged from the fundamentalist cauldron, and question the hegemony of the Orientalists. Only then did scholars such as al-Azmeh (1993) and Sayyid (1997) begin to unpack the label 'fundamentalism'. Modernist, liberal and radical Islamic agendas that have little or nothing to do with terrorism and violence have emerged in Egypt, Jordan, Syria and other locations and, perhaps more importantly for the writing of radical Islam, researchers were at last identifying these expressions of radicalism and questioning the context in which acts of political violence associated with Islamic groups were taking place. Nevertheless, this process of identification and analysis, while now part of research on radical Islam, has so far failed to percolate into the popular psyche. Its challenge to popular culture and discourse on radical Islam may still represent a marginalized research perspective. Such research is still sidelined and dismissed by the mainstream Orientalist cohort led by writers like Lewis, Pipes and Kramer, who are openly critical of researchers like Esposito, whom they label 'apologists'. These Orientalists perceive it as their duty to go to great lengths to discredit the claims of the so-called 'apologists', disproving their arguments by illustrating their points in the words and deeds of the fundamentalists themselves. Such confrontation seems set to continue to characterize the research on radical Islam for a long time to come.

Nightmare on Salah Eddin Street

In recent years the confrontation between the conservative Orientalists and the apologists has taken on new proportions. As a number of authors writing in the field of terrorism studies have turned their attentions to radical Islamist movements, new conflicts over this field of researching Islam have become apparent. The 'holy terror' thesis has been accepted by mainstream media and the popular press, and by many western governments and policy-makers, with scant attention paid to the credentials of those working in this particular field of studies. Any critique of this approach has been dismissed as further evidence of the apologist tendency and as evidence of support for Islamic groups currently engaging in acts of political violence.

While it is true that the discourse of holy terror reflects on other religions, there has been a discernible tendency by the advocates of this approach to single out radical Islam. The discourse, its emergence, and the way in which it is researched have as much to say about current understandings of Islam in the West as they do about contemporary manifestations of radical Islam in the Middle East. This understanding of radical Islam remains the province of traditional Orientalist approaches to scholarship and discourse and is, by and large, unaffected by the Saidian debate and attack on Orientalism. As such, the approach carries the torch for Orientalist scholarship into the discipline of terrorism studies. The motifs that this discourse evokes are drawn from a discrete viewpoint of radical Islam, its relation to violence and therefore terrorism. Such motifs include the demonization and objectification of Islam as a monolith represented by radical Islam. This discourse portrays radical Islam and the religion *per se* in purely fundamentalist terms, and, from this standpoint, argues that violence is a divine duty within radical Islamic circles.

This process of reductionism associated with the discourse has profound implications. For example, the assumption of radical Islam as purely an expression of fundamentalism raises some difficulties that are both implicit and explicit in the approach. In the discourse of holy terror, however, fundamentalist Islam is reductive in the extreme, reflecting a negative signifier, particularly in relation to the West. The motif reigns, and difference in the 'other' is largely ignored. It becomes relatively easy, therefore, to make assertions such as, 'The revolution in Iran, accordingly is held up as an example to Muslims throughout the world to reassert fundamental teachings of the Koran and to resist intrusion of Western – particularly United States – influence over the Middle East' (Hoffman 1995: 279).

The construction and writing of radical Islam established by the discourse on holy terror is, to recall Laclau's (1996) approach, a politics of signifiers in which the empty signifier is filled through 'the subversion of the process of signification itself'. While Laclau illustrates his postmodernist thesis through the example of Hobbes and his notion of the state of nature and order of the ruler, the same points could be illustrated through analysis of the discourse on holy terror. In this context, the signified – Islamic terror/radical Islam – is posited as a negative. Thus, the power of the rulers (secular states in the Middle East), no matter how lacking in intrinsic value, 'has to be accepted', because 'it is an order and the only alternative' to radical Islam/holy terror (Laclau 1996: 51). Radical Islam and Islam in general are represented in contrast to the West, and the West stands for everything that radical Islam is not. This writing of radical Islam, working from Laclau's standpoint, is premised on a process of signification; the notion of good and evil becomes corrupted and simplistic in its presentation. Yet discourse theory relies on an analysis of social antagonisms involving, as Howarth (1995: 120) reminds us, 'an "enemy" or "other" [that] is vital for the establishment of political frontiers', and the discourse of radical Islam constructed through the holy terror thesis relies on the same constructions of social relationships when viewing Islam. Laclau (1996) and Mouffe (1993) deliberate on the construction of antagonism in a variety of settings; identity, its false construction and obstruction assume an importance. Certain signifiers, such as 'freedom', 'democracy', 'the nation', 'terrorism', 'radical', 'Islam', and so on, therefore remain 'vitally important' in reflecting and examining how political subjects are constituted and written. In the case of radical Islam and the holy terror thesis, the signifiers of 'Islam', 'radical', 'the people', 'liberation' and 'violence' are filled with a series of presumptions that lead inevitably to the religion's negative signification, with the result that it can only be written, represented and understood properly in the negative. This renders it impossible to grasp radical Islam in any other way, reducing its complexity.

This process of signification to which the writers of the discourse of holy terror have subjected radical Islam, therefore, contributes further to a Saidian 'other' in a classic Orientalist sense. The authors of this approach have only signified radical Islam in terms of a narrow concept of the political. This concept of the political rests on a view of Islamists as fundamentalists. The essence of Islam in this context is part of a particular monolithic, expression of conflict. As Taheri (1987: 1) states, 'Islamic politics inevitably lead to violence and terror'. These authors, however, fail to address Islam as an ethical signifier, and even begin to empty it (Islam in general and radical Islam in particular) of its religious significance by placing such an emphasis on politics. Holy terror and radical Islam, in their synonymous guise, only obtain meaning because they are different from secular terror, secular radical politics, political violence and warfare. Among these presumptions, the religious terrorists represent an Islam that is perceived as radical, fundamentalist, anti-Jewish, anti-democratic and anti-plural. Yet as Bobby Sayyid (1994: 267) reminds us, there is a danger in writing radical Islam in this manner: 'it makes an understanding of these movements difficult by making them look simple'. In the development of a discourse on radical Islam and holy terror, the authors of this approach fail to understand the antagonism itself. The 'other' is represented in the construction of boundaries and identities that prohibit the development of a full and positive identity for Muslims.

The signification of Islam within the discourse of holy terror and radical Islam has also portrayed the threat of this particular manifestation of Islam as something that is larger-than-life, something 'bigger than the sum of its parts' and out of control. Indeed, the writings of authors associated with the discourse contribute to a belief that radical Islam and its twin, holy terror, threaten western civilization as we know it. It is an absolute antagonism: the identity of Islam *per se* as it is written from this perspective becomes the name of the threat to the West. Yet in reality the Islamic terrorists and radical Islam remain an exceedingly small cohort of disparate groupings and movements that have emerged out of a variety of political contexts. Their power and impact have been exaggerated; they have become the name of Islam. Within the broad spectrum of political Islam, radical groups like al-Gama'a al-Islamiyya and Islamic Jihad are empirically marginal players, yet through their own dramatic deeds and the scholarly and popular writing of radical Islam they are perceived as 'the gospel for the youth', inaugurating a 'new era in Islamic thought' (Rapoport 1984: 672).

In the main, it is the experts who embrace the 'holy terror' thesis who appear in print and in the media as experts on Islamic terror, rather than scholars of Islam or political Islam. Their work is reinforced by predecessors such as Bernard Lewis, whose now infamous *Atlantic Monthly* article 'The Roots of Muslim Rage' (1990) led Halliday (1996) to refer to the former's 'anti-Muslimness'. Many such authors have come to the study of Islam from terrorism studies. Their scholarship of Islam *per se* appears, in some cases, to be questionable to say the least. Yet their approaches filter into and support the widely held but misleading stereotypes of Islam propounded by the American media in particular. As recently as 1996 and 1997, feature articles, television programmes and books authored by respected journalists and academics exaggerated the belief that radical Islam threatens the American public on a daily basis. Steven Emerson's controversial, and largely inaccurate, television documentary *Jihad in America* (1996 US TV); a book on Islamic fundamentalism (Jansen 1997) that blamed Muslim terrorists – radical Islamists – for the Oklahoma bombing; and a series of Associated Press feature articles entitled 'Jihad USA' (1997) – all reiterate the message of threat from radical Islam. Such writing is also often inaccurate; for example, the 'Jihad USA' articles variously mis-labelled groups as politically diverse as the Kurdish PKK, Palestinian George Habash's secular socialist DFLP and Palestinian Abu Nidal's secular fighters as 'Islamic terrorists' intent on conducting a 'holy war' in the USA.

The contribution made to writing radical Islam by the current discourse on holy terror cannot, I would contend, be said to represent a version of Islam that is either familiar, known or relevant to Islamists or Muslims. The discourse works from an understanding of Islam that is familiar in the West, not in the Muslim world. It highlights the gap between the West and the represented 'other', and while purporting to rethink Islam, it leads instead to a familiar picture of the faith drawn by the classical Orientalist approach to the religion. That a modern field of studies like that on terrorism is open to such old-fashioned prejudices should be surprising. Nevertheless, it remains a fact that without such a reductive and hostile view of Islam *per se* and radical Islam in particular, the discourse would never work or allow its proponents to reach the conclusions they reach. Through the process of signification, the discourse creates a new 'quilting point' (Laclau 1996), pulling together a variety of threads, which, although relevant to the worldview of the authors of the holy terror thesis, say more about radical Islam as a signifier of western insecurity and anti-Muslim prejudice than about Islamists and those among them who are 'radical' or engage in acts of political violence.

The religious terror thesis fails to explore the other causes of political violence in societies that have experienced totalitarian government, socio-economic deprivation, limited political rights and ethno-national conflict. I would argue that the religious terror thesis, by reflecting the monolithic mainstream (read male-stream) vision of Islam, highlights the complicit nature of male construction of radical Islam in a way that actually favours antagonistic attitudes and cultural stereotyping of the world of radical Islam as a rigidly male environment.

Where is the woman's place?

In 1986, feminist theorist Beverly Thiele (1986: 30) argued that 'it is common knowledge among feminists that social and political theory was, and for the most part still is, written by men, for men and about men'. It takes no great leap of the imagination to apply this statement to current research on radical Islam. Like so many other aspects of the study of Islam, work by academics and others on radical Islam has reflected a predominantly male(-stream) agenda and thus 'their subject matter reflects male concerns, deals with male activity and male ambitions and is directed away from issues involving or of concern to women' (Thiele 1986: 30). As such, most 'male-stream' research in politics on radical Islam reflects the hostility to new thinking and postmodern approaches identified above. This in turn emphasizes the macho image associated with the research subject. The notion that researching and writing radical Islam is a 'man's job' is reinforced not only by the cultural and religious attitudes prevalent among the research subjects but also within the discipline by the majority of male researchers who occupy this sphere. Even at the turn of the twentieth century, writing and researching radical Islam is still a male space, and the frontiers of scholarship are jealously guarded by a variety of conservative and liberal patriarchal attitudes. A recent international conference on Islam illustrates the point. Out of six keynote sessions addressing new debates, research paradigms and empirically based thinking, and out of fourteen 'international scholars', only three out of fourteen speakers were women, two of whom spoke in a special session on gender. Despite efforts by women to incorporate themselves into the discipline, it is the men who remain the gatekeepers to this territory and women are usually recognized as scholars only in the sphere of gender and Islam. Indeed, it is a poor reflection on the discipline of politics that most international conferences now have to adopt proactive policies and strategies to encourage women's participation and involvement.

When radical Islam is represented in a way that portrays it as violent, engulfed in webs of terror, and characterized by hostile misogyny, sometimes located in geographically tough terrain, in war zones or remote regions, the work of researching the subject becomes 'man's work'. The male camaraderie that operates in war zones and 'under fire' excludes women and places them on the periphery of the action. The world of radical Islam is, in turn, a world of men, and it is the work of male researchers to describe it, a masculinized description that, to paraphrase de Beauvoir (1975), they then 'confuse with the absolute truth'. Gaten's (1986: 20) claim that 'the history of philosophy is the history of man defining man as having some particular relation to some essential faculty or power' may be extended to research on radical Islam. However, the philosophical point, in terms of a feminist agenda, is problematic. If, for example, one accepts that western political theory and philosophy is a male product, and if the ideas, norms and values associated with it are then used by western men to research radical Islam, what is the role and where is the place for women in this scheme? De Beauvoir's claim to woman as the 'other', invisible and desiring invisibility, creates a bond of commonality between women and the Saidian 'other' of Islam in the researched world of radical Islam. Both are 'others' in relation to the male-defined and masculinized West. Does this make the experience of the woman researcher of radical Islam any easier in relation to the research subjects? The answers to such questions remain elusive, as feminist epistemology is still at the border of researching radical Islam.

The apparently violent and radical nature of Islam leads to a corpus of academic work where the male agenda dominates, where books are sold on the back of the 'macho' nature of the male writer who 'penetrates' the hidden world of radical Islam. Here the western male does as much, if not more, than the radical male Muslim to exclude women in the same way that he accuses the radical Islamists of doing. The roots of such chauvinistic tendencies are not difficult to discern. The 'Orient' always was a predominantly male preserve, and Islam even more so. Male researchers, the figures of western history, Gerard de Nerval, Richard Burton and T.E. Lawrence, are the westerners who forged the bond with Islam, illuminated it, made it akin and romantic to western civilization. It was these men and others like them who 'discovered Islam' and presented it to the West, and in this landscape women were largely invisible: Muslim women were secluded in the harems of Cairo or Baghdad, western women in the strict confines of the society 'harems' of London or Paris. Today, of course, things are a little different, yet equality of treatment, parity of esteem, value of intellect is often not the same for male and female scholars, and the chauvinistic tradition encouraged by Orientalist scholarship of radical Islam persists to the present.

Personal experience will illustrate my argument at this point. In 1989, I returned to the Middle East to carry out fieldwork on the rise of political Islam under Israeli occupation of the West Bank and Gaza Strip. During this time I encountered male hostility within the discipline in a number of ways. Before my departure, some male colleagues within my university dismissed my proposed research with remarks like: 'They'll [Hamas, Islamic Jihad, etc.] never talk to a woman and a westerner to boot,' 'You'll have to wear *hijab* [the Islamic headscarf] or they'll have nothing to do with you,' 'They don't speak to women because they believe they are Israeli-backed mata haris,' 'Maybe if you convert [to Islam] they'll speak to you, but I doubt it.' The sense of powerlessness that these comments provoked in me did little for my self-confidence as a researcher. Some of my male colleagues had dismissed my academic task because of my gender, not my research paradigm. This arrogance towards, even dismissal of, my work has characterized subsequent encounters with some male colleagues in the field of politics and Islamic studies. Such arrogance appears to call into question my competence, abilities, objectivity and balance because of my gender. It reflects a wider opposition to feminism from the conservative-Orientalist scholars whose work dominates research on radical Islam, reinforcing their sense of superiority over the Orient as well as over women.

I believe that such attitudes stem from women's perceived violation of a space that so many male researchers somehow regard as their 'sovereign territory'. Often this attitude is reinforced by the sexual tensions associated with the presence of women in this field. Women cannot hope to 'bond' with their research subjects in the way that male colleagues can, nor can men know how painful it is to remain 'frozen' out from the hyper-male bonding that the cultural status of the Middle East and the Muslim world allows men to enjoy so much. There is no physical contact, there are no meaningful looks or shared confidences; in this the male researcher and research subject are co-conspirators against women. The male research experience of radical Islam is privileged without that privilege ever being acknowledged.

Nevertheless, I was determined to prove the male sceptics wrong. Once in the field, I persisted in seeking out interviews with Islamic leaders and members of the political organizations with which they were associated. For example, for several months I had tried to arrange a series of interviews with Islamists (including a leader from Hizb Tahrir) in Hebron. Given the perceived conservative attitude of Hebronites, the political conditions of the Intifada, and the logistical difficulty in arranging interviews, I was delighted when I secured a morning of interviews with the Islamists. I had, however, been persuaded by a male Palestinian intermediary to allow a fellow American researcher to accompany me to Hebron.

The following day the American and I travelled to Hebron. I had spent the previous days researching the interviews and carefully constructing a series of questions for my interviewees. Upon arrival in Hebron, we were greeted with a degree of reserve appropriate for these situations and quickly settled down to business. I was ushered into the room where the interviews would take place and the American followed uninvited. He sat in on what I perceived to be *my* interview and took a seat directly opposite the two main respondents. I was the only woman in a room of six. Throughout the interviews (which lasted for nearly three hours), I posed the questions but my respondents directed their answers to the American man. When I asked for elaboration of a particular point, the reply remained physically and verbally directed towards my male colleague. My sense of frustration increased as I became further marginalized, although the interview itself was proving to be a great success. As the interview came to an end and I busily scribbled my notes, the Islamists turned to my male colleague and complimented him on the sophisticated level of questioning and his impressive knowledge of Islam. He responded warmly, engaging further in the exclusionary male camaraderie that by now enveloped the whole encounter. So impressed were the Islamists that the American was invited for lunch, an invitation he accepted with grace as kind reward for his work. As these men trooped off to eat, I was left in an empty room, invisible and excluded from the encounter. I felt deeply betrayed, not by the interviewees, but by my so-called 'colleague' for his unabashed chauvinism and sheer effrontery for taking credit for my work.

Maybe my attitude can be excused. I was naïve, and why should I expect a western male to be any more enlightened than his Palestinian counterparts? I realized that while I knew about Islam, could converse about Sayyid Qutb with more authority than some of my Hebronite interviewees, I had, in choosing to engage in ethnographic-based research of a radical Islamic movement, exposed myself to a variety of experiences that ultimately reflected my gender and altered my own subjectivity towards the Islamists, as well as towards the discipline in which my work was centred. Trust, respect and confidence became important issues for me, and increasingly my research support came from other women rather than men. The majority of Islamists with whom I came into contact patronized me and never really took me as seriously as I knew they did my male counterparts. To the leaders and activists of Hamas and other Islamic organizations I was '*ya bint*' (the girl), no matter how many letters I had after my name. I was always aware that rapport was something difficult to attain, and I was never treated as an equal in any sense of the word. Dialogue, no matter how many years it has been sustained, remains centred on my gender. The most frustrating factor in this experience has been that the arena of radical Islam is dominated by men, and they remain the gatekeepers to academic exploration. Western women, like myself, who have entered this space have only been able to play the game successfully by hiding their identity, toning it down, striving to be an honorary male. This is not to say that such researchers embrace masculine identities, for this too is likely to be a disastrous strategy. Rather, they expend much time and energy attempting to gain access to an arena of politics that men (Muslim and non-Muslim) take for granted. In fact, women – whether western academics, western-based academics or those who remain in the Muslim world – have expended so much energy knocking at the door to the research arena that subsequent admission is gratefully received and their continuing invisibility taken for granted.

Women who research radical Islam therefore often remain marginalized, and their work, which admittedly includes some of my own, has gone some way in further representing this world as masculine, male-dominated territory, wittingly or unwittingly accepting, as my Hebron experience highlights, a role on the fringe. Feminist and women researchers of radical Islam – and here I must stress the radical in distinction to other Islamisms – must ask themselves to what extent they conspire in the construction of the Saidian 'other' by accepting the traditional masculine agenda, thus letting Orientalism in through the back door by encouraging the perception of weak, passive women, silenced by their own research agenda. Given methodological, ethnographic and cultural sensitivities, is the status of honorary man the best that women can hope for, à la Madeleine Albright who did not have to wear *hijab* when she met King Fahd during her trip to Saudi Arabia in September 1997? Is this acceptable? Moreover, what future role should women within the discipline of politics and Islamic studies seek for themselves and demand from their male colleagues?

The point, I now understand, is that women researching radical Islam are a minority voice, and will remain so for as long as men within the discipline (as well as the research subjects) continue to understand radical Islam from their 'male-stream' perspective. The male-stream perspective is dominated by the misogynist and myopic tendencies of terrorism studies, as Said (1978: 48) has pointed out:

> The isolation of terrorism from history and from other things in Vico's world of the nations has had the effect of magnifying its ravages, even as terrorism itself has been shrunk from the public world into a small private world reserved tautologically for the terrorists who commit terrorism, and for the experts who study them.

Western and non-western women who research and write about radical Islam may be said to fall into three categories. While it is true that these categories may be arbitrarily imposed, they do give an idea of the direction from which these contributions are generated and, thus, the perspectives evident in particular bodies of writing.

The first category consists of women writing about radical Islam from a feminist (secular or Muslim) perspective. Radical Islam is researched in relation to the impact this has upon the lives of Muslim women, whether through examining the matrix of power between state and radical Islam, the imposition of *hijab* or the Shi'a revolutionary doctrine of Iran. These feminists, including, among others, Mernissi, Kandiyoti and Afshar, have made gender visible in the discourse of radical Islam both in a historical and in a contemporary sphere. Their approach takes issue with the exclusion of women and their marginal role in the study of Muslim society. As Kandiyoti (1997: 192) highlights, 'when Islamist movements become a factor, tighter control over women and restrictions of their rights constitute the lowest common denominator of their policies'. These authors make gender visible by researching the world of Muslim women from a variety of perspectives, including the sociological and anthropological. Hammami (1997), for instance, engages radical Islam in her debate about *hijab* as a specific example of the way in which 'invented tradition' is promoted as authentic Islam in a power struggle between Islamists and secularists in the Palestinian context. The work of these women, however, is not always acknowledged in the literature about radical Islam, and their contribution is pushed to one side. Their ability to theorize another, 'gendered' perspective runs counter to the accepted masculinized norm. Yet this emerging corpus of feminist critical theory that engages with Islamism in its many guises, including the radical, 'involves constructing "knowledge" about the world, not [only] in the interests of social and political control, but in the service of an emancipatory politics' (Steans 1998: 173).

The second category of women writing about radical Islam is not interested in changing the current Orientalist domination of this field of research. These scholars, such as Judith Miller (1993), are 'honorary members of the club' and uncritically compliant with current research patterns into radical Islam. For these authors, there is a rigidity and traditionalism to their scholarship that maintains and upholds the status quo. In researching and writing radical Islam they remain, for the most part, geographically and culturally removed from the research subject, essentializing the 'other' from their western-based boltholes. Their methodological approach remains largely unmoved by ethnographic debate or cultural relativism. Instead, these intellectual transvestites cling to the male-centric universe constructed by their male colleagues and allow their work to reinforce the cultural and gender stereotypes, something that ultimately weakens its value.

The third and final category of scholarship consists of female scholars from the Middle East who have focused their work on radical Islamists in a variety of contexts from Algeria to Lebanon, Jordan to Palestine, and who represent a new way of researching and writing radical Islam that is gendered, and predicated on a new discourse. In particular, the work of authors such as Hala Mustafa and Hala Jaber is testimony to a vibrant new method of research and discourse on radical Islam that is unfettered by the Orientalist tradition of associating so-called 'movements of violence' with notions of masculinity, of warriors, and of women as subjects to be brought under control and subjugated. They highlight the diversity and debates within radical Islam and do not let their gender get in the way of the researched subject. Nevertheless, their approaches to 'writing radical Islam' inherently reflect a gendered focus, which is apparent in the new perspectives they offer of the subject. They avoid the essentializing of radical Islam that is so prevalent elsewhere in the field. While researching the radical, they privilege the subaltern voice, a voice that frequently stands in stark contrast to the stereotype so often reproduced by reductive analyses.

Concluding the subject

At the beginning of the twenty-first century a certain pessimism pervades the research and writing of radical Islam and the movements that are manifest in this guise. The self-destruct button has been pressed and radical Islam, as represented in such writing, is on a crash course with western civilization. The future of this way of writing Islam remains embedded in the 'threat' such movements pose; it is the threat of violence that encourages governments to fund think-tanks and studies assessing, calculating and devising means of successfully combating this phenomenon. Knowledge of Islam is important and will remain so to scholars of this subject, but so too will expertise in strategic, national security and defence issues. Knowledge of Islam and radical Islam in particular, therefore, will be predicated on the defence and security agenda, and studies that challenge this agenda will find it difficult to be accepted into the mainstream of the discipline. Until the connections between the phenomenon of radical Islam and the socio-economic, political and cultural contexts within which it occurs are dealt with more seriously, Muslims all over the world will be objectified through the 'radical' prefix. Nevertheless, there is some hope that gendered perspectives on radical Islam, together with discourse analysis and the current work by authors like Eickelman and Piscatori (1996) and Muslim authors such as Ahmed (1992), Arkoun (1994) and Choueiri (1990) on Muslim politics (with a small p), will encourage a move from a high culture approach to one that questions current labels and ascriptions in the context of the politics of signifiers in a postmodernist age. Indeed, the work of many Muslim and Arab scholars researching the field of radical Islam has often been ignored in the West, yet their contribution points to a valuable methodology from which many western observers could learn. Current researchers and scholars writing radical Islam should be encouraged to engage in long-term fieldwork projects that bring them into close contact with the researched. Hizbollah, al-Gama'a al-Islamiyya or Islamic Jihad will never be understood unless researchers, male and female alike, spend time in the field, or with as much archive material as possible. The 'other' will always remain a threat and be described as such unless we touch upon each other's lives in the true pursuit of understanding.

References

Ahmed, A.S. 1992. *Postmodernism and Islam: Predicament and Promise.* London: Routledge.

Anderson, B. 1983. *Imagined Communities: Reflections on the Origin and Spread of Nationalism.* London: Verso.

Arkoun, M. 1994. *Rethinking Islam.* Boulder, CO: Westview.

Ayubi, N. 1991. *Political Islam: Religion and Politics in the Arab World.* London: Routledge.

al-Azmeh, A. 1993. *Islams and Modernities.* London: Verso.

al-Azun, S.J. 1981. Orientalism and Orientalism in reverse. *Khamsin* 8: 5–26.

Choueiri, Y. 1990. *Islamic Fundamentalism.* London: Pinter.

de Beauvoir, S. 1975. *The Second Sex.* Harmondsworth: Penguin.

Eickelman, D. and Piscatori, J. 1996. *Muslim Politics.* Princeton, NJ: Princeton University Press.

Esposito, J. 1992. *The Islamic Threat.* New York: Oxford University Press.

Gaten, M. 1986. Feminism, philosophy and riddles without answers. In C. Pateman and E. Gross (eds), *Feminist Challenges: Social and Political Theory.* Sydney: Allen and Unwin.

Haddad, Y., Voll, J.O. and Esposito, J.L. (eds) 1991. *The Contemporary Islamic Revival: A Critical Survey and Bibliography.* New York: Greenwood.

Halliday, F. 1996. *Islam and the Myth of Confrontation: Religion and Politics in the Middle East.* London: I.B. Tauris.

Hammami, R. 1997. From immodesty to collaboration: Hamas, the women's movement, and national identity in the Intifada. In J. Beinin and J. Stork (eds), *Political Islam.* London: I.B. Tauris.

Hoffman, B. 1995. Holy terror: the implications of terrorism motivated by a religious imperative. *Studies in Conflict and Terrorism* 18: 271–84.

Howarth, D. 1995. Discourse theory. In D. Marsh and G. Stoker (eds), *Theory and Methods in Political Science.* London: Macmillan.

Hunter, S. 1995. The rise of Islamist movements and the western response: clash of civilizations or clash of interests? In L. Guazzone (ed.), *The Islamist Dilemma: The Political Role of Islamist Movements in the Contemporary Arab World.* Reading: Ithaca Press.

Hussein, A., Olson, R. and Qureshi, J. (eds) 1984. *Orientalism, Islam and Islamists.* Battleboro, VT: Amana Books.

Jansen, J.J.G. 1997. *The Dual Nature of Islamic Fundamentalism.* London: Hurst.

Kandiyoti, D. 1997. Women, Islam and the state. In J. Beinin and J. Stork (eds), *Political Islam.* London: I.B. Tauris.

Kramer, M. 1980. *Political Islam.* Beverley Hills, CA: Sage.

Kramer, M. 1993. Islam versus democracy. *Commentary* January: 35–41.

Laclau, E. 1996. *Emancipation(s).* London: Verso.

Lewis, B. 1990. The roots of Muslim rage. *The Atlantic Monthly* September: 47–60.

Marty, M. and Appleby, S. (eds) 1993. *Fundamentalisms and the State.* Chicago: University of Chicago Press.

Miller, J. 1993. The challenge of radical Islam. *Foreign Affairs* Spring: 201–15.

Mouffe, C. 1993. *The Return to the Political.* London: Verso.

Naipaul, V.S. 1981. *Among the Believers: An Islamic Journey.* New York: Random House.

Pipes, D. 1983. *In the Path of God: Islam and Political Power.* New York: Basic Books.

Rapoport, D. 1984. Fear and trembling: terrorism in three religious traditions. *American Political Science Review* 78: 658–77.

Roy, O. 1994. *The Failure of Political Islam.* London: I.B. Tauris.

Said, E.W. 1978. *Orientalism.* Harmondsworth: Penguin.

Sayyid, B. 1994. Sign o'times: kaffirs and infidels fighting the ninth crusade. In E. Laclau (ed.), *The Making of Political Identities.* London: Verso.

Sayyid, B. 1997. *A Fundamental Fear: Eurocentrism and the Emergence of Islamism.* London: Zed Books.

Sivan, E. 1985. *Radical Islam, Medieval Theology and Modern Politics.* New Haven, CT: Yale University Press.

Steans, J. 1998. *Gender and International Relations.* Cambridge: Polity.

Taheri, A. 1987. *Holy Terror: The Inside Story of Islamic Terrorism.* London: Sphere.

Thiele, B. 1986. Vanishing acts in social and political thought: tricks of the trade. In C. Pateman and E. Gross (eds), *Feminist Challenges: Social and Political Theory.* Sydney: Allen and Unwin.

4
ISLAM IN THE MEDIA

Malise Ruthven

Death of two princesses

On the evening of Sunday, 31 August 1997, as the body of Diana Princess of Wales was flown from Paris to London to await the funeral service in Westminster Abbey that would attract the largest audience in television history, her companion Imad ('Dodi') al-Fayed, who died with her in the same automobile accident, was buried with a minimum of publicity after a short but simple ceremony at the Central London Mosque. The imbalance in news coverage between the two sets of obsequies was inevitable. The divorced wife of the heir to the British throne has been widely described as the 'most famous woman in the world'. She was an international media star who was paradoxically seen as being both a victim of the media and one of its most accomplished manipulators. Compared to the Princess, Dodi al-Fayed was a nonentity. Before the tabloid press brought his relationship with the Princess to popular attention using long-lens photography to capture moments of shared intimacy on yachts and powerboats, he was virtually unknown, a shadow in the entourage of his famous father, Muhammad al-Fayed. The latter, a controversial Egyptian businessman, was arguably the best-known Muslim in Britain. The allegations of 'sleaze' he made against ministers in the Major government contributed significantly to the massive defeat suffered by the Conservatives in the General Election in May 1997.

Television mythologizes, and in a certain selective way may be said to resacralize a world 'disenchanted' by print and its associated technologies, which, as Marshall McLuhan (1962, 1964) noted, includes most of the industrial processes of modernity. Despite his initial obscurity, the very presence of Dodi in the final weeks of Diana's life represented a small but significant step towards the inclusion of Muslims in the British national mythology. In her column in the *Guardian*, the novelist Linda Grant speculated ironically on the implications the relationship between Diana and Dodi might have had if the couple had been spared – Dodi being a Muslim 'and what the upper classes used to term (and probably still do) a Wog'.

> If there had been no car crash, if the pair really were in love and had married, then the royal family, in a year or two, would have been confronting the prospect of a Wog half-brother or sister for the heir to the throne. And worse, a mother to the future king who, like Jemima Goldsmith [wife of the Pakistani cricketer Imran Khan], might herself have converted to Islam. ... That great missed opportunity, denied us by the terrible deaths

of the couple and their chauffeur, would have brought to the front of our attention the complicated feelings of non-Muslims about the Muslim faith, our Islamophobia. (*Guardian*, 2 September 1997, p. 10)

The *Guardian* is not everyone's newspaper, and in the acres of reportage and comment that followed the death of Princess Diana, one writer's willingness to confront 'our Islamophobia', to remind her readers that the biggest news story of the decade had a dimension in which a Muslim party played a positive, if tragic, role, hardly amounted to a sea-change in media attitudes to Islam and Muslims. Nevertheless, in the world of television-driven magazines in which celebrities feature as cultural icons, the symbolic significance of Dodi as a Muslim icon should not be underestimated.

Over two decades ago, in 1980, a drama-documentary, *Death of A Princess*, created a major diplomatic row between Saudi Arabia, Britain and the United States. The princess in question, a minor member of the ruling Saudi dynasty, was executed after attempting to leave the country with her lover, with whom, as a married woman, she was having an illicit relationship contrary to Islamic law and tribal custom. Despite her royal status, Princess Mishal was reported to have been beheaded on the explicit instructions of her grandfather, a senior member of the royal family, for the dishonour she brought on her clan. Anthony Thomas's film, acknowledging that the truth could not be established factually, used a series of interviews with exiles and dissidents (including the Lebanese ex-wife of one Saudi prince) to reconstruct a semi-fictional version of what might have happened. The 'execution' was shot in Egypt; the film included a sequence, to which the Saudis took particular objection, of wealthy Saudi women cruising the streets of Jeddah with a view to luring young men into the backs of their chauffeur-driven limousines. *Death of a Princess* contained a potent mixture of two Orientalist themes: 'medieval' barbarism and cruelty, and the sexual allure of the mysterious East, symbolized by veiled women in the backs of smoked-glass limousines. The film, and the row it generated, did not appear out of the blue. As Edward Said (1981: 69) argued in *Covering Islam*, the cultural milieu in which it appeared had for a long time been 'literally teeming with overt anti-Islamic and anti-Arab slurs', with insulting and racist caricatures of Muslims represented as generic, one Muslim seen to be typical of all and of Islam in general. The showing of the film, as Said (1981: 67) pointed out, demonstrated the massive imbalance of cultural power between even wealthy Saudi Arabia and the 'West'.

Islam as 'medieval barbarism'

Images of 'medieval barbarism' continue to dominate the struggle over representations of Islam in an increasingly globalized media in which Muslims are the consumers as well as generators of news. Commenting on the *Death of a Princess* affair in April 1980, the *Economist* stated: 'Islamic law to most Westerners means Islamic punishment: a simplified myth that this film will have fostered' (cited in Said 1981: 67). A similar row over the representation of 'Islamic' executions in Saudi Arabia ended the short-lived collaboration between Saudi money and the

BBC, whereby the BBC adapted part of its television news and current affairs output for transmission to the Arab world through a satellite channel funded by a Saudi consortium. The arrangement broke down when the BBC chose to defend its editorial independence by transmitting a documentary that included secretly filmed footage of a public execution in Riyadh. Images of similar executions or public floggings caught on amateur cameras loomed large in the story of the two British nurses, Deborah Parry and Lucille McLauchlan, found guilty by a Saudi court of the murder of Yvonne Gilford, an Australian nurse, at a hospital complex at Dhahran in 1997. Photographs of red-capped Saudi police administering public floggings dominated the front pages of the tabloids along with a less distinct black and white image of a Saudi executioner bringing a curved scimitar down on the neck of his victim, dating from 1985. The timbre of tabloid reportage is well represented by the following extended caption from the *Daily Mail* under the headline: 'Crowds flock to Friday bloodbath':

> Saudi executions are carried out with military precision. Thousands of eager spectators flock to see them take place outside provincial palaces each Friday. At 12.10 pm, the executioner will arrive wearing a white skullcap embroidered with gold and silver. He will have spent hours honing his technique – it is important for an executioner's reputation that the captive is killed with one blow. Next at the scene will be a judge reading from the Koran. It is a ritual which adds extra torture to the prisoner, who may not have known the day was to be his last until the guards burst into his cell. Finally he is dragged before the swordsman and forced to kneel. The executioner will prod the base of the victim's spine, to make him arch his back, before the 4ft curved blade whirls in a glittering arc and descends. (*Daily Mail*, 28 September 1997)

Islamophobia: the substitution test

Do such descriptions contribute to Islamophobia? A commission headed by Gordon Conway, then vice-chancellor of the University of Sussex, describes Islamophobia as 'a useful shorthand way of referring to dread or hatred of Islam – and therefore to fear or dislike of all or most Muslims' (Runnymede Trust 1997: 1). A useful touchstone for journalists and editors, as the Runnymede Trust Commission argues in its chapter on media coverage, would be to substitute the terms 'Islam' and 'Muslim' with 'Christianity' or 'Christian', 'Judaism' or 'Jew', and to see if the article or passage in question would still pass muster for publication. 'Editors may ask themselves: "Would I print this article or cartoon, or make this juxtaposition of text and illustration, or slant this story in this way, or make this generalisation, if it were about any other topic besides Islam? For example, if it were about a Jewish person or community?"' (Runnymede Trust 1997: 27). As the Runnymede Trust's report points out, the substitution test is no guarantee that editors will necessarily mend their ways. The Press Complaints Commission (PCC) dismissed a complaint against an article by Robert Kilroy-Silk published in the *Daily Express* in January 1995 that contained the following passage:

> Moslems everywhere behave with equal savagery [to the Iraqis who were reported to be publicly cutting off the ears and hands of thieves and army deserters]. They behead

> criminals, stone to death female – only female – adulterers, throw acid in the faces of women who refuse to wear the chadar [*sic*], mutilate the genitals of young girls and ritually abuse animals. … No matter. We have to treat them and their religion with respect. Of course we must. That is what the new dogma of political correctness demands of us. (Cited in Runnymede Trust 1997: 26)

In rejecting the complaint, the PCC took the view that the column in which it appeared 'clearly represented a named columnist's personal view and would be seen as no more than his own robust opinion'. The article was not deemed to be 'prejudicial or pejorative' in what it said about Muslims, nor 'inaccurate, misleading or distorted'. Despite the PCC's ruling in this case, the complainant was surely correct in arguing that 'had a similarly vulgar piece of writing been aimed at the Christian faith the blasphemy laws would have been invoked', and that 'in the case of the Jewish faith the article would have been considered antisemitic as well as a criminal offence against the race relations legislation' (Runnymede Trust 1997: 27).

What offends in this passage is not that Kilroy expresses his repugnance for certain practices prevalent in parts of the Muslim world, but that he magnifies them rhetorically into broad, blanket generalizations about Muslims and the Islamic faith. In *Covering Islam* Said makes a similar point: executions and atrocities committed during the revolution in Iran were uniformly attributed to 'Islam' in the crudest form of 'us-versus-them' analysis. Atrocities or disorders committed in western countries are rarely if ever attributed to the religion of the majority (Said 1981: 8).

It is instructive, however, to subject the *Daily Mail* description cited above of a typical Saudi execution to the substitution test: would it pass editorial muster, for example, if similar details were applied to the execution of, say, a British-born criminal in the United States? Executions – along with the murders that usually precede them – have had an enduring appeal to editors ever since 'penny dreadful' police reports began circulating early in the nineteenth century. Ghoulish attention to the details of execution belongs to a long tradition of reportage of which Charles Dickens was a distinguished exemplar.[1] American executions that attract the attention of British news editors may not actually show the victim in the electric chair or gas chamber as the prison rules do not allow this; but tabloids frequently show pictures of 'Old Sparky' accompanied by detailed descriptions of what happens to the human body when subjected to a current of several thousand volts. Applying the same standard to coverage of the criminal justice system in Saudi Arabia, it would be wrong to assume that dwelling on the details of beheading will necessarily invoke feelings of Islamophobia. However, the *Daily Mail* caption cited above fails the substitution test in one significant detail, in its comment that the reading from the Qur'an adds 'torture' to the execution (as distinct from offering comfort to the victim or, more neutrally, contextualizing the execution within a culturally accepted religio-judicial framework). Would the *Mail* have described the final prayer or Bible reading by the prison chaplain who normally attends an American execution as an addition of 'torture'?

Islam and extremism

The burden of Muslim complaint against the media in Britain is that coverage is unfairly weighted towards extremism, especially on issues involving gender and violence. Among the negative headlines cited in the Runnymede Trust report is one from the *Guardian*: 'Muslim rebels massacre 93 in overnight raid' (*Daily Mirror*, 25 September 1997), with no hint that the people who were murdered were also Muslims. One of several correspondents cited by the report complains that

> when an atrocity occurs in Ulster the journalist/cameraman will regularly cut to a picture of a church leader denouncing the crime, but when Muslims carry out sectarian violence the British media never interview a Muslim leader who denounces the act, although, as any reader of the Arabic press must realise, such denunciations are frequently made. (Runnymede Trust 1997: 21)

One response to this complaint (not made in the Runnymede Trust report) is that neither republican nor loyalist terrorism invokes Christianity to legitimize itself, whereas Islamist and Jewish terrorists are only too willing to invoke their respective religions. Behind this difference lies another: both Judaism and Islam have become politicized, or re-politicized, after long periods of *de facto* (and, in the case of Islam) unacknowledged separation between religion and state, whereas Christians, with some exceptions, have continued to maintain a distinction between religious and political agendas. Paramilitaries in Northern Ireland describe themselves not as Catholic and Protestants, but as 'republicans' or 'loyalists', a style of nomenclature that distances them from their respective churches and adds weight to denunciations by church leaders, although the victims of shootings and bombings have usually been targeted solely on the basis of perceived religious identity. Nevertheless, a superficial glance at coverage of an atrocity that occurred in November 1997 – the massacre of more than sixty tourists, including several British men, women and children, at Luxor in Egypt by a faction of al-Gama'a al-Islamiyya – seems to substantiate the widely held perception among Muslims in Britain that double standards exist in the association of Islam with violence. Condemnations of the Luxor massacre from (among others) Akbar Ahmed were reported on national radio (*The World At One*, BBC Radio 4, 18 November 1997), but the more significant condemnations by the Iranian government, by Sheikh Ahmed Yasin, the leader of the Palestinian Hamas, and by the Lebanese Hizbollah were widely ignored in the broadcasting media, the tabloids and broadsheets. (Important exceptions were Martin Woollacott's article in the *Guardian* on 19 November 1997 and the front-page story in the *Daily Telegraph* on the same day.) There can be little doubt that had these condemnations from other organizations involved in attacks on civilians in other contexts been included in the coverage, readers and viewers would have received a much less 'monolithic' impression of Islamic militancy. If, for example, the *Daily Mail* had contained the headline 'Hamas condemns temple massacre', the way that Islamic discourse is used to legitimize violence in a variety of different conflicts by groups with varied political agendas would have become much more apparent. By contrast, the condemnations by Israeli and Jewish leaders of the massacre of Muslim worshippers by Baruch Goldstein at the Tomb of the Patriarchs in Hebron in February 1994 were widely and prominently reported, as have been the subsequent efforts by the Israeli religious authorities to prevent Goldstein's tomb from becoming a shrine for Jewish extremists. Even the inevitable charges of hypocrisy that would flow from reporting the condemnation of the Temple Massacre by the alleged architect of the suicide bombings that had killed several dozen Israeli civilians would have focused readers' minds on the complexity and diversity of the Islamist movements. Instead, both tabloids and broadsheets directed their readers' attention to evil machinations of Sheikh 'Ümar Abdul Rahman, 'Sheikh of hatred' (*Daily Mirror*, 19 November 1997), 'Fanatic who kills for Allah' (*Daily Mail*, 19 November 1997), currently serving a life sentence in the United States for his part in the World Trade Center bombing in 1994. The reason for including Sheikh 'Umar in the story was a statement from al-Gama'a al-Islamiyya blaming Egyptian police for the civilian casualties, stating that their objective had been simply to take foreign hostages to use as bargaining chips for the release of Sheikh 'Umar. Nevertheless, the inclusion of Sheikh 'Umar in the coverage and the exclusion of Sheikh Yasin tended to reinforce public perception that '"Islam" has some uniform essence' (unlike 'Roman Catholicism' or 'Protestantism'), and that it generally sanctions violence (Runnymede Trust 1997: 5).

Muslims in Britain justly object to being tarred with the terrorist brush. The image of militancy, in the eyes of many Muslims, is a distortion by the western media. Few report on, or make television documentaries about, the Muslim family that runs a corner shop or the peaceful evangelical activities of the Tablighi Jamaat, a large but explicitly non-political Islamic organization with large followings in the West (Dassetto 1988; King 1993). By contrast, marginal groups such as Hizb al-Tahrir, or its off-shoot, the Muhajiroun, are given the full 'media-treatment', either because they seem to confirm western fears about 'militant' Islam or, in the case of the *Tottenham Ayatollah* described below, because they provide material for a 'de-bunking' exercise. In either case, the broader picture of Islamic faith and life tends to be ignored.[2]

Coverage of the Muslim Parliament, established in the wake of the Salman Rushdie affair, is a case in point. The leading light behind it was the late Kalim Siddiqui, a radical Islamist thinker and supporter of the Iranian revolutionary cause. Siddiqui professed to see the media as playing an important role in the conspiracy against British Muslims. The 'silent moral majority' of Muslims who were offended by *The Satanic Verses* were 'oppressed by the mass media, the political parties and the publishing and commercial empires' (*Guardian*, 3 April 1989, cited in Burrell 1994: 3). A former sub-editor on the *Guardian*, Siddiqui had the contacts and skills to 'beat the media' at its own game. In July 1990 a poll conducted by the BBC programme *Public Eye* found that a majority of British Muslims disapproved of the Ayatollah Khomeini's *fatwa* (legal ruling) declaring Salman Rushdie an apostate and therefore deserving of death. Siddiqui promptly invited the BBC cameras to a meeting of more than 500 Muslims in which he asked the audience to raise their hands in support of the *fatwa*. The unanimous vote in support of the *fatwa* was broadcast on the national news (Burrell 1994: 12). As a supporter of the *fatwa* who nevertheless was careful to stay within the bounds of British law (several attempts to prosecute him for incitement to murder failed for lack of evidence), Siddiqui was in constant demand from news and current affairs programmes as the 'voice of militant Islam'. I myself had used him in that capacity in 1986, when making a series of programmes about religion and politics for the BBC World Service. I was, of course, fully aware that he was a controversial figure: originally accused of being in the pay of Saudi Arabia, he had switched his allegiance to Iran after the 1979 revolution, and headed the Muslim Institute, which was widely seen as an Iranian 'front' organization. For my programmes I needed someone who could speak eloquently in favour of the Islamic revolution and the Islamist aspirations it represented. Siddiqui fitted the bill to perfection: as countless researchers and producers would find in the aftermath of the Rushdie affair, he was a media-friendly militant, always good for the radical sound-bite.

Does the very deftness with which Siddiqui 'used the media to attack the media' support, or call into question, the widespread accusation of anti-Muslim bias in the British media? Focus groups drawn from religious and ethnic minorities consulted by Gunter and Viney (1994) in their research into British religious broadcasting accused the media of 'all too often using spokespeople with extreme viewpoints' when seeking the responses of particular communities. Specific examples cited included coverage of the Rushdie affair 'when it was perceived that the voices of an extreme minority within the Muslim community were heard giving an unrepresentative impression of Muslim opinion' (Gunter and Viney 1994: 112). Siddiqui's Muslim critics accused him of being unrepresentative of British Muslims, of providing 'post-facto intellectual, revolutionary and theoretical justification for the excesses and extremism of the Iranian regime' (Sardar and Davies 1990: 143). The unanimous show of hands in the assembly that eventually became the Muslim Parliament contrasted with the more sober figure (42 per cent) of British Muslims who supported the *fatwa* according to the BBC poll. In establishing the Muslim Parliament (the very term implied a challenge to British sovereignty), Siddiqui and his colleagues consciously set out to create a separate legal and institutional identity for British Muslims against the wishes of a majority who simply wanted to get on with their lives unmolested by politics. Arguably, the very attention paid to Siddiqui and the Muslim Parliament, an unrepresentative body in which 'MMPs' were elected by a small minority of radically minded Muslims, had a distorting effect, creating the impression that British Muslims were more alientated from British society and inclined towards separatism than was actually the case. If coverage of British Muslim affairs had been confined to the Muslim Parliament and its spokespersons, there can be little doubt that it would have conformed to the stereotypical or 'closed' views of Islam condemned by the Runnymede Trust as contributing to Islamophobia (Runnymede Trust 1997: 5).

However, as Burrell (1994) points out, the impact of Siddiqui had precisely the opposite effect. Media coverage of the Muslim Parliament's most extreme statements and activities was consistently counter-balanced by references to 'moderate' Muslim spokespersons, such as Dr Zaki Badawi of the Imams and Mosques Council, Dr Aziz Pasha of the Union of Muslim Organizations and Dr Hisham al-Essawy of the Islamic Society for the Promotion of Religious Tolerance. As a result of the overall media coverage of the parliament, Burrell argues, the British public became more, not less, aware of 'different groups and shades of opinion in the British Muslim community' (Burrell 1994: 18). Even the tabloid press, in its campaign against Siddiqui, who became something of a popular hate-figure, emphasized the differences between 'moderates' and 'militants'. The *Sun* (18 January 1992), whose headline 'Sod off back home if you don't like it here' is cited by the Runnymede Trust (1997: 20) as a glaring example of Islamophobia, used a poll of Muslims who wrote to the paper or phoned in on its special hotline to produce an anti-Siddiqui article under the heading 'Muslims tell Siddiqui: go home you bigot' (Burrell 1994: 19). Burrell points out that the 'moderates' were approved of since they adhered to 'respectable British values'. *The Times* (7 January 1992) referred to them as the 'restrained and decent majority'; the *Sun* (6 January 1992) described the 'overwhelming mass' of Muslims as 'decent, hard-working people who only want to live in PEACE with their fellow citizens' (both cited in Burrell 1994: 23).

Press coverage of the Muslim Parliament may have been biased, but it was not inaccurate. After interviewing Siddiqui and other members of the Muslim Parliament, Burrell concluded that coverage was 'factually correct'. 'The aggressive quotes were all taken from Siddiqui's speeches, and were not changed in any way' (Burrell 1994: 30). The parliament did not declare primary allegiance to the British state, but to the 'non-territorial Ummah'; members of established political parties were barred from becoming MMPs. Its foundational document, the Muslim Manifesto (widely reported in the British press), stated explicitly that 'British law does not, and cannot be expected to provide an adequate framework for our survival. The only survival kit that will work is entirely community based and integrated with a global Islamic movement.'[3] The institution explicitly referred to itself as undemocratic – a term used about it in the media – (cited in Burrell 1994: 22). In his inaugural speech, Siddiqui dismissed as unacceptable 'dictatorship of the majority dressed up as democracy' and threatened to break the country's laws if necessary (Burrell 1994: 34). Burrell (1994: 35–6) points out, however, that the Muslim Parliament's more constructive plans, its efforts 'to help the professionals, traders and industrialists among us become more numerous and successful', its project (which subsequently failed) for a Hallal Meat Authority accepted by the whole British Muslim community, its plan for an Islamic university and its encouragement of community work were generally overlooked by the media. Had these aspects of Siddiqui's speeches and the Muslim Parliament's activities been highlighted instead of the confrontational rhetoric, 'a different image of the parliament could have been created', leading to a 'picture of a law-abiding, pro-British and peace-loving body' (Burrell 1994: 36). That the former militant and hostile image, rather than the latter constructive and accommodationist one, became paramount was partly the responsibility of the parliament and its spokespersons, particularly Siddiqui; but it was also due to the nature of the media. Militant statements – as Siddiqui well knew from his experience as a *Guardian* sub-editor – were more likely to grab the headlines than well-meaning social projects. Muslim affairs were more likely to be covered in the media and press – particularly the national media and press – when they were seen to pose a challenge to mainstream British society (Burrell 1994: 18).

TV news: the message and the audience

In the worlds of newspaper and broadcasting journalism, events compete for attention. 'Events', however, are not simply neutral facts 'out there'. As Raymond Williams (1980: 114) observed, 'we cannot draw any firm line between events and their presentation. A very large number of events now presented are in fact interpretations by a small group of highly privileged voices, directly transmitted or read out by hired celebrities.' The processes by which events are deemed to be newsworthy are complex, subjective and not easily susceptible to analysis. Most analysts would probably agree with Golding and Elliott (1996 [1979]: 409) that 'Bad news is good news. As is often observed, there is little mileage in reporting the safe arrival of aircraft, the continued health of a film star, or the smooth untroubled negotiations of a wage settlement. News is about disruptions in the normal current of events.' 'Things are newsworthy because they represent the changefulness, the unpredictability and the conflictful nature of the world' (Hall et al. 1996 [1978]: 425). The normative rhythms of Islamic life are only featured when they are disrupted, for example when fires or other accidents create casualties during the *hajj*.

It does not follow, however, that news is either random or arbitrary, a reflection of wider cosmic disorder or social anomie. News is a product to be marketed. It is assiduously manipulated by governments, corporations and other powerful interest groups as well as by individuals who or groups that perceive themselves to be dispossessed or powerless. Governments, parliaments, courts, sports organisations, business corporations and other institutions feed the news with material by pre-scheduling events for the convenience of news organisations and maintaining regular contacts with editors and journalists. The news industry supports an army of press officers and public relations companies dedicated to spreading 'good news' about their employers or clients, or putting a positive 'spin' on events concerning them. Attempts to manipulate or control the news by determining its content are far from being confined to those who are wealthy, powerful or institutionally organized. The spectacular hi-jackings conducted by Palestinian guerrillas in the early 1970s were highly successful in dramatizing Palestinian grievances and arguably placed Palestinian rights – a previously neglected issue in the wider Arab–Israel dispute – at the heart of the international agenda. Terrorist acts, such as suicide bombings in Israel or the massacre of tourists in Egypt, are used by today's Islamist militants to dramatize their insistence that *jihad* is an integral and necessary part of the faith. The very western prejudices about which Muslims complain, namely the widespread perception that 'Islam is an inherently violent religion', is testimony to the success of those self-styled *mujahiddin* in getting their point of view across. 'News' consists not of events-in-themselves, but of the *account* of events as presented by the media. News gathering is an art, not a science; its rules are understood by its practitioners who tend to operate in accordance with an undeclared subjective consensus or, to use a favourite journalist's expression, 'by feel' (Gans 1980: 82). Essential to any definition of news is the idea of novelty-plus-narrative, encapsulated in the word 'story'. 'Unlike sociologists, who divide external reality into social processes, and historians who look at these processes over long periods, journalists see external reality as a set of disparate and independent events, each of which is new and can therefore be reported as news' (Gans 1980: 167).

Where political agendas are themselves driven by public responses to news (for example, in the case of mass murder or famine, where governments may be pressured into interventions they would otherwise have avoided, as in Somalia, the Kurdish enclaves in Iraq or the Serbian province of Kosovo), news coverage may itself be instrumental in creating or modifying events. The primary role of the media is to confer meaning or value on the otherwise arbitrary succession of events that 'cannot be allowed to remain in the limbo of the "random"' (Gans 1980: 167). The secondary, sometimes unacknowledged, role is to create events by influencing public opinion, events that can act as exercises in the uses of social power. The drama over the nurses in Saudi Arabia is a case in point. According to Amnesty International, several hundred non-western or non-white foreigners have been executed in Saudi Arabia after being convicted of capital crimes: only when white British nurses were involved, whose cases were taken up by the media, was world attention directed at the kingdom's criminal justice system. The pressure thus generated undoubtedly secured the nurses' release in May 1998 following a royal pardon by King Fahd. The king's recompense was the sale by the nurses of their stories to different Sunday newspapers, in which the details of alleged tortures and sexual abuse were given additional publicity. Despite the power of petrodollars, the Saudis were in a 'no-win situation'. If the nurses remained in jail or were executed, they were hapless victims of a medieval tyranny; if they were released, they damaged the kingdom by selling their stories. Meanwhile, in Algeria thousands of civilians were being massacred in the conflict between a western-backed government and Islamist insurgents, many of them, apparently, victims of government forces. Television images were conspicuous by their absence. As Amnesty International pointed out in its November 1997 report, owing to successful press censorship and press harassment, 'the world had hardly noticed'.

Gans (1980) has discussed different theories of news gathering, based on fieldwork he conducted in the 1970s in the newsrooms of two American television networks – CBS and NBC – and the news magazines *Newsweek* and *Time*. He briefly surveys a number of theories of news selection, including: the 'journalist-centred' theory favoured by politicians and journalists; social science approaches favouring selection according to the organizational requirements of the news service; the 'mirror theory', also popular among journalists, according to which it is 'events' themselves that determine story selection; and the 'technological determinism' favoured by McLuhan and his followers, according to which the message is largely determined by the technological requirements of the medium.

Gans does not reject any of these theories outright, but opts for a theory of news selection as primarily driven by sources.

> By 'sources' I mean the actors whom journalists observe or interview, including interviewees who appear on the air or who are quoted in magazine articles, and those who only supply background information or story suggestions. … The most salient characteristic of sources is that they provide information as members or representatives of organized and unorganized interest groups, and yet larger sectors of nation and society. (Gans 1980: 80)

Gans stresses the symbiosis or mutual dependency between the news organization and its sources. The sources cannot provide information until they make contact with the news organization; but the organization does not operate in a vacuum: '[I]t will choose the sources it considers suitable for the audience, even as it is chosen by sources who want to transmit information to the audience.' Sources, journalists and audiences coexist in a system that Gans describes as being 'closer to a tug of war than a functionally interrelated organism'. Such 'tugs of war', he argues 'are resolved by power; and news is, amongst other things "the exercise of power over the interpretation of reality"'. Even readers and viewers have some power in this equation, expressed by their ability to protest against and/or their refusal to accept what they read and see (Gans 1980: 81).

Two criteria, in Gans' view, underpin story selection: the first determines the availability of news and relates journalists to their sources; the second determines the suitability of news, which ties journalists to audiences. The economically and politically powerful have easy access to news. Those lacking power are harder to reach by journalists, and are generally not sought out until their activities produce what Gans calls 'social and moral disorder news'. Story selection is also subject to the important limitations of time and space. Journalism may be distinguished from literary and social science studies by the imperative of the deadline. This is immutable in broadcasting and can be extended by magazines only by high additional expenditures. The same criteria determine the speed and informality of the decision-making process: journalists and editors are forced by the pressure of deadlines to act on the basis of 'quick virtually intuitive judgements which some ascribe to "feel"' (Gans 1980: 82). Many of Gans' insights are echoed by other analysts. Both Golding and Elliott (1996 [1979]) and Hall et al. (1996 [1978]) interpret as ideologically conservative the tendency of news, especially broadcast news, to represent events as discrete moments unrelated to each other rather than as markers in the unfolding of social or historical processes. 'What is provided is a topping up of the limited range of regularly observed events in the world with more of the same. A reassuring sameness assimilates each succession of events to ready-made patterns in a timeless mosaic' (Golding and Elliott 1996 [1979]: 413). The 'evacuation of history' finds its correlative in the masking of power.

> News is about the actions of individuals, not corporate entities, thus individual authority rather than the exertion of entrenched power is seen to be the mover of events. … Groups which may exert power but which do not make news disappear, by definition, from view, and with them the visibility of power itself. … Of all the institutions which contribute to social process none is so invisible to broadcast news as the world of the company boardroom. (Golding and Elliott 1996 [1979]: 413)

Hall et al. (1996 [1978]) argue that the news and its interpretation, by conferring meaning on events, serves to reinforce the myth of a society as built on consensus. News presentation assumes that the audience shares a common stock of cultural knowledge. The news serves to reinforce the assumed consensus by framing the unexpected and unfamiliar within 'maps of meaning' that tend to have a reassuring effect. Not only do the media present information about events that lie outside the direct experience of the majority of people; they are often the only source of information about important events and topics. By mapping 'problematic' events within the frame of society's conventional understandings, the media define for society at large what events are happening and how they should be interpreted (Hall et al. 1996 [1978]: 426). The murder of a nurse is a 'domestic' event that occurs within a familiar 'map of meaning' even in a country as distant as Saudi Arabia, particularly for a public taste conditioned by the popular 'whodunnit' genres, or months of live coverage of the O.J. Simpson trial. Not all the tabloids assumed the nurses' innocence. After their release it was noted that the papers that were outbid for their stories were the ones most likely to express their doubts. The horrors of Algeria, by contrast, may be too alien, even too terrible, to be accommodated within the maps of meaning with which western audiences are familiar. The spectacle of several hundred people lying with their throats cut – showing the 'big smile' as it is known in Algeria – is difficult to accommodate within the experience of ordinary quotidian life. The same considerations apply in the case of the massacres in Rwanda: the scale of the atrocities may be too vast to be encompassed by the domestic imagination. The most effective television pictures from zones of war and famine invariably involve children, because children are emblems of domesticity and normality with which ordinary people can empathize.

The generally critical approach towards the media outlined above shares some broad assumptions with the Frankfurt School associated with the work of Horkheimer and Adorno in the 1940s. The tone of their critique was conveyed in a chapter of their 1947 book *Dialectic of Enlightenment*, entitled 'The culture industry: enlightenment as mass deception'. Just as the rational forces of the Enlightenment had been misappropriated by capitalism to advance mere technical expertise instead of the wider goal of human emancipation, so culture itself, rather than reflecting the wider aspirations of the human spirit, was being commoditized for mass consumption, as in other areas of manufacturing. According to Adorno, 'the entire practice of the culture industry transfers the profit motive naked into cultural forms'. Whereas in true works of art 'technique is concerned with the internal organisation of the object itself, with its inner logic', technique in the culture industry 'is from the beginning one of mechanical reproduction, and therefore always remains external to its object' (Adorno 1996 [1991]: 25, 26). Habermas, who stands in the Frankfurt tradition, argues that the development of the media and entertainment industries represents a corruption or 'refeudalization' of the 'public sphere', the forum (including the press, debating societies, and so forth) where 'open rational debate' has been fostered since the eighteenth century. For Habermas, broadcasting and the press have been adulterated by consumerism and the public relations industry, with public authority effectively drained of its truly democratic component and returned to the condition of mere public display characteristic of the pre-Enlightenment or feudal era. As Thompson (1995) points out, however, Habermas's conception of the public sphere bears little relation to the kinds of action and communication that have become increasingly common in the modern world. Broadcasting is neither a one-way nor a two-way street, but a form of 'mediated quasi-interaction', something much less predictable than either:

> Unlike the interlocutors in a face-to-face situation, the producers of media messages are not in a position to monitor directly the responses of recipients and to modify their action in the light of this feedback. … By providing individuals with images of and information about events that take place in locales beyond their immediate social milieux, the media may stimulate or intensify forms of collective action which may be difficult to control with the established mechanisms of power. (Thompson 1995: 116)

Baudrillard detects a similar unpredictability and ambiguity in what he terms 'the end of representation'. Contemporary culture is a culture of 'simulation' in which reality virtually disappears. 'The situation no longer permits us to isolate reality … as a fundamental variable. … [B]ecause we will never in future be able to separate reality from its statistical, stimulative projection in the media.' The result is a 'state of suspense and definitive uncertainty about reality' with the media increasingly filling the space once constituted by society and politics; indeed, it is the media themselves that constitute the 'hyperreal spectacle that is society and politics today' (Baudrillard 1996 [1988]: 12). Like Thompson, Baudrillard (1996 [1988]: 67) perceives the fundamental ambiguity of what he calls the 'implosion of the social in the media':

> About the media you can sustain two opposing hypotheses: they are the strategy of power, which find in them the means of mystifying the masses and of imposing its own truth. Or else they are the strategic territory of the ruse of the masses, who exercise in them their concrete power of the refusal of truth, of the denial of reality. Now the media are nothing else than a marvellous instrument for destablizing the real and the true, all historical or political truth (there is thus no possible political strategy of the media: it is a contradiction in terms). … Obviously there is a paradox in the inextricable entanglement of the masses and the media: is it the media that neutralize meaning and that produce the 'formless' (or informed) mass; or is it the mass which victoriously resists the media by diverting or by absorbing without reply all the messages that they produce? Are the mass media on the side of power in the manipulation of the masses, or are they on the side of the masses in the liquidation of meaning, in the violence done to meaning? Is it the media that fascinate the masses, or is it the masses who divert the media into showmanship? The media toss around sense and nonsense; they manipulate in every sense at once. No one can control this process.

Numerous analysts, including Eco and Hall, have pointed out that the combination of sound and visual images in television does not make it a suitable medium for beaming unambiguous, one-dimensional views on any subject. 'The communication chain', according to Eco (1987: 138),

> assumes a Source that, through a Transmitter, emits a Signal via a Channel. At the end of the Channel the Signal, through a Receiver, is transformed into a Message for the Addressee. Since the Signal, while traveling through the Channel, can be disturbed by Noise, one must make the Message *redundant*, so that the information is transmitted clearly. But the other fundamental requirement of this Chain is a Code, shared by the

> Source and the Addressee. A Code is an established system of probabilities, and only on the basis of the Code can we decide whether the elements of the message are intentional (desired by the source) or the result of Noise. (original emphasis)

Challenging McLuhan's famous aphorism that 'the medium is the message', Eco concludes that 'the medium is not the message' because 'the message depends on the code'. Generally speaking, the 'variability of interpretation' is a random factor. With few exceptions, '[n]obody regulates the way in which the addressee uses the message'. The medium therefore 'transmits those ideologies which the addressee receives according to codes originating in his social situation, in his previous education, and in the psychological tendencies of the moment' (Eco 1987: 141). In a similar vein Hall follows Barthes in distinguishing between the denotative and connotative levels at which televisual signifiers are decoded. At the denotative level a sweater always signifies a 'warm garment'; at the connotative level it may signify a fashionable style of *haute couture* or, alternatively, an informal style of dress. Interpretation at the connotative level is more open to variation than at the level of denotation. The connotative range of interpretations may as a rule operate with a dominant or hegemonic code; but alternative readings are possible based on pre-existing codes. In addition to a hermeneutic operating from within a dominant code, Hall (1992) advances the hypotheses of a 'negotiated version' containing a mixture of adaptive and oppositional elements, and a 'fully oppositional' version in which the viewer decodes messages both literally and connotatively in a globally contrary way. 'He/she detotalizes the message in the preferred code in order to retotalize the message within some alternative framework of reference' (Hall 1992: 131). The degrees of symmetry – that is, the degrees of 'understanding' and 'misunderstanding' in the communicative exchange – depend on the relations of equivalence established between the positions of producers and receivers. These are both highly variable and difficult to predetermine. 'What are called "distortions" or "misunderstandings" arise precisely from the lack of equivalence between the two sides in the communicative exchange' (Hall 1992: 131).

A few examples should suffice to demonstrate the problematic nature of audio-visual encodings with regard to Muslim viewers. In the case of the 1990–1 conflict in the Gulf, Werbner (1994: 123) has ably demonstrated how Hall's 'fully oppositional' model came into play among British Muslims of mainly Pakistani origin.

> Of course, the television images beamed into British Pakistani homes in Manchester already constituted, for the most part, a moral fable, seen from a Western perspective. The fable cast Saddam as a vicious, tyrannical, insane villain. In Britain, support of the international alliance was very high, one of the highest in the Western world. Against this appropriation, however, Pakistanis created a counter-narrative, a 'resistive reading', an alternative fable, which cast Saddam Hussein in the role of hero. This same fabulation of the events and cast of characters was repeated by different ideological constituencies throughout the Muslim world, from Algeria to Pakistan. … Like its Western counterpart, it was a global fable, globally fabulated.

My own research into BBC World Service Television (WSTV) coverage of the Ayodhya riots in India in 1992 shows how the 'messages' conveyed by sound and images may contradict each other. The problem is rendered more acute by the fact that most South Asian viewers of WSTV would have been unable to follow the English-language commentary.[4]

The trouble began on 6 December 1992 as Hindu leaders held religious ceremonies at the site of the temple. In his commentary, the BBC reporter Mark Tully points out that the leaders 'had called for no violence': the camera shows Hindu holy men sitting peacefully on open ground in front of the mosque. Tully then goes on to explain that the trouble broke out in one corner when a number of young men were seen climbing over the mosque wall and into the mosque enclosure – a few of them are briefly caught by the camera in a long shot. Tully points out that 'the police didn't seem to make any effort to stop them'. There are pictures of the police looking idle and indifferent. (Whether the particular policemen caught by the camera were aware of what was going on, the viewer cannot tell.) Tully goes on to relate that 'some of the young men climbed onto the roof of the mosque and started demolishing one of the domes'. The camera shows them grouped triumphantly on the dome with a banner, striking a heroic pose. Fighting then breaks out among the crowd, with photographers and film crews attacked.[5] The camera shows people shouting 'Long Live Lord Ram' in Hindi. The report continues in similar vein. Tully points out that the central government had tried to secure the mosque with some thirteen thousand paramilitary police camping nearby. But their plans were thwarted by the density of the crowds: '*It is impossible to estimate the bloodshed there would have been had they attempted to force their way through*...' (emphasis added).

Tully was one of the BBC's most experienced reporters, and his commentary on the pictures is a model of balance and objectivity. Switch off the sound, however, or assume that his commentary cannot be understood, because it is delivered in English, and one gets a very different impression. The sequence of camera shots moves from Hindu holy men praying in their saffron robes, to young men climbing over the fence and onto the roof of the mosque. The information that the Hindu leaders 'called for no violence' and that the violation of the mosque was perpetrated by a minority extremist element will have been lost. The same applies to the role of the paramilitary police. The only police the viewer sees on screen are lounging about indifferently. The possibility that police reluctance to act may have been prompted by a concern to avoid bloodshed will have been lost if the viewer speaks no English. The camera sequences, moving from holy men to triumphant mosque violators, to indifferent policemen, to fighting in the crowd, tell a different story from Mark Tully's, one that suggests that the holy men encouraged, and that the police connived at, the violation of the mosque.[6]

After the destruction of the mosque, another BBC reporter, Daniel Lak, reported on the repercussions in Pakistan, where Hindu temples were ransacked and hundreds of Hindu homes burned down. His introduction showed pictures of Muslim militants – identifiable by their beards – demonstrating, calling for a national day of protest. The Pakistani government, Lak explains in his commentary, 'will be determined to prevent more attacks on Hindu temples and property. In Lahore, Quetta, Hyderabad and other cities, armed police were sent to guard the Hindu temples and property, and some attacks were prevented, but so widespread was the unrest that twenty-five holy sites were damaged.' The camera shows a damaged idol in the corner of a burned-out temple. As in Tully's report, the politically significant information – that the Pakistani authorities are doing everything they can to lower the temperature by protecting the property and temples of the Hindu minority – is conveyed exclusively in words. Apart from the reporter and a brief shot of police and firefighters hosing a burnt-out car, the pictures are confined to images of Muslim militants and a desecrated Hindu idol. The viewer without English would be most likely to draw the conclusion that 'Pakistan' was out to 'get' Hindus, just as 'India' was conniving at the destruction of the Muslim temple.[7]

Regardless of the intentions of the producers or the reporters' commentaries, the reporting of these events had a polarizing effect. On a visit to Bombay in 1994 I was told that during the subsequent riots, in which hundreds of Muslims lost their lives, video replays of the Ayodhya incident were used to stir up the emotions of both Hindus and Muslims.

'Balance' in British domestic output: some examples

Given the nature of the medium, it is perhaps inevitable that producers will seek to emphasize the sensational aspects of any subject. Militant soundbites and dramatic confrontations make more exciting viewing than visions of harmony and concord. An example of the way in which the documentary format can have a polarizing effect on the subject of Islam is provided by three *Planet Islam* programmes shown on BBC2 in the summer of 1997.[8] The first, on Islam in France, explores the situation facing that country's Muslims following the bombs in the Paris metro in July 1995 in which eight people were killed and more than a hundred injured. Against close-ups of agonized faces, the commentator William Shawcross explains that the growth of militant Islam imported from Algeria is 'putting tolerance and freedom under strain in the heart of Western Europe'. Police video shows the fatal shooting of one of the suspects, Khaled Khalkal, whose fingerprints are said to have been found on one unexploded bomb. The film uses Khalkal as a symbol of Muslim alienation in France. There are depressing shots of mainly Muslim-inhabited tower blocks where alienated youths describe police harassment. The same message is repeated by the imam of a small mosque in Lyons, where local worshippers are frightened of being branded as terrorists. The images are complemented by interviews with a candidate who is filmed canvassing support for the National Front (NF). He talks about the incompatibility of Islamic and Christian values and meets with a sympathetic response from his potential white constituents. Confrontations between Muslims and members of the NF are described as taking place almost daily. The picture of polarization is accentuated by scenes from a dramatized portrait of Khaled Khalkal as a martyr/hero. Ordinary French people are horrified that such a murderer could be seen as a hero by some of their supposed fellow-citizens.

The second half of the programme concerns the successful legal challenge mounted by two female pupils at the Jean Moulin secondary school in Albertville who had demanded the right to wear their headscarves in class. They are shown arguing with the school authorities, who insisted on excluding them on the ground that the 'veil' is a religious symbol forbidden in state schools under rules of secularity, as well as an unacceptable symbol of female oppression. The students' motive for wearing the veil is never explored. It is presumed, *a priori*, to be 'religious', Islamic by definition. In the country of Roland Barthes and Michel Foucault, the semiotics of veiling is neither explored nor discussed. A highly complex question involving social meanings, individual identities and group identities is reduced to a confrontation between two non-negotiable positions, two 'fundamentalisms' – that of an (uncontested) Islam that insists on veiling, and that of a secularist French educational establishment.

Planet Islam's second programme, about Russia, takes a similarly confrontational approach. The film's tone is set by an opening sequence of shots of police stopping cars in Moscow to look for weapons. 'Fear of terrorism in the heart of Russia', says the commentary, 'has revived old animosities between its different peoples. Viewed from Moscow, the old Soviet empire is a series of dominoes which could fall one by one. And what could topple them, some fear, is Islam!' Shots of the Orthodox Patriarch arriving in Red Square are accompanied by a brief historical excursus about the triumph of Orthodoxy over Islam, symbolized by the Cross superimposed over the Crescent on Russian cathedrals. An Orthodox priest demands closer ties between the church and the new post-communist state in order to overcome the threat posed by Islam. Bearded Muslim worshippers complain of harassment: the authorities will not allow them to open mosques, the police regard them as Chechen terrorists. A segment on Tabaristan focuses on tension between Muslims and Christians in the city of Kazan. It includes an interview with Fawzia Baramova, leader of the small Tartar nationalist party, who protests vociferously against the war in Chechnya, which she sees as a war against Muslims. 'There are people outside Russia who want to kill Muslims,' she says on camera. 'Just look at Tajikistan, Abkhazia and Chechnya. Wherever there are Muslims there is war.' The film includes footage of the war in Tajikistan shot from helicopters as the Russians scour the Pamir valleys for rebels. The commentary presents a generalized picture of Russian–Muslim conflict.

> Russian soldiers patrol the frontier between Afghanistan and the former Soviet republic of Tajikistan where Russian troops support the Tajik government in a war against Islamic militants based across the frontier in Afghanistan. … Moscow's army is still heavily involved in a bloody civil war which has divided the Muslim population. On one side are the militant Muslims who are trying to overthrow the government. They're receiving help from Tajikistan's Muslim neighbours. The Tajiks get support from the local Muslim establishment and from the Russian army. The war has threatened to pull Russia into a conflict reminiscent of its biggest humiliation in the twentieth century, in Afghanistan. That was a war in which Tajik Muslims fought for Moscow's Red Army against other Muslims in Afghanistan. Now some of them have changed sides, and are fighting to defend Islam against Moscow's armies.

The religious character of the conflict is highlighted by footage of Russian soldiers being blessed by a priest. 'Their mission is to stop the flow of drugs, weapons and Islamic militants into Tajikistan. But for Father Alexei they're going to war for their Christian God,' says the commentary over pictures of troops kissing the Cross and being blessed with holy water like medieval knights.

The middle ground in this film is not completely absent. The Muslim leader Abdul Wahid Niazov explains that anti-Muslim hostility is dangerous, and the leaders of Russia should try to defuse it. A lengthy sequence follows Tartarstan's Minister for Religious Affairs as he travels around the city of Kazan with offers of government help to Muslim leaders. Turbanned mullahs express their appreciation for the new religious freedoms that have appeared since the end of the Soviet Union. The minister is presented as being fair and reasonable. Nevertheless, the images of confrontation are those that leave the strongest impression. The persistent theme in both the French and Russian films is that 'Islam' is heading for confrontation with the West. The underlying image is of a monolith called *Planet Islam* whose internal configurations and contradictions are never explored. The possibility that 'Islam' is really a language or set of symbols through which people with widely divergent political and social viewpoints articulate their aspirations is never put forward, or even suggested. This reductionism is most flagrant in the treatment of the war in Tajikistan. The external forces engaged in the conflict are unspecified ('the Tajiks' Muslim neighbours'). The clan rivalries fostered by competition between Moscow and Tashkent – a key factor in any responsible political analysis of the conflict – are completely ignored. The overall impression is that Moscow is defending the Dushanbe government in order to prevent the spread of 'militant Islam' from Afghanistan. At no point is it suggested that there may be a difference between the perception and reality of such a threat. The *realpolitik* perspective widely acknowledged by academic writers, according to which the reconstituted ex-Soviet nomenklatura in Dushanbe deliberately exaggerated the Islamist threat in order to gain Moscow's support against rival factions backed by Tashkent, is discarded or overlooked in favour of the simplicities of 'militant Islam'.

The third film in the *Planet Islam* trilogy follows the rise of the Nation of Islam (NOI) in the United States under its charismatic leader, Louis Farrakhan. Here the lines of confrontation are less sharply drawn, not least because 'Orthodox' Muslims dismiss Farrakhan as 'a fraud'. The struggle between 'Islam' and the rest of the world is more local. Black prisoners are turning to the NOI *en masse.* In inner-city Chicago, says the commentary, 'Islam is a new call to arms in the war against drugs, alcohol and crime.' NOI activists patrol the streets to rid them of dealers in crack cocaine. The film details the story of the NOI and its abrasive relations with the Sunni mainstream.

It would be simplistic to suggest that the *Planet Islam* series expresses Islamophobia or consistent anti-Muslim bias. Its problem is rather that by dramatizing the role of 'Islam' in three countries it becomes hostage to a thesis of confrontation. In the cases of Russia and France, Muslims are presented as the victims of confrontation rather than aggressors. Nevertheless, the implicit message tends to support the 'clash of civilizations' theory popularized by Samuel Huntington (1993, 1996). A high degree of social and political incompatibility is deemed to exist between Islamic and western/Christian life-styles and values. The situation in the United States is treated differently and, in my view, much more accurately. The account of the two wings of the Black Muslim movement – the highly eclectic Nation of Islam and the more orthodox wing led by Warith ul-Din Muhammad – generally conforms to the much more detailed descriptions of academic researchers such as Gilles Kepel (1997) and Matthias Gardell (1996). In France, the thesis of confrontation is sustained by presenting Muslims as terrorists or victims in conflict with the wider society represented by the National Front, the police or the state educational system. Images suggestive of common ground (for example, of non-Muslims and Muslims participating in common activities) are wholly absent. In the film about Russia and the ex-Soviet Union the distortions necessary to sustain the thesis of confrontation are even greater. The war in Chechnya, a few incidents in Kazan and a tendentious account of the civil war in Tajikistan are juxtaposed with the statements by a handful of militant priests and soldiers to create an image of impending conflict.

If Huntington's 'clash of civilizations' thesis provides the subtext for *Planet Islam*, *The Tottenham Ayatollah*, shown on Channel Four's *Witness* slot in 1996, conforms to the thesis sustained by a less influential but far more considered text, Olivier Roy's *The Failure of Political Islam* (1994).[9] The film, written and presented by Jon Ronson, follows the Islamist agitator Omar Bakri Muhamad of the Muhajiroun, a militant faction that broke away from the controversial Hizb al-Tahrir (Islamic Liberation Party), while he plans Holy War in the United Kingdom. 'When the war is won,' says Ronson, 'homosexuals, adulterers and fornicators will be stoned to death.' Despite being boycotted by his fellow Muslims, who see him as a liability, Omar revels in the hostile press coverage he receives. He proudly shows Ronson a wall covered with cuttings from the 'media onslaught against Islam'.

Omar and his deputies travel around north London collecting money in giant Coca-Cola bottles for Hamas, the Palestinian movement responsible for suicide bombings in Israel. Omar's pontificating about corruption of western society, his bloodthirsty rhetoric, contrasts with his engaging personality. There is an element of self-irony about him and about his relationship with Ronson, who is Jewish (a fact with which he confronts Omar at the end of the programme). When Ronson is late for a rendezvous, Omar jocularly threatens him with fifty lashes – playfully confirming the 'bloodthirsty' Muslim stereotype. He takes Ronson and his crew to Wood Green Shopping Centre to show how Britain will change under Islamic Law. The 'Spicey Girls' will not only be banned: anyone selling their discs will be immediately arrested. There will be no night clubs, no mixing of the sexes. The film deflates Omar's windy rhetoric and hence the anxieties expressed in the press and parliament about Muslim extremism. Omar represents no one but himself and a small group of deluded acolytes. The *Tottenham Ayatollah* may not be flattering to Islamist self-esteem, but it domesticates Islamism in a down-to-earth way. In his gently ironic manner Ronson de-demonizes Omar, and, by extension, the whole Islamist movement with its global pretensions and dangerous moral certitudes. The 'clash of civilizations' is reduced from Huntington's grandiose post-Cold War scenario to a semi-jocular exchange of insults in Hyde Park.

Viewed as a film 'about Islam', however, the *Tottenham Ayatollah* is very far from satisfactory. A commissioning editor would doubtless argue that similarly debunking, iconoclastic films have been made about Christian figures, for example the American Evangelist Morris Cerulo, whose claims to heal vulnerable people 'by the power of the holy spirit' were punctured by Joan Bakewell on BBC's *The Heart of the Matter*; or Christopher Hitchens' notorious (but not unmerited) debunking of Mother Theresa (shown on the *Witness* slot in 1994). Some practising Christians, of course, protested at these films; but the overall context in which their protests were made was significantly different. In Britain mainstream Christianity has a privileged place, in society, in religious education and in the national media. A morning service is broadcast daily on BBC radio; Jewish, Catholic and Sikh speakers appear regularly on 'Thought for the Day', a talk with a religious perspective that forms part of the immensely popular *Today* programme running from 6.00 a.m. to 9 a.m. on Radio Four. When I asked a BBC programme editor in charge of 'Thought for the Day' why there were no regular Muslim speakers, he explained (on conditions of anonymity) that two or three had been tried, none of whom 'came up to scratch' in terms of professional broadcasting. The speakers were either 'too hard-edged and dogmatic' or 'too soft' – meaning they had nothing to say that was challenging or thought-provoking. The editor was also aware that they lacked 'a Buddhist or good Hindu'. He added that he was conscious that all faiths should be represented and was actively seeking new speakers who could be given additional training to bring them up to BBC standards.

The established religion also has a privileged position on television. Programmes such as the BBC's *Songs of Praise*, without being overtly propagandist, celebrate the rich repertory of British church architecture and hymnody, against the backdrop of a landscape canonized by saints, poets and mystics, to create a sense of the numinous linked to feelings of patriotism – feelings about what the denizens of an earlier age would not have hesitated to call 'God-and-my-country'. It is difficult to see how Muslims can be made to feel included in the pervasive but hard-to-define sense of Britishness – or, rather, Englishness, Scottishness, Welshness and Irishness – conveyed by productions of this kind.

***Baraka* on television**

Can Muslims find a way of representing their distinctive forms of spirituality through television? Some commentators see television itself as a type of surrogate popular religion, closely linked to the values of consumer capitalism. In the view of Gregor Goethals, western spirituality has become channelled into the elite arts such as painting and sculpture, while the popular religiosity that was once included in the medieval cathedral has now been subsumed into the 'Cathedral of Television' (Goethals 1981, 1990). Others, such as Neil Postman, argue that television tends to assimilate every aspect of public communication to its own distinctive forms – essentially the forms of entertainment and show business.

> In courtrooms, classrooms, operating rooms, board rooms, churches and even airplanes, Americans no longer talk to each other, they entertain each other. They do not exchange ideas, they exchange images. They do not argue with propositions; they argue with good looks, celebrities and commercials. For the message of television as metaphor is not

> only that all the world is a stage, but that the stage is located in Las Vegas, Nevada. (Postman 1987: 95)

The 'showbiz' model, however, need not imply that religious broadcasts must of necessity be frivolous, merely that in order to succeed with audiences accustomed to the conventions of television they must assimilate some of the conventions and forms of the entertainment industry. Straight religious broadcasts (preachers with 'talking heads') may be popular because of their novelty value in countries new to television, but they make less than compelling viewing for more sophisticated audiences. In America during the 1980s the New Christian Right was able to mount a partially successful cultural revolution against the secular humanist monopoly it perceived to be holding sway in the media. Conservative and fundamentalist preachers proved more adept than their liberal counterparts in adapting their liturgies for television and tailoring their interpretations of Christianity to its requirements (Hadden and Shupe 1988; Hadden and Swann 1981; Ruthven 1991: 255–76). In Britain, such religious propaganda is inhibited under the Broadcasting Acts, which have deliberately tried to avoid importing American-style 'televangelism' (Gunter and Viney 1994: 2–3). Public service broadcasting is in some respects the electronic counterpart of the established church. The counter-cultural model prevailing in America is rejected and religious broadcasting generally reflects the wider secular ethos.

> There has been a shift away from the direct promotion of religious beliefs towards a more or less detached exploration of religious beliefs, behaviours and values. … The stories told about religion tend to be about its institutions, politics and personalities. … The religious claim to truth, especially to an exclusive truth, is difficult to assimilate in a media system that has elevated professional tolerance and impartiality above nearly every other virtue. (McDonnell 1993: 93)

Shabbir Akhtar, the Muslim philosopher, described media treatment of Muslim concerns over the Salman Rushdie controversy as a 'liberal inquisition': while his account of the dogmatic intolerance with which Muslims were treated is definitely overdrawn,[10] the phrase is aptly suggestive of the threat posed to liberal values by Muslim demands. For the secular humanist 'church' represented by the media, the suppression of a book on religious grounds amounts to 'heresy' and must be suppressed accordingly.

In an effort to reflect a more balanced and positive image of Islam – partly, no doubt, in response to the Rushdie affair – the BBC in 1992 produced *Living Islam*, a series of six fifty-minute programmes presented by Akbar Ahmed. Although the series did not impress everyone,[11] it was widely welcomed in the British Muslim community. It makes an adequate introduction for students approaching Islam for the first time.

Television excels at personal narrative, and one of the more successful ways of presenting a religious outlook is by building viewer empathy, something that *Living Islam* conspicuously failed to do. A degree of viewer empathy was achieved even in the case of the *Tottenham Ayatollah*: what emerged was a likeable if absurdly self-deluded man wholly at odds with the stereotypical 'terrorist fanatic'. For the British viewer operating within the dominant cultural paradigm, a narrative approach exploring the lives of one or perhaps two Muslim women (including, perhaps, one of the many recent female converts to Islam) would have been far more effective in penetrating the myths surrounding gender in Islam than a series of unconvincing 'talking heads'. A BBC series *Faces of Islam* broadcast early in 1998 to coincide with Ramadan, adopted this approach, with sympathetic profiles of the boxer Chris Eubank (a convert to Islam) and the 'born-again' Muslim cricketer Imran Khan.

Abdullah Schleifer, an American television reporter who converted to Islam and now lives in Cairo, doubts if the distinctive forms of Islamic spirituality can ever be shown on television. Unlike Christianity, with its rich repertoire of iconographies and miracle plays, the icons of Islam, its 'representations of the sacred inner essence of all things', are aural rather than visual, focusing as they do on the centrality of the Word.

> Spiritual grace (*baraka*) does not 'track'.[12] … However obvious and almost palpable it may be to those vast outpourings of the faithful on pilgrimage to sacred centres or at miraculous sites, *baraka* cannot be recorded electronically on video tape for 'live' transmission. Television may induce trances, but it is intrinsically anti-meditative. (Schleifer 1993: 173)

Muslims see beautiful moonlit landscapes or the grandeur of a desert as 'signs' (*ayat*) of God, '[b]ut put these same scenes on video, or even high-definition TV and after a few seconds they pale, and we become bored. The electronic recording that is video simulates the image without its invisible aura of spiritual grace' (Schleifer 1993: 173). By the same technological token, it is impossible to create the 'aura of holiness of a holy man' on television. All you get is 'the image of some nice old guy with a pleasant friendly smile'. Schleifer (1993: 174) concludes that television inevitably desacralizes and despiritualizes the world: 'If God, the angels, heaven, hell and spiritual grace are not visible, then in a tele-technological understanding of ontology, they do not exist. Sex and violence, however, certainly do.' The point is well made and opens up the suggestion that it is not just the western-controlled media, but the technology as such, that drains Islam of its distinctive spirituality. 'Sex and violence' (veiled women and terrorism) dominate images of Islam, not just in the West, but across the globe. Schleifer laments that the news media that have arisen as part of the 'Islamic Revival' rarely concern themselves with 'the rich fabric of traditional Islamic life that still remains (for all modernity's unravelling of the social fabric)'. In reporting on the world of Islam, he argues, '"Islamic" or Islamist journalism appears to be disturbingly similar to the very same secular press it theoretically confronts – similar both in its self-perception as the "scourge of princes" and in its perception of the world of Islam' (Schleifer 1993: 174).

However, Schleifer's critique of the way in which Islamist journalism reflects the broader world of Islam is far from being the last word on the representation of Islamic art and spirituality in the media. As already suggested, a sense of the numinous can be sustained by the combination of sounds and images linked to religiously suggestive motifs, as in the best examples of *Songs of Praise*. If generations of Muslim architects and craftspeople were able to express the complexities of the divine order they perceived in nature – their understanding of the 'signs of God' – in the intricacies of arabesque and geometrical patterning, it should not be beyond the wit of Muslim film-makers to express the same spirit or sense of order in, say, documentaries that helped to bridge the gap between the arts and science. Television *secularizes* the world by challenging received dogmas and certainties and by juxtaposing conflicting traditions, neutrally proclaiming each to be as good as the other. It need not *desacralize* it: on the contrary (as Goethals, McLuhan and others have recognized), there is an element of 're-enchantment' about the medium, to adapt Weberian terminology. 'News', commoditized and marketed in regular predictable segments, decontextualizes human experience, routinizing the exceptional, formatting horror into Art. The explanatory discourses through which reflective literate people seek to address the problems of the day are overlaid by images. As Jean Seaton (1997: 4) observes, 'political communication becomes less and less based on information, and more and more on the ingredients of image-making', a fact with far-reaching implications as policy becomes 'media-driven'. For Muslims, the majority of whom share an aniconic tradition in which images are equated with paganism or *jahiliya*, gaining entry into such a world represents both dangers and opportunities. A world mediated through images may strike the traditionalist as 'pagan', and there have been several examples of television-smashing by militants in Egypt and Afghanistan in recent years. It is highly unlikely, however, that the Islamists will succeed in protecting the Muslim public from profane images emanating from the West. Efforts to ban TV satellite dishes in Iran and Saudi Arabia have been less than successful. As the technology advances, detection and policing become more difficult. However hostile Islamists may feel towards images emanating from the West (and in Algeria engineers accused of installing TV satellite dishes have been murdered), they do not, with some exceptions, have the will to invade private homes. All Islamists, by definition, claim to uphold the Shari'a. As Olivier Roy (1994) has noted, the Shari'a (in all of its versions) protects the sanctity of family and home.[13]

If censorship becomes increasingly difficult under today's technological conditions, the only alternative must be for Muslims to challenge western cultural hegemony by competing in the electronic marketplace. The expertise is available. A recent initiative by the European Union, MedMedia, which facilitated the training of journalists from (mostly) Arab countries and helped finance co-productions between the wealthier and poorer sides of the Mediterranean, offers a potentially fruitful example. Television production is becoming increasingly expensive and there are no compelling political or cultural reasons why Muslim governments, companies, individuals or broadcasting networks should not collaborate with western governments and media in order to secure greater access to the global airwaves. The challenge for Muslim journalists and producers will be to formulate Islamic perspectives in ways that make them sufficiently attractive to the executives and commissioning editors who control access to the airwaves. The Muslim diaspora living in the West, equipped with its skills and aware of its cultural prerequisites, could be the vital link in any such process of cultural exchange.

Notes

1. See, for example, Dickens' account of a public execution by guillotine in Rome from *Pictures from Italy* (1846), reprinted in Carey (1987: 313–16).

2. Omar Bakri Muhammad was interviewed on Radio 4's *Today* programme on the day after the Luxor Massacre about his fundraising activities for Hamas. See Madeleine Bunting, 'Islamophobia: pronouncing a fatwa on extremes', *Guardian*, 20 November 1997.

3. Burrell (1994: 31), citing *The Muslim Manifesto* (London, 1990), p. 22.

4. I should like to express my appreciation to the late Johann Ramsland, editor of WSTV news, for allowing me to watch this footage.

5. Why the rioters should not want their heroic reconquest of the Babri mosque filmed is not entirely clear. The most likely reason is to avoid identification by the police.

6. BBC WSTV main bulletin, 2200 hrs GMT, 12 June 1992.

7. WSTV 2200 hours GMT, 12 July 1992.

8. *Planet Islam*, Menton Barraclough Carey Productions 1997. I am grateful to John Blake for providing me with tapes of these programmes.

9. *Tottenham Ayatollah*, RDF Television, 1997.

10. 'The next time there are gas chambers in Europe there is no doubt concerning who will be inside them' (Shabbir Akhtar, *Guardian*, 27 February 1989). While the context in which Akhtar was writing was the anti-Muslim prejudices manifested in the Rushdie affair, his much quoted remark gained weight and poignancy from the subsequent massacres of Muslims in Bosnia. However, the contexts of these two events are only connected in the most distant way. Muslims in Bosnia were not only victims but also perpetrators of massacres.

11. See my own review in *The Times Literary Supplement*, 14 May 1993, p. 19.

12. To 'track' is to record a sound or picture electronically on tape for reproduction.

13. Roy (1994) brilliantly describes the 'empty social space' resulting from the impositions by Islamists of neo-fundamentalist social norms. As in Saudi Arabia, religious militias can enforce prayer and fasting but cannot invade private homes. No longer the locus of work, the Muslim household is mainly a place for the consumption of television, videos, and so on. Roy argues that the Islamists will never be able to stop the flow of this consumption, precisely because the Shari'a sets such store by protecting the family. The life-style of the modern urban Muslim family, he argues, is the opposite of the Islamic way of life. It is a product of the West. There are no 'Islamist leisure activities'. The new cultural models – videos – are blossoming into the very heart of Islamic identity, even though the result is never a westernization of modes of behaviour but a juxtaposition, in which neither system can be reduced to the other (Roy 1994: 11, 195f.).

References

Adorno, T.W. 1996 [1991]. *The Culture Industry: Selected Essays on Mass Culture.* In P. Marris and S. Thornham (eds), *Media Studies: A Reader.* Edinburgh: Edinburgh University Press.

Baudrillard, J. 1996 [1988]. *Selected Writings.* In P. Marris and S. Thornham (eds), *Media Studies: A Reader.* Edinburgh: Edinburgh University Press.

Burrell, A. 1994. Media, muslims and manipulation. Unpublished MA dissertation, Goldsmiths College, University of London.

Carey, J. (ed.) 1987. *The Faber Book of Reportage.* London: Faber and Faber.

Dassetto, F. 1988. The Tabligh organization in Belgium. In T. Gerholm and Y.G. Lithman (eds), *The New Islamic Presence in Western Europe.* London: Mansell.

Eco, U. 1987. *Travels in Hyperreality* (trans W. Weaver). London: Picador.

Gans, H.J. 1980. *Deciding What's News.* London: Constable.

Gardell, M. 1996. *Countdown to Armageddon: Louis Farrakhan and the Nation of Islam.* London: Hurst.

Goethals, G. 1981. *The Television Ritual: Worship at the Video Altar.* Boston: Beacon Press.

Goethals, G. 1990. *The Electronic Golden Calf: Images, Religion and the Making of Meaning.* Cambridge: Cowley Publications.

Golding, P. and Elliott, P. 1996 [1979]. *Making the News.* In P. Marris and S. Thornham (eds), *Media Studies: A Reader.* Edinburgh: Edinburgh University Press.

Gunter, B. and Viney, R. 1994. *Seeing is Believing: Religion and Television in the 1990s.* London: John Libbey.

Hadden, J.K. and Shupe, A. 1988. *Televangelism: Power and Politics on God's Frontier.* New York: Henry Holt and Co.

Hadden, J.K. and Swann, C.E. 1981. *Prime Time Preachers: The Rising Power of Televangelism.* Reading, MA: Addison-Wesley Pub. Co.

Hall, S. 1992. Encoding/decoding. In S. Hall et al. (eds), *Culture, Media, Language.* London and New York.

Hall, S. et al. 1996 [1978]. *Policing the Crisis: Mugging, the State and Law and Order.* In P. Marris and S. Thornham (eds), *Media Studies: A Reader.* Edinburgh: Edinburgh University Press.

Huntington, S. 1993. The Clash of Civilizations? *Foreign Affairs* 72 (3): 22–49.

Huntington, S. 1996. *The Clash of Civilizations and the Remaking of World Order.* New York: Touchstone Books.

Kepel, G. 1997. *Allah in the West: Islamic Movements in America and Europe* (trans S. Milner). Cambridge: Polity.

King, J. 1993. Tablighi Jamaat and the Deobandi Mosques in Britain. Paper presented at conference on Muslims in Britain, King's College London, December.

McDonnell, J. 1993. Religion, education and communication of values. In C. Arthur (ed.), *Religion and the Media.* Cardiff: University of Wales Press.

McLuhan, M. 1962. *The Gutenberg Galaxy: The Making of Typographic Man.* London: University of Toronto Press.

McLuhan, M. 1964. *Understanding Media: The Extensions of Man.* London.

Postman, N. 1987. *Amusing Ourselves to Death: Public Discourse in the Age of Show Business.* London: Methuen.

Roy, O. 1994. *The Failure of Political Islam.* London: I.B. Tauris.

Runnymede Trust 1997. *Islamophobia – A Challenge for Us All.* London: Runnymede Trust.

Ruthven, M. 1991. *The Divine Supermarket: Shopping for God in America.* London: Hogarth Press.

Said, E.W. 1981. *Covering Islam: How the Media and the Experts Determine How We See the Rest of the World.* London: Routledge and Kegan Paul.

Sardar, Z. and Davies, M.W. 1990. *Distorted Imagination: Lessons from the Rushdie Affair.* London: Grey Seal Books.

Seaton, J. 1997. Sovereignty and the media. Paper delivered at the Sovereignty Seminar, Birkbeck College, London.

Thompson, J.B. 1995. *The Media and Modernity: A Social Theory of the Media.* Cambridge: Polity.

Werbner, P. 1994. Diaspora and millennium: British Pakistani global–local fabulations of the Gulf War. In A.S. Ahmed and H. Donnan (eds), *Islam, Globalization and Postmodernity.* London: Routledge.

Williams, R. 1980. *What I Came to Say.* London: Hutchinson.

5

INTERPRETING ISLAM IN AMERICAN SCHOOLS

Susan L. Douglass and Ross E. Dunn

Twenty-five years ago it was quite possible for a citizen of the United States to grow up, graduate from a major university, and pursue a career without knowing anything about Islam or the Muslim world. The entire school curriculum made no more than passing reference to Muslims in history, in connection with the Crusades, perhaps, or the fall of Constantinople to the Turks. A smattering of innovative programmes beginning in the 1960s introduced students to Indian, Chinese or Mesoamerican culture at the secondary level, but Islam was excluded. Until the 1960s, few American universities offered courses on Asian, African or Middle Eastern history. Consequently, most history and social studies teachers entered the profession possessing no systematic knowledge of these regions to pass on to youngsters, even if they might have been predisposed to do so. World history was defined largely as synonymous with the history of Greece, Rome, medieval Christendom and modern Europe. Apart from small numbers of university specialists interested in Asia or Africa, the vast majority of Americans acquired what scant information they had on Islam and Muslims from television, films, advertising and print journalism.

Stereotypes and misrepresentations of Islam have been deeply ingrained in American culture. Just as the legacy of slavery has shaped popular images of Africa as a continent of heathen tribes and impenetrable jungles, so the western medieval and colonial heritage of hostility to Islam has underlain modern mis-education about Muslim society and history. In the mass media, cultural bias in coverage of the Muslim world has been so pervasive as to merit academic study (Friedlander 1981; Shaheen 1980, 1984). American public reactions to the Suez Crisis, successive Arab–Israeli conflicts, the Arab oil embargo, the seizure of the US embassy in Tehran and the political activism of such leaders as Qaddafi, Hafez al-Assad and Ayatollah Khomeini have shaped journalistic treatment of all Muslim societies. On the whole, teachers have been poorly equipped to examine critically the faulty assumptions and misunderstandings that infect this coverage. Consequently, the popular media's interpretation of Islam and the Muslim world has flowed freely into schoolrooms and then back out again to the wider public without being subjected to much critical analysis and correction.

The cultural and social conditions for learning about Islam and Muslims in American schools slowly began to change in the 1970s. This pattern is most conspicuous in the instructional materials that teachers and students read. To the extent that young Americans are exposed to interpretations of Islam and Muslim history independent of the mass media, they get them from the commercial textbooks that schools adopt, as well as from ancillary print and visual materials selected by teachers. Teachers also receive guidelines for instruction about Islam from national, state and local educational agencies. It is no exaggeration to affirm that commercial textbooks, together with the academic standards documents that most states have recently developed, are the intellectual tools with which most young Americans undertake any study of Islam and Muslim societies.

Whatever scholars may think of the results, schools teach children interpretations of Islam, the ideas that most high school graduates will carry into their careers and community lives. A look at factors in the US education system that affect the presentation of Islam and Muslim history, as well as the approaches to this subject in textbooks and curriculum, is an indicator of the general quality of Americans' knowledge of Islam and helps gauge how these understandings are changing.

The context: international education in American schools

Most American children learn about Islam only in connection with their schools' social studies curriculum. Since the 1920s, educators have defined social studies to embrace history, geography, economics, government, and occasionally social sciences such as sociology and anthropology. Social studies has never developed as a distinct academic discipline, and the various subjects grouped under this rubric have traditionally been taught separately in universities. Elementary and secondary schools, however, often utilize interdisciplinary, cross-curricular approaches to social studies that may include literature, art, science and technology, as well as social ethics, national values and world religions.

What and how much students learn about Islam in public (that is, publicly financed) schools depends generally on the commitment of their particular state or school district to what professional educators commonly call 'global education'. In other words, educational reformers who urge improved instruction about world societies, religions and history have not generally singled out Islam as deserving especially meticulous investigation. Rather, they have implicitly included Islam and Muslim regions in their calls for a more geographically and culturally inclusive curriculum and for world history education that is not limited to the Christian peoples of Western and Central Europe.

In the 1970s, media representations of Islam and Muslims were growing steadily more negative and cliché-ridden, owing to the fourth Arab–Israeli war, the oil embargo and the Iranian revolution. Ironically, it was in this same decade that educators built a persuasive case for improving global history, foreign language training and knowledge of world affairs. A number of developments inspired this campaign. One was recognition that political multi-polarism, the proliferation of new nation-states, global economic complexities and the electronic revolution required that young Americans know much more about the world around them than they appeared to know. For global educators of the 1970s, the most compelling symbol of the new international order was the 'big blue marble': the earth photographed from the moon. Planetary unity demanded an ecumenized citizenry.

Another factor in curriculum reform was the extraordinary growth of knowledge in history and the social sciences. This phenomenon included new research in American and European social history and an explosion of knowledge about African, Asian and Native American peoples. Internationally minded reformers called for inclusion of this new knowledge in school curricula. Surely, they argued, the American public recognized the importance of this research, because in 1958 it supported the National Defense Education Act, which generously funded scholarship on the history, economy and languages of developing countries. As the corpus of scholarly publication grew, school texts that limited African history to the story of European imperialism, had nothing to say about China before 1840, or took Muslim history seriously only up to the tenth century seemed behind the times.

A third impetus for curriculum reform was the rapidly changing demographic profile of the United States. As new immigration patterns of the 1970s and 1980s dawned in American social and political consciousness, educators called for a multicultural curriculum that would take into account the backgrounds and identities of schoolchildren freshly arrived from Guatemala, Vietnam, Iran and other corners of the world. Insistent demands for multicultural studies came from African American, Latino, Native American Indian and feminist organizations in the wake of the civil rights movement. Advocates argued that affirmation of the social and cultural identities of all groups within the American body politic required inclusion of their ethno-racial ancestors – and women of all backgrounds – in the elementary and secondary curriculum alongside the traditional pantheon of white male luminaries.

Multiculturalist strategies for history education, which at first appeared sensible and pragmatic to most Americans, became increasingly controversial in the 1980s. This happened because multiculturalism entailed reconstruction of Americans' collective memory, as well as competition among numerous contending groups. Many educational leaders argued that the United States was religiously and ethnically the most diverse country in the world and should therefore put forth a model of social education that addressed the struggle for 'a more perfect union'. Recognizing various groups' roles in this common endeavour would encourage toleration and understanding among citizens. By contrast, traditionalists on the political right asserted that from the founding of the nation to the 1960s, or, as Congressman Newt Gingrich put it, 'from de Tocqueville to Norman Rockwell's paintings', all Americans shared and should appreciate a single consensual vision of the national past. These critics feared that critically analysing and then rewriting the existing story of one nation, one people would ultimately tear the country apart (Bennett 1992; Gingrich 1995; Gitlin 1995; Nash et al. 1997; Schlesinger 1991). Public debates in the 1980s and early 1990s over proposals for improved international and world history education were less controversial because they touched nerves of national identity less than did debates over US history.[1] Even so, leaders on the right worried that too much study of 'other cultures' besides Europe and North America would discourage young Americans from embracing a common heritage and diminish their commitment to traditional western ideals and values.

Multiculturalists argued that the curriculum should include Islam and other world religions, not because world history does not make sense without them, but because Muslims and others now form significant groups within the American population. Though multiculturalists consistently ranged themselves against the dominance of western heritage studies, the issue of which ethno-religious communities should be included and how much time should be allotted to each took on a reductionist logic: as immigrant constituencies of various origins multiplied and had to be accommodated in the curriculum, the school year would have to be sliced into finer and finer bits. Critics on the right responded to this social calculus by crying 'Enough!' The curriculum is slipping into chaos, they warned. Fragmentation of social education, and ultimately the fabric of the nation, can be averted only by returning to the unitary narrative of western civilization, wellspring of democracy and universal values. Room might be found for detailed study of a few 'non-western cultures', but students who do not see themselves and their forebears reflected in the mainstream version of the past should just be grateful for the chance to adopt the western heritage as their passport to the American way of life. On the other hand, the educational community was quietly winning the struggle for a history curriculum that included more social history of minority groups, working people and women, and that had a more internationalist scope.

Another factor affecting coverage of Islam among world religions has been the successful movement to forge a national consensus on teaching about religion within a legal and social framework that honours religious diversity. After the Second World War, majority sentiment among educators favoured the idea that ignoring religion in schools was a good way to avoid conflict. Consequently, religions were nearly written out of many social studies programmes altogether. This trend contrasted sharply with the situation in post-war Britain, where religious education was the one subject required by parliamentary statute in all state-maintained schools.

Public discontent in the US over this trend came to a head in the 1970s. Critics charged that school policies designed to avoid religious issues were based on faulty interpretation of the First Amendment to the US Constitution, the clause forbidding establishment of religion. Gradually, consensus developed among historians, theologians and educators that study of religions is not only constitutional but highly desirable: it promotes understanding among peoples of diverse faiths and takes account of the significance of religion in history and culture. The most important factor in achieving consensus was the promulgation of classroom criteria that clearly differentiate between teaching religion and teaching *about* religion (Nord 1995; Piediscalzi and Collie 1977). A milestone in this project was the 1988 Williamsburg Charter, a public statement that set forth principles regarding the meaning and social implications of the First Amendment. Two US presidents, two chief justices of the Supreme Court and over two hundred political and civic leaders attended the charter's signing ceremony. One of the signatories was Warith Deen Muhammad, a Muslim who had brought most of the body of the Nation of Islam into the fold of Sunni Islam (Haynes and Thomas 1994: 2:1–8).

Also in 1988, seventeen religious and educational organizations, including the Islamic Society of North America, approved guidelines that articulate the distinctions between 'teaching religion' and 'teaching about religion' (Haynes and Thomas 1994: 6:1, 10:1). In brief, these criteria require an academic, not devotional, approach to religious study, the goal being student understanding of various belief systems and their history. Schools may sponsor study, but not practice of religion; assign sacred scriptural texts as primary source readings and discuss them within appropriate historical and cultural contexts, but not simulate religious observances; and teach about various beliefs and practices, but not reduce them to sociological or psychological phenomena or explain them away as manifestations of 'cultural relativism'. The 1988 guidelines have become widely accepted in American schools, and they provide standards for assessing educational materials (Douglass 1994: 79–122). There is no doubt that since the 1960s American educators have made enormous progress in reintegrating education about religion into the schools (American Textbook Council 1994: 32–4; Nord 1995: 138–59; Douglass 2000: *passim*).

Characteristics of the American education system

The decentralized character of American education greatly influences how curriculum officials, teachers and textbook publishers decide what students will be taught about Islam. The United States has no curriculum policy-making structure at the federal level, in other words, no ministry of education. The US Department of Education has no authority to set curriculum or assessments for schools.

In 1989, however, President George Bush and the governors of the fifty states launched an initiative to establish national standards of achievement linked to national assessments. Groups of educators in all the basic school subjects started projects to set voluntary national standards of competency for children. Federal agencies funded several of these projects, though no federal office directed or managed them. A national curriculum comparable to the one legislated in Britain in 1988 was not envisioned.

By 1995, however, this approach to standards setting had encountered difficulty. In the aftermath of the Republican Party's Victory in the 1994 Congressional elections and its vow to terminate the Department of Education, the Clinton administration rapidly abandoned support for a federal role in funding or certifying academic standards. This wholesale retreat was prompted in part by a raucous media controversy over publication of the National Standards for History, which came under searing attack from the political right for being negative, 'ultra-liberal' and excessively enthusiastic about ethnic, gender-related and non-western history.[2] The Republican congressional agenda, combined with a campaign of disinformation to sabotage the history standards, inspired politicians to reaffirm the long-cherished American tradition of decentralized educational policy.

Until very recently, the absence of official assessments or qualifying exams in most states has encouraged teacher independence in formulating strategies for attaining general state and local curriculum objectives. Following the official rejection of National Standards, most of the states have passed legislation mandating the setting of academic standards and development of state exams. The short-term result of these policies has been to curtail both local autonomy and teacher independence as to what students are taught. Promulgation of fifty different state standards documents has also disturbed the remarkable uniformity that had existed in the scope and sequence of study in US schools, which had amounted to a default national standard in basic courses like US and world history. University education degree and certification programmes have generally done little to help teachers provide accurate or effective instruction on Islam or any other religion. In most American universities, the weight of history programmes falls heavily on the side of US and modern Europe. Few young teachers get much exposure to the content and pedagogy of global history, and fewer still take introductory courses on Islam and Muslim history.

On the other hand, American teachers as a group, like their British counterparts, are more amenable to innovation than are government educational agencies. Teachers who interact daily with students, parents and colleagues representing various cultural backgrounds often learn to implement more globally inclusive conceptions of the past, teaching first-hand about cultural diversity in matters of dress, custom, language, ritual and beliefs. They often invite guest speakers from the local community, who share their religious and cultural perspectives.

Islam has become something of a 'hot topic' in American classrooms. Both the remarkable growth of the Muslim community in the US during the past few decades and the continuing flow of news from Muslim regions have brought teaching about Islam and Muslims under closer scrutiny. Criticism of faulty instructional material is more effectively reaching the ears of teachers and administrators, sometimes resulting in correction or deletion of inaccurate content. Dedicated teachers take advantage of workshops and conferences sponsored by educational associations, universities and civic groups, as well as in-service programmes on issues of cultural diversity. Moreover, the Internet provides a universe of knowledge sources at no cost.

Despite teachers' efforts to expand their intellectual horizons, it is probably fair to say that in the average history classroom the textbook *is* the curriculum, largely determining the scope and sequence of day-to-day teaching. Fewer than ten major publishers produce the textbooks used in tens of thousands of schools across the country. These companies resist moving out in front of what state textbook adoption boards will tolerate in the way of innovation. They claim that until states demand genuinely globe-encompassing world history, including substantive integration of Islam and Muslim societies into the human drama, they cannot restructure their books, as much as in-house development teams might like to.[3]

Islam in world history textbooks

The time an average student spends studying about Islam and Muslim history in American schools amounts to just a few weeks in twelve years of schooling. This instruction usually takes place in the context of world history or world culture/geography surveys between grades six and twelve (ages 11–18). The prescribed textbook sets forth not only the factual information students are expected to learn but also the conceptual framework by which they will relate history involving Islam and Muslims to the history of their community, their nation, western civilization and the world as a whole. Even the sequencing of chapters influences the degree to which students perceive Muslim history and culture either as a dimension of the human community to which young Americans belong or as antiquarian, essentialist and exotic. It guides students toward or away from the Orientalist paradigm, which disconnects the history of Islam from the Judaeo-Christian tradition.

In the past thirty years, no publishing firm has marketed a textbook entitled '*World History*' that recounts exclusively the history of western countries. In the 1970s, publishers quickly hoisted sail to catch the breezes of educational ideology favouring internationalism and multiculturalism. Consequently, world history textbooks had to include more than cursory coverage of major African, Asian and American 'cultures'. Recent textbooks therefore reflect educators' demand for increased sensitivity to cultural or ethno-racial diversity, including all the cultural and religious traditions whose absence might be noticed by interested groups.

On the other hand, textbooks do not stimulate social studies educators to rethink conceptions of world history or to integrate the narrative along more global-scale lines. Texts have paid little attention to major processes of change that cannot be confined within the experience of one 'culture group' or another. Such a unitary approach, what André Gunder Frank (1991) has called 'humanocentric history', might effectively satisfy the inclusionary demands of multiculturalists and at the same time be more relevant to the interactive, deterritorialized, globalizing world in which we live.

If a coherent and engaging paradigm for a more unified version of the human past is some years off, the victory of multiculturalist sentiment and the movement to include teaching about religion has meant that all widely used textbooks include lessons on Islam and Muslim history. This is also true of the eleven textbooks reviewed here, including their most recent revisions (Armento et al. 1991, 1994; Banks et al. 1997; Beck et al. 1999; Bednarz et al. 1997; Boehm et al. 1997; Ellis and Esler 1997; Farah and Karls 1997, 1999; Garcia et al. 1997; Hanes 1997 and 1999; Krieger et al. 1997; Wallbank 1997). In these books the introductory chapter on Islam and early Muslim civilization appears somewhere in the second third of the book, but in varying juxtaposition to narratives on the breakup of Rome, the Byzantine empire and medieval Europe. This placement tends to inhibit attention to world-scale chronologies or connections among peoples across space.

For example, lessons on Byzantium usually end with the 'fall' of Constantinople to the Ottomans in 1453, though introductions to Islam, the Abbasid Caliphate and the Turkic expansion may come much later in the book. Consequently, historical explanations of events in the Eastern Mediterranean–Black Sea basin that incorporate the entire aggregate of peoples and social forces of that region are sacrificed to coverage of Byzantine civilization as a self-contained phenomenon. In the older books, students may even study the Crusades and Italian maritime expansion in the Mediterranean before they read about Islam. In three of these texts the Ottoman Empire is sent into decline before students read about the early modern Iberian expansion or the development of bureaucratic states and religious wars in sixteenth-century Europe. Most books contain information about the growth of Muslim communities in East and West Africa, but not in connection with interregional factors of cause and effect (such as the maturing of the Indian Ocean commercial economy or long-distance gold trade). Rather, students read a chapter on 'Africa', which includes paragraphs on Neolithic farming, Nok sculpture, Christian Ethiopia, Zimbabwe, Mali, Songhay, Benin, the East African city-states and various other subjects in a single sequence. This largely incoherent chapter, which in two of the eleven books is grouped in a unit with pre-Columbian America, meets the multicultural requirement for an answer to the question 'What was happening in Africa?' but leaves peoples of the continent disconnected from wider spheres of world-historical meaning.

Coverage of Muhammad, Mecca and the rise of Islam

The 1988 guidelines for teaching about religion challenge textbook authors to explain 'how people of faith interpret their own practices and beliefs', using language that clearly attributes these tenets to their adherents. Though introductory chapters on Islam in the world history books have improved considerably in this respect over the past decade or so, most still fall short of the guidelines. Our review of these books reveals that Islam is generally not interpreted as its adherents understand it but as the editors believe will be acceptable to textbook adoption committees. Moreover, certain fundamental facts are ignored, while other details are selectively emphasized.

Most of the textbooks address similarities among Judaism, Christianity and Islam. They point out links, common elements or shared scriptural understandings that do not necessarily imply Islamic 'borrowing' from the two antecedent faiths. Six of the eleven books include a few sentences on interfaith linkages, and three of them compare and contrast beliefs of the three religions fairly extensively (Armento et al. 1994; Ellis and Esler 1997; Hanes 1997 and 1999). Most of the books explain that all three faiths share a common monotheism, that is, belief in 'one God' (two books) or 'the one true God' (two books). Four books declare that

Muslims believe in 'the same God' as Jews and Christians. Most of them define the Qur'an as a scripture held by Muslims to be the word of God. Seven of the books contain direct quotations from the Qur'an.

On the whole, however, the texts do not demonstrate continuity among the monotheistic faiths or invite direct comparison and contrast. Rather, coverage seems to compartmentalize the three traditions. Abraham, Jesus and Muhammad are characterized as founding figures, scriptures are mainly viewed as discrete, and the history of the traditions is described as following separate paths. Intentionally or otherwise, Judaism, Christianity and Islam each appear as autonomous cultural packages. Moreover, subtle and not so subtle statements denigrate or 'explain away' Islam in clear violation of the 1988 guidelines.

In discussing major world religions (including Buddhism, Hinduism, Confucianism and others), the texts generally avoid references to continuities and connections that might cause discomfort to parents, officials or interest groups that oppose religious ecumenism in public schools. Typically, the books characterize each world religion in terms of a founder figure, an origins story, a holy scripture, a set of basic tenets and practices, and identification with a particular historical period or cultural tradition. This approach accords well with multicultural precepts, the aim being mainly to stress how these religions differ from one another and to encourage understanding and toleration of dissimilar worldviews and practices. These objectives are not undesirable, but they do produce troublesome by-products. Treating each religion as a cultural entity situated within a bounded period of the past leads easily to its being perceived as homogeneous ('all Muslims do this, all Christians do that'), essentialized ('If you are a Muslim, here is how you will think and act') and made ahistorical ('Muslims think and behave this way because they have done so for fourteen hundred years').

Textbooks often use the term 'new' to introduce the origins story of monotheistic belief systems. Five of the eleven books describe Islam as a 'new' religion. In the other five books the implication is the same, since none of the texts make clear Muslims' belief that Islam is religion *per se* or that it is the faith of Adam and all the subsequent prophets, despite the clarity of Islamic doctrine on this point. In fact, Adam and Eve are virtually excluded from all world history texts, even as cultural referents. This primordial pair is presumably of little use when the aim is to dwell mainly on the dissimilarities among Judaism, Christianity and Islam. The origin of Islam, rather, is described not as Muslims would likely do it but in relation to two historical matrices that intersect in the seventh century. The first matrix is the society and culture of the Arabs. The second is the life, beliefs and actions of Muhammad as 'founder' of Islam.

Explanations of Islam as the religion of the Arabs typically begin by describing an arid, harsh physical environment inhabited by nomadic camel herders, traders and townspeople. The Arabian Peninsula is depicted as a remote, bounded locality, and nomadic culture is made the root of Islam. Some texts use romantic language, as in this extreme example: 'They lived as desert wanderers, these Arab traders. … Lacking a permanent home, these nomads, or wanderers, called themselves Arabs' (Armento et al. 1991: 50, 53). All of the books emphasize nomadism as a primary lifestyle of the Arabs, some older texts barely mentioning towns. Text illustrations offer images of modern Bedouin survivals and camels projected backward fourteen hundred years. The dry Arabian steppe is featured over arable or rain-watered terrain, and little reference is made to interactions between Arabs and peoples of Syria, Persia, East Africa or India before Islam. Only three of the books mention Roman or Sassanid relations with Arabia or with the cities of Petra and Palmyra. Some books describe the symbiotic relationship between sedentary and nomadic Arab groups, and four mention, or illustrate on maps, the long-distance trade routes that crossed Arabia (Armento et al. 1991: 53; Banks 1994: 267).

Some accounts note a Jewish and Christian presence in Arabia but do not elaborate this point, except to set up the possibility that Muhammad, at home or on his trading journeys, might have become familiar with some of the beliefs of these faiths and subsequently absorbed their ideas into 'his' new religion. The religious context of Arabia, and particularly of Quraish as the leading tribe, is described in most of the accounts as pagan, paganism being part and parcel of nomadic Arab culture. Two of the texts mention the *hanif* monotheistic tradition, one with strong ethnic overtones: 'Holy men known as *hanifs* denounced the worship of idols. ... They rejected Judaism and Christianity, preferring to find a uniquely Arab form of monotheism' (Farah and Karls 1997: 271). The origins of Islam and Judaism are characterized in distinct but also parallel ways – the story of an ethnic group's spontaneous departure from a prevailing polytheistic belief system.

Mecca is the focal point of information on the Arabian religious context, the texts typically describing it as an oasis on the trade route between the Arabian Sea and the major cities of the Middle East. Some texts explain that Mecca was becoming a more prominent commercial centre around the time Muhammad lived. All the texts describe the town as the location of a religious shrine housing the Arabs' tribal idols. One book states that the Ka'ba was 'like the Pantheon of Rome'. Another asserts that Islamic monotheism in some way grew out of Meccan polytheism:

> Before Muhammad, the Bedouins and the townspeople worshipped hundreds of gods and spirits. Spirits called jinn were thought to reside in rocks and other natural objects. Mecca was the home of the most sacred of these rocks. The Black Stone of Mecca was [and still is] embedded in the wall of a shrine called the Kaaba. ... The Kaaba also contained idols representing 360 gods, including one deity called Allah. (Krieger et al. 1997: 186)

Most of the texts draw attention to the Black Stone as an important and distinctive Islamic symbol. Some books even suggest that it is an object of worship. The emphasis is on the stone's quaintness and obscurity – one of the icons that makes Islam 'different' – rather than on its symbolism or spiritual meaning.

Seven of the eleven accounts acknowledge that Muslims believe in the prophethood of Jesus, Moses and Abraham, or mention the doctrine that the Qur'an completes the chain of earlier revelation. This information, however, is often placed in a concluding section on doctrines and practices, rather than being linked to the 'origins story'. Consequently, the texts consistently manage to gloss over the idea that Islam richly shared the Abrahamic tradition with Judaism and

Christianity. Until the most recent editions of these textbooks, and then under repeated prodding from reviewers, discussions of Mecca's origins have excluded references to Abraham, Isma'il and Hajar. Two of the texts allude to the association between Abraham and the building of the Ka'ba, one book noting, slightly incorrectly, that 'Muslims today believe [it] was built by the prophet Abraham' (Banks et al. 1997: 187; see also Ellis and Esler 1997: 256). Another text quotes the cry of modern pilgrims, 'Here I am, O God, at Thy command!,' but fails to note that this cry commemorates Abraham's reply to God's call as quoted in the Bible (Genesis, Chapter 22). The same book states, following the account of Mecca's origins, that 'Muslims believe that Abraham rebuilt the original Ka'abah,' attributing this to Muhammad's saying, or to 'tradition' (Armento et al. 1994: 184). None of the lessons mentions Abraham and Hajar's journey or their connection to Mecca. None of the texts explains Muslims' belief that Isma'il was the son Abraham was prepared to sacrifice, despite its importance in the major Islamic celebration 'Id al-Adha.

It is difficult to escape the conclusion that the world history textbooks deliberately downplay or exclude connections between Islam and Abraham in order to maintain neat partitions among the symbols, beliefs and major figures of the three monotheistic faiths. Muslim and other scholarly reviewers of textbooks have repeatedly argued that the Abrahamic tradition must be a part of the basic account of Islam's origins and practice. Many publishers continue to disregard the advice, though some new editions indicate that they are beginning to change. Indeed, the omission is made in clear violation of the 1988 guidelines for teaching about religion. Editors may have concluded that the textbook adoption market in politically and religiously conservative states will not bear ambiguity about Abraham's strict identification with the Old Testament and the Judaeo-Christian tradition.

The second matrix for explaining the origins of Islam is the biography of Muhammad, which all the texts recount. None of these narratives expressly describes Qur'anic teachings on the beginnings of Islam. Explicitly or subtly, all the texts define Muhammad as the founder of Islam, just as Abraham, Jesus and the Buddha are cited as the founders of their respective religions. Four of the books apply the terms 'founded' or 'founder' to characterize Muhammad's career (Banks et al. 1997: 271; Bednarz et al. 1997: 78; Hanes 1997: 47; Wallbank et al. 1987: 34, 137). None of them gives a definition of the term, though many students would likely understand it as synonymous with 'inventor', one who brings something into existence, rather than one who established something or caused it to be recognized and accepted. None of these books reflects the Muslims' belief that God is the source of revelation, rendering the concept of a founder extraneous, or the fact that Muhammad is not considered the first prophet of Islam. This presentation of a foregone conclusion about Muhammad's role belies an intrusion of irreligious assumptions that contradict the guidelines by failing to portray the views of believers neutrally. Similar assumptions apply to coverage of other religions in these texts.

The biographic details in the books are fairly uniform. Most make Muhammad's orphanhood, mercantile profession and marriage to the older, wealthy Khadijah as the defining features of his life before prophethood. A few mention his reputation for honesty and simplicity and his dislike of the idols that the Arabs worshipped. All of the books relate the story of the cave of Hira' as the site where Islam 'began'. On this point, most of the accounts are quite authentic, though brief. They quote the Iqra' verses or the words of Jibril as recorded in the *hadith*, carefully attributing these statements to Muslim beliefs. Some of the books directly acknowledge Muhammad's prophethood, though others distance the reader from the concept that God conferred revelation on him. The distancing term of choice in some of the books is 'vision', a word that is not used to describe revelation or contact with God in the discussions of early Judaism or Christianity. One account features multiple repetitions of the term.

> At the age of 40, Muhammad's life was changed overnight by a vision. ... In his vision, the angel Gabriel told him that he was a messenger of God. Muhammad had other visions in which Gabriel appeared with messages from Allah (Arabic for God). Who was Allah? Muhammad believed Allah was the same God worshipped by Christians and Jews. (Krieger et al. 1997: 186)

Islam, presented as separate from the Abrahamic tradition, is shown to have picked up similarities with Judaism and Christianity through alleged imitation or borrowing. Three of the accounts state unequivocally that the earlier traditions were absorbed into the later religion as doctrine. One of the statements is particularly crass, 'explaining away' Islam in violation of the guidelines: 'In his travels [Muhammad] met many people of different cultures, including Jews and Christians. These contacts were to have a profound influence on the religion that he later developed' (Wallbank et al. 1987: 188). Other statements imply unambiguously that Muhammad incorporated certain Jewish or Christian beliefs into Islam simply to fulfil some worldly motive. The decision to change the Kiblah (orientation when praying) from Jerusalem to Mecca for example, is often explained in such a way that divine revelation and political manoeuvre become thoroughly confused:

> In Mecca, Muhammad had emphasized that he was continuing the tradition of Jewish and Christian prophecy. When Jewish tribes in the oasis of Medina refused to acknowledge him as a prophet, however, he began to move away from Jewish and Christian practices. Instead of facing the holy city of Jerusalem while praying, for example, in Medina a new revelation commanded the Muslims to face Mecca and the Ka'abah instead. (Hanes 1997: 249)

Such simple turns of phrase can be loaded statements, because if true, they mean that the religion is false.

Though all of the texts present the Hijra in 622 CE as the consequence of intense persecution by the Meccans, the writers often portray Muhammad's acts in Medina as wilful, artful and calculated. A few of the accounts, after admitting that Muslims endured persecution in Mecca for their beliefs, imply that the subsequent battles were motivated by Muhammad's aggression. In these same texts, this theme forms the central motif in the account of Islam's spread. The newer texts tend to sidestep the issue of Muhammad's motives while he was in Medina, either by ignoring the question altogether or by invoking the young Muslim community's faith, effort and struggle without attempting to explain what happened between 622 and 630 CE. The texts miss many opportunities to describe the dynamics of tribal relations or the events by which the Muslims checkmated the Quraish. Most accounts skip quickly to the victory over Mecca and the end of Muhammad's life.

The problem with these accounts is not that they characterize Muhammad as a political and military leader, which of course he was. The objection, rather, is that they present the conclusion that political wilfulness, calculation, and purely personal ingenuity on Muhammad's part are sufficient explanations for these events, contradicting the Muslim belief that God guided His prophet to make particular decisions through revelation. Such assumptions or conclusions about Muhammad's motives are therefore anything but neutral. They support a between-the-lines interpretation that Muhammad's personality and will power are sufficient to explain the origin of Islam, and that his assertion of will was not tempered by his principles or even linked in any way to actions by the opposing side, as in these examples:

> With Medina now under Muslim control, Muhammad set about conquering his enemies at Makka. For eight years, Muhammad's small forces fought the larger Meccan forces. (Armento et al. 1991: 60)

> From Medina, Muhammad began to convert the desert tribes. With their help, Muslims raided Meccan caravans. In 630, after several years of warfare, the people of Mecca gave in. (Hanes 1997: 249)

Another remarkable feature of the texts is that they relegate the community of Muslims and especially the companions (*sahabah*) to the background until after Muhammad's death. Apart from Khadijah, who acquires some vital dimension in the accounts, no figure in the community comes to life. The reader barely senses the presence of a community at all. The narratives focus relentlessly on Muhammad and his acts, decisions and responses. Because they must cover so much world history, textbook narratives on the early *ummah* are necessarily brief, but the uniformity of this approach across the whole range of books suggests a particular interpretative slant. Islam is portrayed as the work of a 'great man' leading a group of murkily defined Others, rather than a community of real human beings expressing their Abrahamic faith and struggling to defend it.

Coverage of Muslim history after Muhammad's death

Placement of basic Islamic teachings varies, but all of the books present the 'five pillars' as the centrepiece of Islamic doctrine. The descriptions are fairly accurate, though simplistic. None of the texts situates the pillars in a cultural context, showing how each had strong communal aspects or gave rise to lasting institutions. They are described simply as ritual acts of worship in which the personal obligation predominates. Other frequently mentioned Muslim practices are dietary prohibitions, *jihad*, slavery, marriage, divorce and male and female rights. Some of the older texts imply that Islam sharply circumscribes women's roles, but newer ones list their rights and duties, a few offering a more differentiated discussion within the context of the early centuries. All of the books indicate in some way that Islamic practice embraces a way of life. Indeed, some praise values such as racial equality, help for the poor, respect toward parents, and women's rights as compared with their status in other societies in these early centuries, though not today.

Descriptions of the Qur'an and *hadith* as the two major sources of Islamic knowledge and practice vary widely in quality. Many provide murky or inaccurate definitions of the *hadith* and the *sunnah*, and only one book describes how the Qur'an or the *hadith* were transmitted to succeeding generations. The most common statement regarding the transmission or transcription of the Qur'an is that it was essentially fragmentary and oral during Muhammad's lifetime, being collected into a book only some time after his death. An example of strategic omission, and one firmly grounded in the Orientalist sources, is the practice of telling readers that the Qur'anic *suras* were put in order (often described as longest to shortest) after Muhammad's death. The unsuspecting reader is not told about the important role of those who had memorized the Qur'an during Muhammad's lifetime, or the fact that most of the chapters were not revealed at a single time, so that ordering individual *ayat* (verses) into *suras* would have been by far the greater task. Readers are not encouraged to consider that if the ordering had not been accomplished before Muhammad's death, the chances of the community's agreeing on one version of the Qur'an would have been virtually nil. By subtle means, the textbooks give students the impression that the Qur'an's manifestation need not be considered as taking place any differently from the way the Bible and Torah evolved. Moreover, none of the textbooks notes the consensus of scholarship that the Qur'an remains essentially unchanged today.

The question of religious tolerance among Muslims is often portrayed in muddled terms that may reinforce cultural stereotypes. The topic is usually covered as part of the narrative on the spread of Islam. Some books describe the right of People of the Book to worship and live according to their religious law as an initiative of individual rulers rather than as a permanent feature of the Shari'a. Some narratives offer a confusing picture, indicating in some passages that other religions were tolerated, and in others that Muslims forced people to convert (Armento et al. 1991: 62, 64, 66, 80). Much of the mystification over the significance of both tolerance and *jihad* in the seventh and eighth centuries results from failure to draw a chronological or conceptual distinction between the rapid territorial expansion of the Muslim state, and the actual spread of Islam among populations within the state, a much slower process that went on for centuries. The texts rarely draw attention to Islam's minority status in the early period but rather conflate the military expansion of Arab armies and conversion to the faith as part of a single, conquest-driven process.

A broad interpretative thread in all the textbooks is use of the terms 'Islam' and 'Islamic'. In most of the books the word is applied to all manner of historical phenomena: 'Islamic empire', 'Islamic trade routes', 'Islamic art and science', 'Islamic men and women' are some examples of usage suggesting that anything that happened in regions where Muslim populations predominated may reasonably be attributed to religion. This practice is of course fairly pervasive in the scholarly literature generally. None of the texts uses the term 'Christian' in the same way. In critically reviewing textbooks, Muslim scholars have tried to impress on publishers the marked difference between Islam – its beliefs, practices and principles – and the shared cultural and historical experience of both Muslim believers and non-Muslims who lived among them. Marshall Hodgson defined societies where Muslims were preponderate and set the cultural and social style as 'Islamicate'. In the most recent revisions, many textbook writers have acquiesced to using 'Muslim' as an adjective to convey a similar meaning to Hodgson's term, 'Islamicate' being too abstract or unconventional for young readers.

Particularly misleading is the practice of assigning religious causation to historical developments that must largely be explained in other ways. For example, a few of the texts attribute early scientific advances in Muslim culture almost exclusively to the need to pray at accurate times, establish the direction of prayer and *hajj* routes, calculate inheritances, and fulfil various other conditions of Islamic practice. Similarly, certain social attitudes and behaviour toward women are framed in terms of Islam, though their roots may lie in cultural habits that contradict Islamic teachings. Some Muslim historical figures whom the texts characterize as villains are associated with Islam, but their acts are not dissociated from it. A good example of this type of mixed attribution of Islamic-ness is an account of Shah Abbas the Great of Persia that appeared in a draft textbook manuscript. In one sentence, the Shah is described as the greatest leader of his time, his lawgiving and his construction of beautiful mosques offered in evidence. On the next page, he is shown touring the bazaar in the interest of economic and social justice. Finding a butcher who cheated his customers, Shah Abbas is said to have ordered him roasted on his own charcoal spit. The inference? Such punishment was perfectly acceptable practice for 'Islamic' rulers. Religious teachings regarding such behaviour remained unexamined. Though the editors omitted the story in the published text, the incident illustrates how textbooks can be minefields of misinformation and Orientalist stereotyping. Obviously, the whole range of human flaws – militarism, greed, cruelty, corruption – are easy to find in the historical record of any religious or social group. The guidelines for teaching about religion, however, require that the distinction between the tenets of religions and the acts of their adherents be clearly made.

All of the books assign one chapter or less to the origins of Islam, with a second section on the high culture and achievements of Muslim civilization. They follow political developments from the early successors of Muhammad to the period of the *fitna* and the establishment of the Umayyad state, ending with an account of the Abbasid state. In all of the books, the lesson on Muslim history concludes with cultural events, usually under the rubric of the 'golden age' of the Abbasid Caliphate and often including al-Andalus. For eras of world history following this 'golden age', Muslims walk on to the textbook stage mainly in small roles in accounts of the European Crusades or West African empires and in larger roles in brief narratives of the Ottoman, Mughal and Safavid empires. Most texts still conform to the traditional Orientalist habit of defining Islam as the civilization of the Arabs of the 'Near East', that is, the people and territory immediately next door to Christian Europe. As Marshall Hodgson pointed out many years ago, this tendency has detracted attention from the larger-scale patterns of conquest, trade, conversion, intellectual life and urbanization that characterized the emergence of Muslim civilization as a trans-hemispheric phenomenon between 1000 and 1500 CE (Hodgson 1974: 96–7).

A conspicuous aspect of the 'golden age' approach in these books is a listing of each civilization's special achievements. Ever since the 1970s, when multiculturalist ethno-racial critics protested the common schoolbook claim that Europe possessed a monopoly on scientific genius, publishers have included mention of inventions and other achievements as standard fare in chapters on premodern, non-western cultures. The most commonly cited Muslim achievements are astronomical knowledge, medical advances, algebra, bank cheques and lateen sails, described in many books as 'Arab'. Some recent texts now credit India with 'Hindi-Arabic numerals' and the concept of zero, though this innovation is said to have 'passed through' the Muslim Middle East *en route* to Europe. Students are given a list of items 'we' got from 'them', but they learn little about the setting, circumstances or individuals involved in the transfer of ideas and technology. Because the multicultural model treats each civilization's narrative in isolation, few cross-references to seminal inventions and discoveries are made in adjoining chapters on Europe.

An exception is the transfer of Greek philosophical and scientific works to the West by way of Muslim scholars and their enlightened patrons. Revised 1999 editions of a few textbooks demonstrate change in this direction, including discussion of Ibn Rushd's influence on Thomas Aquinas's work, for example, in the chapter on medieval Europe (Beck et al. 1999: 351; Hanes 1999: 297). Even here, however, most of the books give students the impression that scientific and philosophical documents were merely refrigerated in Muslim libraries until rationalist European thinkers thawed them out. Reference to Muslims might appear in a chapter on the European High Middle Ages or Renaissance but not in connection with the Scientific Revolution. One text explains how Thomas Aquinas managed successfully to join faith with reason, while Muslim thinkers suppressed such investigation and chose faith – and consequently backwardness over progress – for all time (Hanes 1997: 258, 297–8, 402). The most recent revision omits these overt misconceptions (Hanes 1999: 258, 297). None of the books, however, has caught up with the current academic view that Muslim scholars, drawing on Indian, Persian and Greek sources and questing for knowledge in fulfilment of one of the prime values of their own faith, achieved a sweeping new synthesis of the mathematical sciences between the eighth and the fourteenth century.

Almost all the textbooks state or at least imply that the Muslim 'golden age' exhausted itself by about the eleventh century; few texts acknowledge any contributions thereafter except tiles and tulips. One recent secondary book is a notable exception. The chapter on Islam closes with an essay entitled 'Author's commentary: A dynamic civilization', which notes how recent historical studies have revised the earlier notion of an Abbasid 'golden age'. Historians, concludes the essay, now acknowledge that Muslim civilization has played an expansive role in world history (Hanes 1997 and 1999: 268). The essay is all the more remarkable because it is the only such feature in the book, and because no other publisher has seen fit to draw attention to such changes in the field of scholarship. More typical is the statement in one of the older texts: 'Under the Abbasids, the Islamic Empire enjoyed a brief but brilliant golden age in arts and sciences' (Krieger et al. 1997: 192). Ironically, that statement is juxtaposed against an image of Muslim scholars using astronomical instruments, though the caption fails to identify the illustration as a seventeenth-century Ottoman miniature.

Most of the books have little to say about shifts in the direction of Muslim history, or about world-historical developments involving Muslims during the period from 1000 to 1500 CE. The most common exceptions are paragraphs on the Crusades, the Mongol Empire, the Ottoman state, West African empires and East African city-states. These topics appear discontinuously and incoherently in several different chapters, so that the dynamic growth of the Dar al-Islam, as well as the transformative actions of Muslims across the entire central two-thirds of the Afro-Eurasian region, is almost totally obscured. For example, the fourteenth-century Muslim traveller and legal scholar Ibn Battuta appears in almost all the recent texts. Publishers have recognized his story as a multicultural counterpoint to Marco Polo, a major icon in the conventional narrative of western exploration and discovery. The record of Ibn Battuta's adventures serves mainly as a source of interesting but brief primary document quotes inserted to describe one non-western region or another, often the sultanate of Mali. Writers miss the opportunity to show students how Ibn Battuta was a world-historical figure whose venture illustrates trans-hemispheric patterns of communication, trade, scholarship and urban cosmopolitanism. Rather, the point made is culture-specific: Europe has its Marco Polo, Islam has its Ibn Battuta, and in the newest books, China has its Cheng Ho (whose Muslim affiliation usually escapes mention). Only one book places these three travellers in the context of hemispheric trade during the period from 1000 to 1500 CE and exemplifies an integrated account of cultural transfers and interconnections (Boehm et al. 1997: 336–94).

The multiculturalist scheme of textbook writing rests on the premise that once a major civilization or region (Africa) has been introduced and its formative era and cultural achievements set forth, then not much more need be said about it, leaving the authors free to devote the second half of the book to the history of Europe and Europeans abroad. Developments in Muslim regions, or even more importantly the historical agency of Muslims in effecting world-scale change, earn virtually no discussion for the period from the sixteenth to the mid-nineteenth century. Most of the books offer lessons on the Ottoman, Safavid and Mughal states within a lesson on 'three empires'. Coverage is devoted almost exclusively to political developments, with cultural achievements confined to court-sponsored arts. The content is nearly always framed in terms of a telescoped sequence of rise, decline and fall, ending with a summary of events to the twentieth century. These lessons appear before the reader has been exposed to developments in Europe beyond the Renaissance. As a result, these states come across largely as historical artefacts lacking any concrete connection to main trends of the fifteenth through to the seventeenth century, such as demographic transformations, developments in the world economy, the rise of 'gunpowder empires', advancements in bureaucratic organization, or the continuing growth of Islam in parts of Asia, Africa and Europe. Most of the texts present these Turkic-ruled states as the executors of a latter-day Muslim 'golden age' centred on the early sixteenth century, exemplified by the Blue Mosque and the Taj Mahal as iconographic illustrations of high cultural achievement. Social history in these chapters is limited to portrayals of religious conflict between Hindu and Muslim, Turk and Christian, Sunni and Shi'a. This discussion lays the groundwork for later coverage of ethno-racial and religious animosities among non-western groups in the twentieth century.

Lessons on 'three Muslim empires' bring to a close almost all discussion of Muslim peoples as independent agents of change in the modern world. Muslims appear haphazardly in chapters on the nineteenth century as minor characters in the drama of Europe's overseas enterprises and the 'new imperialism'. The texts describe nineteenth- and early twentieth-century colonialism in Africa and Asia in a generic way, with little specific focus on Muslim regions. Muslim personalities such as Selim III, Muhammad Ali, Abd al-Qadir or Samori Turé may appear as ethnic leaders, militant figures or political failures, but not as significant historical agents. European overseas expansion and settlement are seldom set in the context of change in the world economy or in terms of encounters among different peoples. Rather, paragraphs on Europe's imperial expansion take the form mainly of sentences with transitive verbs whose grammatical subjects are Portugal, Spain, France, Britain or some other European power.

In the chapters devoted to the twentieth century, Islam figures mainly in connection with the themes of world war, modernization, oil politics, women's roles and Islamic resurgence. Departing only modestly from the 'sick-man-of-Europe' formulation of Orientalist inspiration, recent books usually relate the demise of the Ottoman Empire to the diplomatic and political arrangements that followed the First World War. The Arab–Israeli conflict is given considerable space in all the books, but the depth of coverage varies widely. A few newer texts provide some background on the Zionist movement, while others portray the creation of the Israeli state and the influx of Jewish settlers almost solely as a result of the Holocaust. The Mandate period is often mentioned only briefly as background to this issue. Coverage of the Arab–Israeli conflict is mainly a recital of wars and disturbances – including the Intifada – interspersed with milestones in the US-sponsored peace process. The hallmark of these lessons is avoidance of thought-provoking questions and critical thinking, though coverage has become more even-handed in recent books.

As a world religion in the twentieth century, Islam comes across as a traditional holdover, as anti-western, and often as merely militant and extremist. By contrast, the westernizing secularization programmes of Atatürk, Nasser and the Shah of Iran are more positively portrayed. The status of women in contemporary Muslim societies is usually described within the framework of a dichotomy between tradition and modernity. The culture-bound structure of textbooks and the intellectual commitments reflected in the sources used by textbook researchers make interregional and global patterns of the century, especially since the Second World War, appear irrelevant to Muslim countries. The twin foci of Middle East conflict and Islam dominate coverage in such a way that they almost symbolize the entire region. Nor is the resurgence of Islam placed in comparative context with trends in Buddhism, Judaism and various Christian churches, despite the importance of these patterns as world-scale cultural developments.

Improving teaching practice

Ongoing curriculum reforms in the fifty United States and in major metropolitan school districts mean that increasing numbers of American children are exposed to world history. While instruction will probably retain its emphasis on western history, it will include a basic introduction to Islam and Muslim history. The status of world history in American schools is already a good deal higher than in England, where the statutory National Curriculum for history, which is temporarily under suspension, includes no mandated study of Islam, only optional recommendations (Department for Education 1995). On the other hand, children in state-maintained schools must take Religious Education, which normally involves introductions to all the major world religions, including Islam.[4]

Over the years, Muslim organizations and academic experts have attempted to help improve textbooks and other subject matter documents (Barlow 1994). Although most publishers have traditionally consulted area specialists during a new textbook's development, only in the later 1980s did any publisher include a Muslim consultant or author on its development team (Ahmad et al. 1995; Farah et al. 1994). Beginning in 1989, the Council on Islamic Education (CIE), a national, scholar-based resource organization based in California, began to build relationships with major publishers to improve both accuracy and scope of coverage in teaching about Islam and Muslim history. A panel of scholars and teachers affiliated with CIE act as academic reviewers and consultants on textbook projects. By the mid-1990s, CIE's relationship with the publishers and with some state education agencies had become systematic. In working with nearly all the major companies supplying world history books to the US school market, CIE has adopted an effective strategy of committing itself not only to better teaching about Islam but also to more effective approaches to world history (see Council on Islamic Education 1995).

The single most ambitious project in recent years to rethink the ideological and pedagogical assumptions in world history education has been the National Standards for World History. Published in 1994 by the National Center for History in the Schools at the University of California, Los Angeles, these academic content standards for both United States and world history were the product of three years of development involving about thirty professional and public interest organizations and hundreds of classroom teachers and academic scholars. CIE was one of the organizations that participated in the project as a reviewer of draft materials. The Department of Education and the National Endowment for the Humanities funded the project, but Washington civil servants took no part in directing or managing it (Nash et al. 1997).

The world history standards spoke in two important ways to the issue of interpreting Islam and Muslim history in schools. First, this copiously detailed document laid out broad goals for the study of history, precise knowledge standards and numerous classroom exemplars to help educators bring a high level of scholarship to classroom teaching. Second, the standards suggested an innovative and equitable framework for teaching global history, replacing both 'Western Civ' and multiculturalist dogmas with a thematic framework of world-historical eras, each embracing events trends and cultural processes across the globe and emphasizing interactions among peoples. The standards also incorporated the serious thinking of scholars of world, comparative and interregional history.[5] Though as soon as the guidelines were published, they sustained a lengthy attack from the political right, they have also been widely scrutinized by schools, education agencies and publishers. By early 1999, two-thirds of the states had published or were actively developing their own academic standards for history and social studies, and over one-third of those documents incorporate the National History Standards into their standards in some measure.[6] Since the year 2000, these curriculum reforms have begun to bear fruit in redesign of textbooks, and would appear to have encouraged publishers to offer at least a few products that incorporate an integrated world-historical model.

To the degree that world history education is restructured to incorporate a valid global framework, the overall significance of Islam and Muslim history in the human venture will be thrown into higher relief. Examination of the state documents shows an overall trend toward quantitative and qualitative improvement in instruction about Islam and Muslim history. Many state documents mandate study of the interaction of societies and the process of cultural transfer from one part of the world to another. Such a stipulation opens the way to teach about Islam and the Muslim experience in wider contexts of regional, hemispheric or global change rather than as an isolated, static 'culture'. Study of Islam as a world faith may also benefit, since all state documents require instruction about major world religions, and all but a few adhere to the 1988 guidelines for teaching about religion. Most state the requirement in neutral, even-handed language like this typical example: 'Compare the origin, central ideas, institutions, and worldwide influence of major religious and philosophical traditions including Buddhism, Christianity, Confucianism, Hinduism, Islam, and Judaism' (New Hampshire Department of Education 1997).

Conclusion

Though textbook authors and editors bring considerable good will to the process of portraying religions, many of them fail to paint a consistent or thoroughly accurate picture of the faith or its adherents' history. The willingness of publishers more systematically to seek the advice of knowledgeable reviewers is a hopeful sign. While significant improvement has taken place over the past decade or so, the most important condition for achieving further progress is to convince publishers and curriculum writers to adopt a humanocentric structure for world history that helps students understand particular peoples and religious traditions not as homogeneous and separate 'worlds' of historical reality, but as embedded in contexts of change across time and space that ultimately include all of humanity. Another condition for progress is to raise the level of scholarship upon which textbook accounts are based, including critical use of primary source documents and fundamental understanding that all historical writing, including textbooks, inevitably involves interpretation, judgement and social reconstruction of the past. Finally, if educators attend carefully to accepted standards for teaching about religion, more authentic and less confusing accounts will result. Textbook authors should write about Islam and all other faiths not to induce belief or disbelief, but to record as accurately as they can both the findings of modern scholarship and the understandings that Muslims have of doctrine, moral behaviour, spiritual aspiration and the origins and establishment of their faith. The US Supreme Court argued that the central reason for teaching about religion is that without it neither the long run of human history nor contemporary global culture will make sense to future generations. This is a simple and obvious proposition, but putting it to a full test will require abandoning the current habit in American education of essentializing religions, civilizations and ethno-racial groups in the interests of either patriotism or cultural self-esteem. A human-centred and dynamic global history in the schools holds some promise of counteracting and ultimately bringing to an end the caricatures and misrepresentations of Islam that flow from the popular media.

Notes

1. An important exception has been public contention over Afrocentric claims of ancient Egypt's 'blackness' and its primacy in the diffusion of ancient civilization (see Nash et al. 1997: 117–22).

2. *National Standards for United States History: Exploring the American Experience* and *National Standards for World History: Exploring Paths to the Present*, expanded edition (1994). A revised edition of these guidelines was published in 1995. For discussion of the controversy over the standards, see Nash et al. (1997: 188–258).

3. Council on Islamic Education, unpublished proceedings of World History Conference, Buena Park, California, 2 October 1994; and Colloquium on World History, Orange, California, 22–3 February 1997.

4. On teaching non-western and minority group history in British schools, see Pankhania (1994). An example of a high-quality text for use in religious education classes in British schools is Heywood (1997).

5. The *National Standards for History* are posted on the Internet at http://www.sscnet.ucla.edu/nchs/standards

6. State academic standards in all disciplines may be monitored on the Internet. See the web page 'Developing Curriculum Standards', Putnam Valley Public Schools, Putnam Valley, New York, at http://putnamvalleyschools.org/StSu/social.html. For a politically conservative assessment of state standards, see the Thomas B. Fordham Foundation report 'The State of State Standards' at http://www.edexcellence.net/library/sos2000/2000ssos.html. See also the council on Islamic Education and First Amendment Center report *Teaching About Religion in National and State Social Studies Standards* at http://www.cle.org

References

Ahmad, I., Brodsky, Crofts and Ellis 1995. *World Cultures: A Global Mosaic*. Upper Saddle River, NJ: Prentice Hall.

American Textbook Council 1994. *History Textbooks: A Standard and Guide*. 1994–5 edn. New York: Center for Education Studies/American Textbook Council.

Armento, B.J., Nash, G.B., et al. 1991. *Across the Centuries*. Boston: Houghton Mifflin.

Armento, B.J., Klor de Alva, J.J., et al. 1994. *To See a World: World Cultures* and *Geography*. Boston: Houghton Mifflin.

Banks, J.A., et al. 1997. *World: Adventures in Time and Place*. New York: Macmillan McGraw-Hill.

Barlow, E. (ed.) 1994. *Evaluation of Secondary-Level Textbooks for Coverage of the Middle East and North Africa: A Project of the Middle East Studies Association and the Middle East Outreach Council*. 3rd edn. Ann Arbor, MI: Center for Middle Eastern and North African Studies, University of Michigan.

Beck, R.B., et al. 1999. *World History: Patterns of Interaction*. Evanston, IL: McDougal Littell.

Bednarz, S., et al. 1997. *Discover Our Heritage*. Boston: Houghton Mifflin.

Bennett, W.J. 1992. *The De-Valuing of America: The Fight for Our Culture and Our Children*. New York: Summit Books.

Boehm, R.G., et al. 1997. *Our World's Story*. Orlando, FL: Harcourt Brace.

Commonwealth of Virginia Board of Education 1995. *Standards of Learning for Virginia Public Schools*. Commonwealth of Virginia Board of Education.

Council on Islamic Education 1995. *Teaching About Islam and Muslims in the Public School Classroom*. 3rd edn. Fountain Valley, CA: Council on Islamic Education.

Department for Education, Great Britain 1995. *History in the National Curriculum*. January. London: Department for Education.

Douglass, S.L. 1994. *Strategies and Structures for Presenting World History, with Islam and Muslim History as a Case Study*. Beltsville, MD: Council on Islamic Education/Amana Publications.

Douglass, S.L. 2000. *Teaching About Religion in National and State Social Studies Standards*. Nashville, Tennessee: Council on Islamic Education and First Amendment Center.

Ellis, E.G. and Esler, A. 1997. *World History: Connections to Today*. Upper Saddle River, NJ: Prentice Hall.

Farah, M.A. and Karls, A.B. 1997. *World History: The Human Experience*. New York: Glencoe/ McGraw-Hill.

Farah, M.A., et al. 1994. *Global Insights: People and Cultures*. New York: Glencoe.

Frank, A.G. 1991. A plea for world system history. *Journal of World History* 2: 1–28.

Friedlander, J. 1981. *The Middle East: The Image and the Reality*. Berkeley: University of California Press.

Garcia, J.R., et al. 1997. *The World and Its People*. Parsippany, NJ and Needham, MA: Silver Burdett Ginn.

Gingrich, N. 1995. *To Renew America*. New York: HarperCollins.

Gitlin, T. 1995. *The Twilight of Common Dreams: Why America is Wracked by Culture Wars*. New York: Henry Holt.

Hanes, W.T. III (ed.) 1997, 1999. *World History: Continuity and Change*. Austin, TX: Holt, Reinhart and Winston.

Haynes, C.C. and Thomas, O. (eds), 1994. *Finding Common Ground*. Nashville, TN: Freedom Forum First Amendment Center, Vanderbilt University.

Heywood, A. 1997. *The Muslim Way*. London: Hodder and Stoughton.

Hodgson, M.G.S. 1974. *The Venture of Islam*. Vol. 1. Chicago: University of Chicago Press.

Krieger, L.S., Neill, K. and Jantzen, S.L. 1997. *World History: Perspectives on the Pas*t. Lexington, MA: D.C. Heath.

Nash, G.B., Crabtree, C. and Dunn, R.E. 1997. *History on Trial: Culture Wars and the Teaching of the Past*. New York: Alfred A. Knopf.

National Center for History in the Schools 1994. *National Standards for World History: Exploring Paths to the Present*. Expanded edn. Los Angeles: University of California, Los Angeles.

National Center for History in the Schools 1995. *National Standards for History*. Basic edn. Los Angeles: University of California, Los Angeles.

New Hampshire Department of Education 1997. *New Hampshire K-12 Social Studies Curriculum Framework*. New Hampshire Department of Education.

Nord, W.A. 1995. *Religion and American Education: Rethinking a National Dilemma*. Chapel Hill: University of North Carolina Press.

Pankhania, J. 1994. *Liberating the National Curriculum*. London: Falmer Press.

Piediscalzi, N. and Collie, W.E. (eds), 1977. *Teaching About Religion in Public Schools*. Niles, IL: Argus Communications.

Schlesinger, A.M. Jr 1991. *The Disuniting of America: Reflections on a Multicultural Society*. New York: W.W. Norton.

Shaheen, J.G. 1980. *The Influence of the Arab-Stereotype on the American Children*. Washington, DC: American–Arab Anti-Discrimination Committee.

Shaheen, J.G. 1984. *The TV Arab*. Bowling Green, OH: Bowling Green State University Popular Press.

Wallbank, T.W., et al. 1987. *History and Life: The World and Its People*. 3rd edn. Glenview, IL: Scott, Foresman.

6

IDEOLOGICAL DIMENSIONS OF ISLAM

A critical paradigm

Ilyas Ba-Yunus

Despite the pioneering leads by Marx (1867), Weber (1904) and Durkheim (1964 [1912]), the sociology of religion has been until recently one of the least developed areas in sociology. Even at the college level, especially in American sociology, courses in religion are poorly attended and only rarely offered. When it comes to Islam, sociological literature is very limited. This deficiency in sociology did not go unnoticed. Writing over twenty-five years ago, Turner (1974: 1–2) noted that

> An examination of any sociology of religion textbook published in the last fifty years will show … that sociologists are either not interested in Islam or have nothing to contribute to Islamic scholarship. … There is consequently a need for studies of Islam which will raise important issues in Islamic history and social structure within a broad sociological framework which is relevant to contemporary theoretical issues.

Even when they did focus on Islam, western sociologists were often inconsistent in their approach. This is true of no less a sociologist than Max Weber:

> … Weber also made a massive contribution to contemporary sociology by outlining a special philosophy of social science and a related methodology which attempts to present the social actor's constitution of social reality by subjective interpretations. In Weberian sociology, we must start any research inquiry with an adequate account or description of the actor's subjective world … my argument will be that in his observation on Islam and Muhammed Weber was one of the first sociologists to abandon his own philosophical guide-lines. (Turner 1974: 3)

Weber is not alone in being inconsistent. Said's *Orientalism* (1978) points out a widespread flaw in western scholarship when it comes to the study of non-western cultures in general and Islam and Muslims in particular. Said argues that the representation of Islam in western scholarly writings is deeply implicated in the power relations between researcher and researched, and is partly constructed not so much by independent observation and evidence as by the pre-existing biases of the scholars themselves.

Whatever their flaws in studying 'other' cultures, sociologists of religion and the Orientalists have had a rare attraction in the 'five pillars' of Islam. Their interest in this specific aspect of Islam does not seem to be altogether out of place.

After all, these are the five pillars that bring Islam closer to other religions in function if not in form. Religion is often defined as communion with and commitment to the supernatural, with the accompanying acts that promote piety, a sense of selflessness and a degree of empathy with others, qualities that have the effect of promoting internal social solidarity (Durkheim 1964 [1912]). No wonder that religion has been considered to be a crucial social institution, especially in the Parsonian model (Parsons 1951; Wuthnow 1988). Inasmuch as this is the case, a focus on the five pillars fits neatly into a functional analysis, especially into a structural-functional model.

However, in this chapter I depart from rather than support this approach in its entirety. Much of the literature on Islam, by Muslim and western scholars alike, points out that Islam does not distinguish between religion and politics (Kedouri 1992; Martin 1982); and that, far from being just a formula for worship, Islam, in fact, provides an overall societal ideology (Arjomand 1992; Esposito 1984). Sensitivity to similar concerns has prompted some (Kessler 1972) to assert that either Islam is not a religion or that, as a religion, it is in a category all by itself. Following the ideological approach, it is possible, as we shall see, to reject the treatment of Islam as a social institution and yet retain the integrity of the Parsonian model. We may treat Islam as a social system.

Sociological frame of reference

All human beings have two fundamental needs. First, they must have food, clothing and shelter, as well as a means of energy, transportation and communication. These are economic needs that must be satisfied one way or another. Second, human sexual and reproductive needs can only be satisfied by interacting with others.

However, pursuit of these needs can potentially disrupt social relationships unless people are subjected to some sort of normative controls. Polity or the collective exercise of power, then, is a third major element that humans require while living a social life. Exercise of power itself may vary from arbitrary and coercive to responsive and responsible, yet this need for normative controls in society (even to control arbitrary exercise of power) cannot be denied. Humans have also shown a need for the supernatural and for some way of communicating with the being or beings beyond the mortal.

All societies see to it that these four human needs are satisfied through highly regulated patterns of interaction. Parsons (1951) called these patterns of interaction 'social institutions' – of economy, family, polity and worship. Without the first three of these, human society is unthinkable. Without all four of them, society has not existed historically. Taken together, norms governing these social institutions describe most essential ingredients of the culture of human society universally. As dissimilar as these institutional patterns of social interaction are, ideally they must be interdependent and mutually reinforcing. This is the American version of the so-called 'organic metaphor' that has been handed down to us from the beginning of classical sociology through Comte, Spencer and

Durkheim via Parsons. However, with the possible exception of very simple preliterate societies, this harmonious functioning of societal institutions is rarely the case in reality. In fact, as a society becomes more complex, indeed with every new development, its institutions tend to exert centrifugal pressure upon one another.

Last in a long chain of major religions of the world, Islam came at the threshold of accelerating societal complexity. Human population, with few exceptions, had already become sedantary. As horticulture was widely replaced by irrigation-based agricultural civilizations, nomadism and animal husbandry gave way to urbanization and international commercial settlements, while the barter system was slowly replaced by the gold and monetary standards.

At this juncture in human history, Islam came with a full compliment of social institutions (the Qur'an calls it *deen*) essential to human society. We do not know of any other 'ism', religion, philosophy of life or ideology that deals with these four indispensable aspects of human life at once, as a manifestation of the same source that provides them with organic unity. A common ideological root in Islam, obviously, is meant to keep the complex society of human beings from coming apart at its institutional seams. This claim stands in defiance of all other ideologies of the past and the present that have failed to provide a singular design of institutional unity for human society.

When practised in its totality, the *deen* of Islam aims at creating what the Qur'an calls the 'Middle Nation' (2:143). This centralizing tendency in Islam has the potential of negotiating ideological extremes and providing them with a common ground by seeking a median course between, say, ascetic spiritualism and obsessive materialism, between selfishness and altruism, between complete freedom and restriction in mate selection, between monogamy and polygamy; and, in a more modern context, between capitalism and socialism, and between democracy and authoritarianism. From the Qur'anic point of view, humans are prone to taking extreme positions. The Qur'an presents Islam as a *deen* in order to guard against such extremes.

Dimensions of Islamic economy

An Islamic economy has three features: it respects private property, it promotes a free market of exchange of goods and services, and it aims at minimizing the differential between the rich and the poor. Three strategies are used progressively in order to achieve these objectives. First, Islam emphasizes the work ethic, dedication to one's calling and enjoying the fruits of one's labour. Like Weber's 'Protestant ethic' (1904), Islam calls for hard work in order to earn a living and to take care of one's family, rather than forsaking the world or surviving on handouts, donations and charity; but unlike the Protestant ethic, Islam does not necessarily take material success in this world as a sign of God's approval of what one is doing. Material success in this world might just as well be a test – a trial from God – of one's conviction and faith in the Almighty. Consequently, the more successful one is in this world, the more God-fearing one ought to be. Moreover, much as Islam emphasizes hard work in order to make a living, it is averse to materialism, opportunistic profiteering and seemingly unending pursuit of wealth – a bottomless abyss, as Durkheim (1966 [1897]) put it – and an obsession with this-worldly pleasures (Qur'an 87:16).

Second, at the same time as Islam favours acquisition of property and a market economy, it institutes a prohibition on the sources of 'making a fast buck' or excessive accumulation such as gambling, hoarding and dealing in interest (taking as well as giving). The Islamic economy must not deal in *riba* or interest. This does not mean that banking is prohibited. Indeed, Muslim economists (for instance, Siddiqui 1975) recommend banks as highly efficient machines that make large amounts of capital available to the investor. Islamic banks deal in profit- and loss-sharing rather than interest, something thought to be quite feasible (Anderson et al. 1990), and in which there is a growing interest among Muslim and non-Muslim economists alike.

Third, inasmuch as sources of excessive accumulation of wealth are denied by Qur'anic prohibition, dispersion of property is facilitated by Islamic folkways (through various forms of voluntary acts of charity, generosity and hospitality), as well as through explicit Qur'anic commandments of inheritence or *wiratha* (4:7, 11) and the poor tax or the *zakat* (see Benthall, Chapter 9, this volume). In the case of *wiratha*, the property of the deceased should be distributed not only among the nearest surviving relatives (wife, sons and daughters), but also among other near relatives such as surviving parents, and brothers and sisters of the deceased, as well as among other less prosperous relatives, and even among needy neighbours and the chronic poor in the community (Qur'an 4:7, 8). The idea is to distribute the property of the deceased widely, rather than allowing it to remain in a few hands.

Zakat, on the other hand, which is not to be confused with a state-levied tax, is the requirement among Muslims to set aside (or contribute to a fund with a similar objective), for the exclusive use of the poor and the needy, 2.5 per cent of one's property left unused for one whole year. *Zakat* should also not be confused with voluntary acts of charity. It is supposed to be the exclusive *right* of the poor, who deserve a share in one's success. If property is invested, then no *zakat* is payable. In other words, property must not be kept lying idle. It should either be kept in circulation or *zakat* should be paid on it. When property is in circulation, it helps the overall community, including the poor. When not in circulation, *zakat* ensures that it still helps the economy.

When Muslims abide by these requirements, they are free to use their property as they like for the benefit of their family. No human system, whether economic or otherwise, is without restrictions that regulate it. Non-Islamic economic systems have their own regulations. An Islamic economy has its own. Islam encourages worldly success while recommending a redistribution of property far in excess of what modern capitalism would accept, yet far below the level that socialism would tolerate. Briefly, Islam allows capitalism minus material obsessions. While defying any socialist solutions, however, it also restricts accumulation of resources in a limited number of hands.

Dimensions of Islamic family

Although a Muslim does not have to get married, celibacy is not considered to be especially virtuous in Islam. The Prophet Muhammad is quoted as saying that marriage is what makes a man perfect, that one must marry as soon as circumstances allow. Islamic institutions of marriage and the family neither wholly restrict choice of marriage partner, nor permit complete freedom. Marriage in Islam is a social contract, not a sacrament. It is a contract exclusively between the groom and the bride, with full and explicit knowledge and consent of the two, and is in stark contrast to those practices in which a bride has no say in her own marriage or is sold to the highest bidder.

However, this freedom of choice in mate selection in Islam does not permit premarital courting, dating, intimacy or sexual intercourse. In fact, according to the established tradition (*sunnah*) of the Prophet, unrelated men and women cannot so much as even touch one another. Consequently, men and women are supposed to distance themselves from each other through the practice of *hijab* or 'modesty', often manifest in the veil, a practice that divides many Muslim societies into two gender-specific subcultures. In such circumstances, a 'love marriage' is extremely uncommon. As Lipskey (1961: 53) put it, 'the general attitude is that love should grow out of marriage, not precede it. Not romantic love but proper social arrangements and satisfactory material circumstances are regarded as essential foundations for a successful marriage'. In this situation, it is generally left up to the parents and other relatives, even to friends and neighbours, to find a suitable mate for marriageable offspring. Because marriage is a contract, there is generally a protracted period of time during which the two sides are supposed to discuss and finalize the prenuptial conditions. However, in no circumstances should the right of the bride or the groom to say 'no' be denied.

After the bride and groom have agreed to the prenuptial conditions, they proclaim their consent to the marriage contract in the presence of at least two adult and sane Muslim witnesses. The marriage is then solemnized. Marriage in Islam thus brings together two families as well as uniting two individuals. Islam creates a system in which differentiation between the family of orientation and the family of procreation appears to diminish. Indeed, the family of orientation (parental family) necessarily plays a significant role in shaping the family of procreation.

No Islamic marriage is solemnized unless the groom has agreed at the time of the wedding itself to give the bride on demand (*mua'jjal*) or later (*mowajjal*) a piece of property as *mehr.* A number of historians and Orientalists have translated *mehr* as dowry. However, *mehr* must not be confused with dowry, which is generally given to the bride's parents or her family before the wedding takes place. *Mehr*, on the other hand, is the exclusive right of the wife and wife alone. No one else – not her parents, her guardian, nor even her husband – can claim a right to the property that is promised to her in her marriage contract. As its sole beneficiary, she has the legal right to dispose of this property as she wishes.

According to Levy (1962: 5), *mehr* reflects a stage in the emancipation of woman from concubinage and slavery through bride-price to the Islamic stage, where a gift is paid to the bride alone. Evidently, the practice of *mehr* has been instituted in Islam to support women in the event of marital conflict. No wonder that the amount of *mehr* is often much disputed in prenuptial negotiations. Thus, when entering marriage, a Muslim woman not only becomes a wife, she also becomes a propertied person, perhaps for the first time in her life. It is perhaps because of this that even most modern and educated Muslim women seem to favour the practice of *mehr* in their marrriage (Ba-Yunus 1990).

Islam opens the door for polygamy, and yet puts it under severe restriction. Although permitting up to four wives, it all but forbids this in practice:

> If you are afraid that you shall not do justice among them then [marry] only one. (Qur'an 4:3)

> But you will not be able to do justice among them. (Qur'an 4:129)

Muslims thus do not have a free licence to practise polygamy. Because the Qur'an does not oblige believers to practise it, polygamy may actually on occasion be legally prohibited (for example, by civil court justices or by judge or *qadi*). Some circumstances, however, may make polygamy desirable; for instance, in times of war when children are orphaned or left homeless (which are, in fact, the kinds of circumstance specified by the Qur'an in the verses cited above). The sex ratio may also change to favour females in the reproductive age, owing, for instance, to an epidemic that takes a heavier toll of men than of women. Cultural conditions may evolve so that eligible men are more at risk due, for example, to increasing mobility, highway accidents, juvenile delinquency and violent crime.[1] Or a Muslim community may have to accommodate large numbers of female converts to Islam, as in contemporary North America (Shafi 1990).

In modern industrial democratic societies, a falling sex ratio is a well-known demographic phenomenon. After its initial advantage at birth, the male population, especially in developed societies, seems to decline faster than the female population. While the lowest sex ratio is generally in the post-retirement age bracket, it is present among those of marriageable age as well. However, in modern western societies that have adopted a 'new morality' or 'alternative lifestyles' (such as postponement of marrriage, cohabitation and greater freedom in sexual practices), a gradual decrease in the male population may not necessarily pose an immediate social problem. Evidently, Islam would not favour this 'new morality' as a 'solution' to the problem of eligible females remaining unmarried.

In defence of polygamy in Islam, the typical male response, occasionally supported by some jurists, has been to assert that men are sexually more aggressive than women. Thus, as the argument goes, those whose sexual urges are not satisfied by their wives alone are allowed to take additional wives, rather than engage in such disdainful acts as prostitution. As chauvinistic as this explanation may sound, it stresses the fact that in Islam the foremost function of marriage is to regulate the sexual act.

Islam thus does not commit the male believer to monogamy. But it does not commit him to polygamy either. In Islam neither monogamy nor polygamy is supposed to be ideal. Monogamy may remain an ideal form of marriage, with husband and wife, as the Qur'an (2:187) puts it, living like beautiful attire as adornment for one another, with mutual love masking one another's defects. However, at other times this ideal may not be so ideal any more. What is supposed to be ideal in all marriages, whether monogamous, or polygamous is justice; and in the broadest terms justice in marriage means that it has the function (in addition to regulating sexual behaviour) of providing homes and family life full of love and mutual care for women who otherwise may remain unmarried (Qur'an 30:21). Lastly, it may be pointed out that because of her right to say 'no', a Muslim woman cannot be forced to enter into a polygamous union. Consequently, although polygamy is permitted, Islamic society has with few exceptions remained monogamous and mostly chaste throughout history.

Dimensions of Islamic polity

> Obey Allah, and obey the Prophet and those of authority among you. (Qur'an 54:24)

Unlike the Shi'a minority view, which is explicitly dynastic and authoritarian, the majority Sunni view on Islamic polity falls midway between authoritarianism and democratic ideals. After all, Islam functions by virtue of the authority of none other than God, because He is the creator, the sustainer and the law-giver. Polity in Islam, like all other things, derives from His will. Because He is the law-giver, in Islam He is the head of state. Man is only His vicegerent who rules on His behalf according to His directives (as laid down in the Qur'an and as put into practice by the *sunnah*). His directives cannot but result in a form of polity that involves public participation and the right to dissent and criticize.[2] This is how the first Islamic system emerged soon after the death of the Prophet. The system introduced by the Prophet's immediate successors, the *khalifah*, remains the main source of inspiration for today's Islamic ideologues and activists, in essence if not in detail. It is considered to be the embodiment, however rudimentary, of the Qur'anic verse quoted above.

This verse identifies the three parameters of the Islamic polity quite clearly. First is God, who put down the law; second is the Prophet, who put God's commandments into practice; and third are those who rule the community of believers in obedience to the commandments of God and the *sunnah* of the Prophet. But, then, who are these rulers, what are their qualifications, and how do they assume power? These questions are not clearly answered in the Qur'an. The Shi'a point of view is that those with authority are the descendants of the Prophet through his cousin, the fourth khalifah, Ali. The Sunni point of view is that after the Prophet, the men of authority in the Islamic polity come only through a process of *Shura* or mutual consultation as ordained in the Qur'an: 'And Shura is the decision [maker] among them' (42:38). This is one of the most encompassing verses from the Qur'an. It describes in the broadest terms a problem-solving technique for use in daily life as well as for solving issues in society as a whole.

It is unfortunate that the real meanings of *Shura* as reflected in the *sunnah* of the Prophet seem to have been lost during the centuries-long monarchical rule in the Muslim world. Roughly translated into English as 'mutual consultation', this concept was rarely invoked in Islamic juristic discourse for obvious reasons (the dynastic rulers and the sultans would not allow any talk of public participation in politics). It is only lately that the full implications of *Shura* have been explored by Muslim scholars and activists (for instance, Ba-Yunus and Ahmed 1985; El-Awa 1980).

No sociological approach to the understanding of Islam can afford to ignore the meanings and implications of *Shura*, which seems to be a dynamic process of seeking solutions to the problems of living in a plural society. In the political arena, *Shura* is the process through which political authority emerges. This process is further specified by a saying (*hadith*) of the Prophet, emphasizing that after his death the believers should install *arbab alhal wa alaqd* ('men of solution and resolution') as their rulers. Combining the two Qur'anic verses cited above with the saying of the Prophet, a basis for a democratic polity in Islam seems to take shape: believers should elect as their leaders through mutual consultation people capable of making wise decisions, and obey them as long as they obey God and His Prophet. This is how *Khalifah al Rashidun*, or the pious Caliphate, emerged following the Prophet's death.

Does this mean that Islam preaches democracy in its political programme? Although democracy is the only political system that seems to approximate Islam, Islam is Islam. It emerged long before the term 'democracy' came into existence. Hence, Islam must not be confused with democracy as practised in contemporary western capitalist polities. Islam does not preach a 'government of the people, by the people, for the people'. In its political form *Shura* stems from the will of God, by the authority of God and for the pleasure of God. The election in the process of *Shura* is not an election so much as it is an emergence of political *taqwa*, or piety, among the believers. Hence, in *Shura* Muslims do not seek power. They are actively brought forward for the sake of 'stopping what is evil and promoting what is good' (Qur'an 3:101, 110).

Those who come to power in an Islamic polity thus cannot supersede or negate what is ordained in the Qur'an and the *sunnah* of the Prophet. In short, the Qur'an and the *sunnah* describe the constitutional limits or the outer parameters of Islamic democracy. They cannot be amended by public pressure or demand. But who, then, decides whether or not those in authority have acted in accordance with the Qur'an and the *sunnah* of the Prophet? The answer is the *qadi* or the judge. An independent judiciary specializing in *shariah* (law) and *fiqah* (jurisprudence) is a necessary condition of Islamic democracy.

Evidently, an Islamic polity must not be confused with theocracy. Nor does it accommodate monarchy either.

Dimensions of Islamic worship

Worship in Islam has both broad and specific meanings. In its broad sense, worship (*ibadah*) in Islam literally means obedience to all the commandments laid down in the Qur'an, including all institutional and extra-institutional rules of conduct. Thus, when a person avoids involvement in interest transactions, pays *zakat* regularly, refrains from extramarital indulgence, or participates in and promotes Islamic polity, then he or she is worshipping God. Likewise, when a person tries to develop his or her personal character in accordance with Qur'anic injunctions, he or she is worshipping God. In a general sense, then, worship in Islam means obedience to the divine directives.

In a more limited sense, as in its dictionary meanings, worship in Islam means observation of the 'five pillars': the proclamation of faith (*shahada*); observation of the five prescribed daily prayers (*salat*); regular payment of *zakat*; fasting from dawn to dusk in Ramadan; and, lastly, *hajj*, the pilgrimage to Mecca at least once in a lifetime for those who can afford to undertake it.

These micro-dimensions of Islamic worship are not mere supplications. They are not left up to the believer's convenience. They are duties imposed upon the believer by the Creator. These are the duties that must be performed conscientiously at their proper times and in their proper manner as practised and instructed by the Prophet. Not that God needs the believer's worship or sacrifice; on the contrary, what is emphasized is that it is the believer who needs to worship Him in order to strengthen his or her own moral fibre and personal commitment (*taqwa*) to divine injunction and to the Islamic institutional order.

Because both aspects of worship in Islam – the institutional and the personal – belong to the same generic root, that is, the Qur'an, the relationship between the two ought to be close and reciprocal. There is little doubt that without personal commitment or *taqwa*, the institutional order of Islam would not endure. It is equally true that without an emergent Islamic institutional order, *taqwa* would soon be rendered useless and meaningless.

Ritualistic worship at the individual level has the same function in Islam as in other religions: inculcation of personal commitment, piety and altruism. However, where other religions stop at ritualistic worship, they do not provide personal piety with an appropriate environment within which to promote and nourish itself. Consequently, in many contemporary societies personal piety has a short lifespan. In fact, it may even be irrelevant, because the contemporary social institutions of modernized and modernizing societies have no generic relationship with, and often go against, the very spirit of personal piety.

In Islam personal worship and obedience to the rules of other institutions are the two sides of the same coin. One cannot exist without the other. This broadening of the meaning of worship seems to be unique to Islam. Above all, it means that for a Muslim to be pious, altruistic and peaceful within and without, not only is a personal and ritualistic devotion to God a requirement, but also an Islamic institutional environment in which to live as a Muslim.

Conclusion

Islam is perhaps one of the most misunderstood religions in the world. Many non-Muslims do not even seem to know it by its real name. It has been called Mohammedanism, Mohammadism, Islamism, Moslemism or the Moslem religion. Likewise, Islam has become all things to all people. Many equate Islam with esoteric Sufi thought. For others, Islam has meant mobs in the streets or terrorists trying to blow up public buildings. For many others, it invokes images of harems and the exploitation of women. Even in the academia, as Said (1978) and others have pointed out, Islam has sufferred from cultural and political biases. In order to avoid this confusing array of perceptions, a more holistic approach has been adopted in this chapter: if there was a living Islamic society today, what would it look like?

However, the functional theoretical analysis of Islam as presented in this chapter must not be confused with the reality of the Muslim world. In fact, in its totality Islam survived only a few decades after the death of the Prophet Muhammad (peace be upon him). In the centuries that followed, Muslims saw the rise and fall of their civilization, the colonization and domination of their lands by western powers, and the emergence of a dismembered and dispirited Muslim world as it exists today. Although Muslim countries are now mostly free of foreign occupation, they are afflicted with extensive poverty, political instability, inefficient and corrupt bureaucracies, sexist chauvinism, widespread illiteracy and technological underdevelopment. Hence, Ahmed's (1988) argument about the sociology of Islam requiring the juxtaposition of the 'Islamic ideal' with contemporary Muslim realities.

For a long time it was hoped that as colonialism receded, the situation in the Muslim world would improve. However, with few exceptions, it looks like the underdevelopment of the Muslim world will continue well into the twenty-first century. As Avineri (1992) points out, the Muslim world has tried just about every recipe in the book but to no avail. Now there seems to be a growing demand for a return to Islam, especially among the educated and restive youth: where everything else has failed, Islam deserves a chance.

The model of Islam presented in this chapter only represents a sociological rendition of the vision of Islam as reflected in hundreds of Muslim publications often not easily accessible to a western readership. I do not claim that the model of Islam presented here is the last word. There may be a number of unintended omissions. However, in its broadest outlines, this model comes close to capturing the *verstehen* of contemporary Islamic movements. Insofar as this is the case, this model may be used to measure the relative departure of Muslim society – and, for that matter, any society – from Islam.

Notes

1. In 1984, it was estimated that more Americans die on the highways each year than the total American casualties in the Vietnam War. Weeks (1989: 160) writes that in the United States about 5 per cent of all deaths are accidental, with motor vehicle accidents being the single most important cause.

2. The Shi'a trace their origin to Ali, the fourth khalifah or pious Caliph. Ali was a cousin and son-in-law of the Prophet, and one of his most important companions. He was also the first after the Prophet's death to challenge the election of all three of his predecessors, signifying that in an Islamic polity no one except Allah and his Prophet are above question. His actions indicate that those in elected offices are especially subject to scrutiny and criticism.

References

Ahmed, A.S. 1988. *Discovering Islam: Making Sense of Muslim History and Society.* London: Routledge and Kegan Paul.

Anderson, R.R., Seibert, R.F. and Wagner, J.G. 1990. *Politics and Change in the Middle East: Sources of Accommodation and Conflict.* New York: Prentice Hall.

Arjomand, S.A. 1992. *The Turban for the Crown: The Islamic Revolution in Iran.* New York: Oxford University Press.

Avineri, S. 1992. The return to Islam. In *Global Studies: The Middle East.* Guilford, CT: The Dushkin Group.

Ba-Yunus, I. 1990. Muslims in North America: mate selection as an indicator of change. In E.H. Waugh, S. Abu-Labon and R. Qureshi (eds), *Muslim Families in North America.* Edmonton, Alberta: University of Alberta Press.

Ba-Yunus, I. and Ahmed, F. 1985. *Islamic Sociology: An Introduction.* Cambridge, MA.: Hodder and Stoughton.

Durkheim, É 1964 [1912]. *The Elementary Forms of Religious Life.* New York: Free Press.

Durkheim, É. 1966 [1897]. *Suicide.* New York: Free Press.

El-Awa, M.S. 1980. *On the Political System of the Islamic State.* Indianapolis: American Trust Publications.

Esposito, J.L. 1984. *Islam and Politics.* New York: Syracuse University Press.

Kedouri, E. 1992. *Politics in the Middle East.* New York: Oxford University Press.

Kessler, C.S. 1972. Islam, society and political behaviour: some comparative implications. *British Journal of Sociology* 23: 33–50.

Levy, R. 1962. *The Social Structure of Islam.* Cambridge: Cambridge University Press.

Lipskey, G.A. 1961. *Saudi Arabia: Its People, Its Society, Its Culture.* New Haven, CT: HRAF Press.

Martin, R.C. 1982. *Islam: A Cultural Perspective.* Englewood Cliffs, NJ: Prentice Hall.

Marx, K. [1867]. *Capital.* New York: Oxford University Press.

Parsons, T. 1951. *The Social System.* Glencoe, IL: Free Press.

Said, E.W. 1978. *Orientalism.* New York: Pantheon.

Shafi, M.A. 1990. Polygamy among African American Muslims. Paper presented at the 20th Annual Conference of the Association of Muslim Social Scientists, Michigan, Detriot.

Siddiqui, N. 1975. *Islamic Banking.* Leicester: Islamic Foundation.

Turner, B.S. 1974. *Weber and Islam.* London: Routledge and Kegan Paul.

Weber, M. 1904. *The Protestant Ethic and the Spirit of Capitalism.* New York: Scribner's.

Weeks, J.R. 1989. *Population: An Introduction to Concepts and Issues.* Belmont, CA: Wadsworth.

Wuthnow, R. 1988. Sociology of religion. In N.J. Smelser (ed.), *Handbook of Sociology.* Newbury Park, CA: Sage.

7

KISSING COUSINS

Anthropologists on Islam

Charles Lindholm

> If one wants to write an anthropology of Islam one should begin, as Muslims do, from the concept of a discursive tradition that includes and relates itself to the founding texts of the Quran and the hadith. Islam is neither a distinctive social structure nor a heterogeneous collection of beliefs, artifacts, customs and morals. It is a tradition. (Asad 1986: 14)

In the pages to follow, I will briefly discuss the history of and prospects for an anthropology of Islam. This is a difficult and daunting task, and I should say at the outset that I make no claims whatsoever to completeness, nor do I claim to cover the whole vast geographical span where Islam is found. Instead, I have focused on the area from Afghanistan and northern Pakistan across the Islamic heartland and on to North Africa, and have only cited works that I believe are especially ground-breaking or representative of a type. Many worthy books and articles have necessarily been left out. The reader should also not expect too much critical fingerpointing (though I do air a few pet peeves), and I do not make an attempt to put forward the 'best' approach to this formidably complex project; my effort here is simply to describe some of the historical trajectories, vicissitudes, possibilities and limitations of a particular scholarly enterprise.

Obstacles to the anthropological study of Islam

More than any other religious annunciation, Islam has awakened highly charged and negative reactions in the West. Up until relatively recent times the Prophet Muhammad was regularly execrated as the anti-Christ and portrayed with the horns of the Devil, while Islam itself was derided as a primitive religion, at best based on misunderstanding of Judaeo-Christian doctrines, at worst a diabolical plot (Daniel 1960). And although these stereotypes are no longer voiced publicly, nonetheless Islam is still viewed by many westerners as a dangerous and subversive doctrine – one so frightening to modern French bureaucrats that they have prohibited the wearing of Islamic headscarves in public schools.

This over-reaction is partly an artefact of history: the Muslim Ottoman Empire came very close indeed to conquering Europe, and until recently the Muslim Middle East was the nearest and most feared opponent of the West – an opposition expressed not only politically and economically, but also religiously, since the stated ambition of Islam is to fulfil the Abrahamic tradition and bring all the world within its ambit. Many westerners continue to fear these aspirations and are not mollified by the Muslim inclusion of Jesus and Moses as Prophets in the Islamic canon. New tensions have been aroused by the expansion of what is misleadingly called Islamic fundamentalism, and by the connection glibly made in the popular press between Islam and terrorism. On the grounds of protecting Christianity from a *jihad*, Bosnian Serbs have justified the slaughter of their Muslim neighbours, while many Americans assume that any acts of random violence, such as the bombing of a government building in Oklahoma city, must have been the work of 'Muslim extremists'.

Such a pervasive fear of a 'Muslim threat' is ironic given the real political weakness of Middle Eastern states, which have been subjected to long periods of colonial rule or, at the very least, to widespread western influence. Under these conditions, Muslims' own cultural values have been deeply challenged, so that, as Edward Said (1978: 323) remarks, 'the felt tendencies of contemporary culture in the Near East are guided by European and American models', leading to the 'paradox of an Arab regarding himself as an "Arab" of the sort put out by Hollywood'. It is within the context of heightened Muslim self-doubt, and in the name of setting right the imbalance of power, that Said embarked upon his own passionate denunciation of western scholarship on the Middle East as essentialist and reductionist, aimed at producing false and destructive images of the Muslim 'other' (Said 1978). As is well known, his critique led to a wholesale revaluation of the field of Islamic studies, particularly among the historians and theologians whom Said lumped together as 'Orientalists'. The very *raison d'être* of this discipline was harshly attacked by Said and his followers as a form of thinly veiled colonialism, dehumanizing and objectifying Middle Eastern people by turning them into exotic figures to be analysed and classified by western experts. Said's polemic also aroused a strong reaction among anthropologists studying the Middle East, leaving most of them with a deep fear of being accused of 'Orientalizing' or 'essentializing' their subjects.[1]

Given the level of anxiety and controversy aroused in the general public and in the academic community by the relationship between the West and the Muslim world, it seems paradoxical indeed that the anthropology of Islam and Islamic societies – especially work in the heartland of the Middle East – has, until recently, been neither very important nor very controversial in the discipline. Certainly, there have been some important theoreticians who have spent time in the central regions of Islamic culture, such as Clifford Geertz, Ernest Gellner and Pierre Bourdieu, all of whom worked in North Africa. But although Geertz's well-known book *Islam Observed* (1968) tells the reader a great deal about what the author believes to be the respective worldviews of Muslims in Java and in Morocco, it says almost nothing about the doctrines, practices or principles of Islam itself. It is as if a book comparing the attitudes and cultural biases of the English and French were entitled *Christianity Observed*.[2] Bourdieu had even less to say about Islamic theory and practice. Only Gellner paid serious attention to Muslim consciousness, but, as we shall see, his work is primarily a structural contrast between urban and rural social organization.

I believe that in part this vacancy is a result of the austere and seemingly simple nature of Islam itself. In fact, some of my anthropological colleagues who work in other regions of the world have admitted to me in private that for them Islam is simply not interesting to study. Where in Islamic dogma and practice, they ask, does one find the complex symbolic systems, the enigmatic ceremonies, obscure rituals and the mythic narratives that anthropologists love to interpret in order to reveal the hidden underpinnings and contradictions of culture? Where are the depths, the mysteries, the ambiguous metonyms and metaphors revealing deep existential tensions, that render the study of religion and its relationship to culture intellectually challenging? Although I find this vision of Islam to be mistaken, I can understand how it has come to be held.

It is true that elaborate rituals and the narratives that surround them have little place in Islamic practice. Of course, the symbolism of the pilgrimage, for example, is complex and deep, and there are indeed some enclaves where local ceremonial performances are amenable to interpretative anthropological analysis (see Hammoudi 1993 for a recent example). But in general, as Marshall Hodgson (1974) has commented, the dominant mode of Islamic thought disavows exactly the sort of mythic tales and symbolic patterning that western anthropologists have been trained to see as the core of religion. Indeed, orthodox Muslim scholarship on Islamic doctrine, as revealed in the Qur'an and in the transmitted accounts of the deeds and words of the Prophet (*hadith*), strongly affirms that analogy or metaphor cannot be used to interpret scripture, nor can Muhammad's message be submitted to the test of logic; what is said is what is meant – no more, no less. If Allah is portrayed in the Qur'an with his hand reached toward the sinner, the helping hand is not to be taken as a symbol of God's forgiveness; it must be accepted *bila kayf*, that is, without our being able to specify what it signifies. Any absurdities this may seem to entail are taken by orthodox Muslims as indications of human incapacity to grasp the infinite potentiality of Allah's omnipotence. The symbolic analysis so beloved of the majority of anthropologists of religion is here repudiated utterly.

Islam favours instead the kerygmatic mode of revelation; that is, it places the study of sacred history at the centre of its annunciation. Muslims, as Hodgson (1974) notes, do not try to imagine the cosmos, nor do they attempt to develop complex symbolic systems and dense ceremonial performances in order to put themselves in touch with the infinite; rather, they seek ultimate meaning in the datable irrevocable events in the life and times of the Prophet and his companions. For Muslims, such acts of recollection and emulation are the keys to salvation. Islamic scholarly debate is therefore preoccupied with historiography: How do we know that the Prophet actually said or did this or that? How can we measure the probity of witnesses to those great events of the past, and how can we be sure of the accuracy of the chains of transmission of accounts of the Prophet's life and times? These are not questions that seem, at least on the surface, to lend themselves to the type of analysis that has so far dominated the anthropological study of religion.[3]

Instead of a theology that gives a symbolic picture of the cosmos or a portrait of the nature of God, Islam offers the faithful a simple set of performances and prohibitions commanded by Allah and enacted by the Prophet and his companions. These practices mark out for humanity the proper pathway that must be followed over the course of a lifetime in order to behave ethically and thereby achieve salvation. Individual devotional practice in everyday life and acceptance of the Word are what is crucial, not reflection, symbolic elaboration or rationalization. Straying from the path leads not to an inner sense of guilt; instead the sinner is wandering alone and desperate in the moral darkness, without hope of illumination and redemption. Because of its sober and pragmatic emphasis on practical application, Islam has been appropriately described as a religion not so much of orthodoxy as of orthopraxy (Smith 1957), reliant on simple actions that have the straightforward purposes of serving God and demonstrating faith. These include the 'five pillars': regular prayer; public witnessing of the oneness of God and the mission of the Prophet (the *shahada*); undertaking the pilgrimage to Mecca; fasting during the month of Ramadan; and donating alms. In fact, the very word 'Islam' signifies an *act*: the initiatory act of surrender and submission to Allah.

For western anthropologists predominantly interested in disentangling symbol systems, the Muslim emphasis on prescribed action and its principled attachment to historical study and textual exegesis often made the religion appear outside the range of anthropological analysis. What can one say, for example, about the regular practice of prayer, except that it is required? How can interpretation be elaborated within such a pragmatic and action-oriented framework? Nor did anthropologists feel comfortable with or capable of delving into the debates of Muslim scholars over the historical validity of various chains of transmission of *hadith*, or the legal significance of a particular set of terms in the Qur'an. The general lack of interest in Islamic scholarship was augmented by the fact that the doctrines and moral codes of Islam are descended from and similar to (Muslims would say they are 'perfections' of) Judaism and Christianity – the earlier emissary religions of the region. As a result, Islam looked all too familiar to anthropologists raised within, and often agnostic about, their own religious traditions. Owing to these factors, western anthropologists concerned above all with deciphering the unfamiliar beliefs and practices of exotic religions often saw Islam as more or less transparent, and treated it as a taken-for-granted background, not requiring any deep analysis, but merely as something to be mentioned, like climate and soil type, before getting on with more compelling research, which typically concerned the lives and preoccupations of rural people, usually tribesmen.

The tribal paradigm

I can illustrate this characteristic attitude with a case I know very well: my own. When I went to do fieldwork in the valley of Swat in northern Pakistan I certainly knew the people were Muslims, but that meant very little to me. My knowledge of Islam was, in truth, extremely minimal: I realized that Muhammad was the Prophet of Islam, and that Muslims prayed in the direction of Mecca, where they also went on pilgrimage. I realized there was a difference between Sunni Islam and Shi'ism, but had only a vague idea what it was, though I knew my friends were Sunnis. The most I knew about Islamic doctrine came from Sufi poetry I had read as an undergraduate, but that esoteric doctrine apparently had nothing to do with the world of the village or Islam as it was practised by ordinary people. The only Sufis I saw during my fieldwork were the ragged mendicants the dogs occasionally chased through the streets.

As a lapsed Unitarian and former pupil of Oriental Studies as an undergraduate at Columbia, I was much more familiar with the overtly far more alien doctrines of Hinduism and Buddhism than I was with Islam, despite the fact that I had already spent considerable time in Islamic societies, including Iran, Afghanistan and Pakistan. But even though I found Buddhist and Hindu dogmas intellectually fascinating, at that time my fascination did not extend to Islam. During the time I spent in Muslim countries, I never entered any of the local mosques, and I never heard a sermon except brokenly, over a harshly barking loudspeaker; I never had anything to do with religious teachers, nor did I want to spend time with them. Only late in my work did I realize what school of law the people followed; I never did learn how to read Islamic texts and I rarely discussed religion with anyone. By the same token, the subject of religion was rarely broached with me, nor was I ever pressured to convert to Islam, though some village women did tell my wife to repeat the *shahada* after them, so that – as they believed – she could join them in heaven. They roared with laughter when my wife repeated not only the *shahada*, but the rest of their conversation as well.

My attitude can be excused, to a degree, as a reflection of the environment in which I did my fieldwork. My hosts in Swat were Yusufzai Pukhtun khans, fiercely independent tribesmen who took their religion as their natural birthright, just as they took their other customs and habits. For them, Islam was not a matter for comment or questioning, nor did they offer any great respect to piety or learning in others. They had an amused view of local mullahs and preachers, who were required to preside at weddings and funerals, but whose manly honour was tainted by their social inferiority and whose self-advertised virtue was considered more than suspect. No one took them especially seriously, though this was later to change with the upsurge of Islamic revivalism, as local mullahs became powerful political activists. But when I first arrived in Swat in 1969, these changes were far off, and village preachers were still treated with good-humoured condescension, an attitude that I imitated.

The khans had a more ambiguous attitude toward the wildly bearded beggars dressed in Sufi patchwork who sometimes came into the villages asking for food. These men were pitied for their poverty, but were also feared as magicians. Such unsavoury characters were to be avoided, not worshipped, and the Pukhtun had no interest at all in their purported status as holy men. Similarly, Sufi shrines were thought to be rather sordid places where desperate women went to beg for favours from God through saintly mediators, who were suspected of taking advantage of their unhappy supplicants in various ways. For example, children with birthmarks were considered to be the consequence of saints responding a bit too directly to the petitions of women who had come to beg for fertility. In contrast, my friends did honour and respect the families of great Sufi saints of the past who had gained considerable power and land. But their respect was couched in political, not religious terms – the elite saintly families had lost their holiness as they engaged the khans in the never-ending struggle for secular domination. Other men of saintly lineage who were weak or incompetent received no special deference, but were treated like any other inferior.

Of course, the khans themselves were not irreligious – but their religion was one of practice, not discourse. Some of these warrior farmers grew beards and piously dyed them red in imitation of the Prophet, and some who could afford it went on the pilgrimage to Mecca, from whence they returned with new prestige, but without any exceptional sacred qualities. In old age, men who could read Arabic script commonly began to recite from the Qur'an in the mornings and evenings, hoping to forestall God's wrath by the magical act of repeating aloud the sacred words they could only rarely understand. As one told me: 'God must be merciful, because I have committed many crimes.' But outside the obligatory prayers and a strict adherence to fasting, Islam seemed to ride lightly on the people with whom I was working. If custom and religious duty came into conflict, custom usually won. For instance, women were not given their share of inheritance, as demanded in the Qur'an, nor was divorce allowed, though it is permitted in Islam. As many ethnographers have reported, this constellation of attitudes is common among Middle Eastern tribesmen, who see themselves as Muslims much as they see themselves as honourable human beings; that is, without doubt or interrogation.

My own studies therefore directly reflected the way the Pukhtun took Islam as an essential and unquestioned part of their identity. My lack of interest in their religion also echoed their lack of interest in mine. Instead of questioning me about my beliefs, which might have led to my questioning them about theirs in return, they only expressed curiosity about whether Christians buried their dead standing up, as they had been told, and whether our law permitted us to eat frogs. In fact, my only 'encounters' with Islam were outside the village. Once, in Karachi, a merchant refused to return my '*salaam alaikum*', saying it was forbidden for infidels to make that greeting, something no one in Swat had ever mentioned to me, and which made me feel angry and humiliated. And when we went to visit the famous Sufi shrine of Pir Baba a zealous gatekeeper angrily challenged my wife's right to enter, but he was quickly silenced when he was told that real Pukhtuns treat their guests with respect and not hostility, perhaps not a central Islamic principle, but one very dear to the hearts of the tribesmen.

Under these circumstances, Islamic theology and practice was of little importance for my studies. It was simply an ambient noise, buzzing everywhere, but never taking concrete shape. I was consciously aware of Islam only when its manifestations broke my routine: if I was woken in the early morning by the cry of the muezzin, or had to put up with the sullen silence of my friends during the long days of a summer Ramadan fast, or was obliged to wait while someone I wanted to talk to was prostrated in prayer. At those moments, I found myself meditating about the pervasiveness of Islam, and wondering how it managed to penetrate so deeply into daily life, but then I soon returned to my own work of discussing genealogies and talking about politics, which were the topics that obsessed the men around me. Only if religion entered *that* realm did it become really interesting (see Lindholm 1982, 1992 for some of my research on this topic).

I ruefully make these embarrassing confessions with the somewhat exonerating knowledge that my experience as an anthropologist in the Islamic world was not unusual. Other ethnographers of my generation and earlier who worked in the Middle East and its environs have told me similar stories, since they too did research with people who were, like the Pukhtun, usually illiterate and ignorant of the fine points of religious doctrine, but were very knowledgeable indeed about the matters that concerned them most: honourable behaviour, the techniques of survival in harsh circumstances, the making of political and marital alliances, the struggle to gain respect and authority, and, above all, the social structure of the patriline. For the majority of anthropologists of this period, the kin-based social system, with its structured rivalries among equals and its amazing capacity for fission and fusion, appeared to be a key for understanding the way local tribespeople, who lacked ascribed authority positions and institutionalized political structures, managed to organize themselves.[4]

Mirroring the central concerns articulated by the people being studied, a great part of the anthropological fieldwork in the Middle East of the fifties, sixties and seventies centred on the degree to which the indigenous egalitarian segmentary model actually worked (or did not work) in practice in different contexts, and more broadly on the manner in which authority was organized, accepted or resisted not only by independent warrior nomads or mountain farmers, but even by lowland peasants, though tribal studies were more prestigious than studies of peasants.[5] With few exceptions, urban life, where a more confrontational relationship with Islamic practitioners might have taken place, was left out of the picture, despite the fact that a majority of Middle Easterners already lived in cities. As in my own fieldwork, any discussions of Islamic texts and practices were usually entirely absent from anthropological inquiry during this period. For example, Emmanuel Marx's exemplary study of the Bedouin of the Negev (1967) hardly mentions Islam; nor does Robert Fernea's highly regarded work on Iraqi Bedouin (1970) have anything in particular to say about religious knowledge or practice, though he does discuss at length the political role of religious leaders. Even if they might agree with him on little else, these writers, like most other ethnographers of the period, would probably concur with Geertz's statement that for most Muslims 'religious truth is so little subject to argument and so little responsive to temporal concerns that it ought not to hinder practical activities'; and, by implication, need not be analysed (Geertz 1979: 141).

Sufis : *Ulema* :: Anthropologists : Orientalists

When mentioned at all by ethnographers of this era, Islam – manifested in the presence of Sufi saints and in the cults that surrounded their tombs – was understood primarily as a moderating force in the segmentary system of the people of the hinterlands. According to segmentary lineage theory (as developed in Evans-Pritchard 1940, 1949; Sahlins 1961), rival kin groups could not, in principle, negotiate settlements between themselves, since they only gained solidity and cohesion in competitive relationships of 'complementary opposition' with lineage groups of equivalent genealogical depth. To ameliorate the violence and disunity such opposition implies, Middle Eastern tribal lineages often required the mediation of Sufi 'saints' whose power came not from kinship (though they might claim descent from the Prophet to ratify their sacred status), but from God.

The saint's special quality was legitimized among the warring tribes as much by his public austerities and his garb and demeanour as by his purported knowledge of and adherence to the rules and demands of Islamic law. (It should be recalled that reading, among illiterate tribesmen, was considered to be a magical act.)[6] These saintly men could also serve as occasional leaders, bringing together rival tribesmen under the banner of God in order to resist the encroachment of external authority. In this sense, saints were generally in opposition to the central state, though in their enclaves and surrounded by their loyalists they could sometimes evolve peripheral proto-states of their own.

Such sacred mediators were discovered and described in many regions of the Middle Eastern hinterlands. In my own research area of Swat, for example, Fredrik Barth had already found that local Muslim Sufi 'saints' were symbolically marked off from the tribal warriors who surrounded them; they wore special robes and turbans, grew impressive beards, avoided violence, were ostentatiously abstemious and pious, and so on. They also were separated spatially, living on strips of land set aside for them between the villagers whom they served. As men of God who stood outside the ordinary strife of lineage rivalry, they were sought out as judges in tribal disputes and sometimes led the united tribesmen in wars against encroaching enemies. The most successful of these saintly lineages provided the first (and last) rulers of the region (Barth 1965).[7]

Similarly, research by Ernest Gellner (1969) in highland Morocco revealed a pattern of saintly lineages occupying land between rival tribes who used them as arbitrators and potential leaders.[8] But unlike other fieldworkers who remained within the circle of their tribes and the saints who served them, Gellner extended his understanding to encompass the cities as well. Although much debated, his model remains the most powerful yet produced for the analysis of Middle Eastern society as a whole.[9] Innovatively marrying the theories of Ibn Khaldun with those of David Hume, he argued that the Middle East was characterized by a dialectical relationship between rural and urban social structures and the religious styles appropriate to them. According to him, in a pattern that is the converse of Europe, low-culture 'Catholic' saint-worship prevails in the tribal periphery of the Middle East (for example, among the Berbers he studied), while high-culture 'Protestant' egalitarian scripturalism dominates the urban centres. The history of the Middle East, Gellner contended, is in large measure the history of the continuous antagonistic dialectic between these two polar opposites, as saint-led tribesmen sought to avoid, or to conquer, the central state. However, Gellner argued, modern conditions, which favour the ascendance of the city over the country, have necessarily spelled the end of tribal saint religions. Austere scripturalism is the wave of the future (Gellner 1981, 1983, 1990).

Although he produced a model that brought the ethic of urban clerics into anthropological purview, and although he noted the Puritan and textualist character of that ethic, Gellner actually had little to say about the content or inculcation of 'Protestant' Islam. He admitted that 'the Muslim world is pervaded by a reverence for the high-culture variant of Islam – egalitarian, scripturalist, puritan, and nomocratic', and concluded that 'this ethos seems to have a life and authority of its own, not visibly dependent on any institutional incarnation' (Gellner 1990: 112). However, he gave no proof of his claim that institutional explanations were inadequate for grasping the nature and powerful influence of high-culture Islam, nor did he make any great effort to discover from whence the authority of urban Islam actually did arise.

That task was left by default to the Orientalist scholars who had already been engaged for at least a century in the historical reconstruction of Muslim cosmopolitan culture. For them, books, not people, contained the essential truths about Islam; they took it for granted that retrieval of the textual arguments of the academic, urban and courtly medieval Muslim scholar-administrator-jurist-cleric (the *ulema*) would reveal the core of Islamic society; anything else was purely secondary and derivative. As we have seen, anthropologists, in contrast, took as their field the ethnographic study of the lives and customs of contemporary tribesmen and their relationships to the Sufis who served as their arbitrators and leaders. This division of labour meant that Orientalists were uninterested in tribal studies or even in living people, while anthropologists avoided cities and rarely read texts.

It was not ever thus. Much of the classic ethnographic literature of the century or so prior to the appearance of the academic discipline of anthropology was far more varied and traversed with ease the boundaries between city and country, written and oral, Orientalist and ethnographer. Some of the best of it was written by adventurous travellers who had journeyed to the Middle East in order to make their fortunes as writers. Probably best known of these was Sir Richard Burton, a brilliant Orientalist scholar whose colourful and sometimes scurrilous version of his adventures in disguise among ordinary Muslims on pilgrimage (Burton 1964 [1855]) was one of the most widely read of nineteenth-century 'ethnographic' travellers' accounts. But other travellers, notably Doughty (1888) and Niebuhr (1994 [1792]), spent far more time in the Middle East, and presented more balanced accounts of their travels to their readers.

These travellers' adventures were complemented by descriptive 'folkloric' monographs such as Musil's great work on the Rwala Bedouin (1928), Hanoteau and Letourneux on the Kayble (1873), Westermarck's work on Moroccan customs (1926), and Burckhardt's account of the Wahhabis (1831). The latter two are especially noteworthy for the anthropological study of Islam. Westermarck's *Ritual and Belief in Morocco* (1926) provided what remains the most detailed account of the 'folk religion' of Morocco that lies outside the high literate tradition, that is, the popular worship of saints and the use of amulets and magical charms. His voluminous account consists primarily of lists, but remains a more or less untouched goldmine of data for researchers interested in exploring this usually hidden world. Burckhardt had a completely different agenda: producing a first-hand historical record of the puritanical Wahhabi movement as it evolved before his eyes. His work includes detailed description of their doctrines, and also the way those doctrines were perceived by other Arabs. Though rarely cited by anthropologists, it nonetheless remains an exemplary model for the ethnographic study of contemporary Islamic political movements, which all look back to Wahhabism as their precursor.[10]

During this early period the anthropological fascination with the tribal periphery, while already predominant, was balanced by important ethnographic research in urban areas, most notably Lane's study of Cairo (1871) and Hurgronje's masterly portrait of Mecca (1931 [1888–9]). These latter works, located as they were in the centres of clerical piety, were the first complex portraits of the manners and customs of urban Islamic practice to appear in the West. Hurgronje was especially important in that he was a serious Orientalist scholar, whose textual work remains seminal in the origins of that discipline.[11] But in contrast to later practitioners, he saw no contradiction between doing fieldwork on the religious brotherhoods and the intellectual life of Muslim scholars in contemporary Mecca while also continuing his research on ancient Islamic texts and practices. For Hurgronje, studying the present social context of Islam offered a unique insight into the past and was also necessary for gaining any real understanding of Muslim religious experience.

A similar 'proto-anthropological' approach, but this time in a tribal context, was taken by another great scholar of ancient Semitic religion, R.R. Robertson-Smith, who was expelled from his professorship at Aberdeen University for his unorthodox theories about the historical origins of Christianity. To test his ideas, he journeyed several times to Arabia, where he temporarily took on an Arab identity in order to investigate in person the actual social organization of the tribesmen, which he then extrapolated – sometimes with rather dubious results – into the pre-Islamic era (Robertson-Smith 1972 [1889]). His research led as well to a seminal work on Arab kinship and marriage (Robertson-Smith 1967 [1885]), which Émile Durkheim later used as the type case for 'mechanical' solidarity, and which inspired Evans-Pritchard's portrait of segmentary society – a case of Orientalist influence on anthropology that is usually ignored.[12] But more important for our purposes, Robertson-Smith was the first Orientalist scholar to develop a theoretical approach linking Islamic beliefs and practices to tribal social organization and ecology. For him, the study of contemporary Muslim tribes was central for historical scholarship.[13]

Unfortunately, only a few later Orientalist researchers followed in the footsteps of these early explorer-scholars and sought information about the nature of Islam by doing ethnographic research among tribesmen. One notable exception was R.B. Serjeant, who used material from his time spent in South Arabia among the Bedouin to argue that a characteristic form of sacred space and a social organization associated with that space had existed in that region from time immemorial. According to Serjeant's research, among the Bedouin these sacred spots, called *hatwah*, are governed by a member of a saintly lineage who collects taxes and arbitrates disputes among his followers. The *hatwah* is also the centre for a marketplace that is protected by the presence of the holy man. The tribesmen who accept the authority of the saint are obliged to fight for him, and, in times of political strife, can form the core of a powerful army.

Using his Bedouin data, as well as historical material, Serjeant then argued that Muhammad's leadership at Medina was not as innovative as had been previously supposed, but was well within the traditional pattern he had discovered; the success of Islam in expanding was not due to the novelty of Muhammad's message, but derived from the unstable political setting of the time (Serjeant 1981). This is a claim that, like Robertson-Smith's reading back of present Bedouin life into the pre-Islamic past, can be contested,[14] but whether or not Serjeant was correct about the historical continuity of Muhammad's mission, it is very clear that the configuration he describes is much like the one that anthropologists had already described among other Muslim tribal peoples. Serjeant shows no awareness of any of this anthropological work; similarly, few anthropologists have ever cited Serjeant's research, though he had a great deal to say about contemporary Bedouin religio-social organization. Clearly, once the disciplinary division of labour between Orientalist and anthropologist had become institutionalized, there was little, if any, cross-fertilization between the disciplines, even when there was an obvious convergence of interests.

Perhaps part of the reason for the impermeability of the barrier between the two fields is the fact that a similar distinction is to be found within Middle Eastern culture itself, as oral tribal traditions and the scholarly records of the learned are sharply differentiated from one another, with the latter presented by the dominant *ulema* as 'civilized' and 'true' and the former disparaged as 'primitive' and 'false'. Edward Said has argued that this pattern of 'hegemonic textuality' is a western product, but, as Andrew Shryock (1997: 18) has recently noted, the privileging of the written word in the Middle East had been assiduously promoted long before the colonial period by 'the interregional (and unequal) collusion of learned elites heavily invested in their own textual authority'. Western Orientalists, as inheritors of the urban *ulema*'s literate tradition, gladly embraced the Muslim scholars' denigration of oral knowledge from the periphery and followed them in reifying written texts as the sole form of legitimate information. In contrast, most anthropologists, following their own moral tradition of support for the downtrodden, naturally felt themselves to be on the side of the excluded and illiterate tribesmen and against the elitist and lettered clerics. Unhappily, the anthropologist's position, however laudable in impulse, had the practical consequence of making textual ignorance into a virtue, and further solidified the already existent wall between the two disciplines.

However, the rift between tribe and city, oral and written, anthropologist and Orientalist, is not a necessary prerequisite for Middle Eastern scholarship, any more than it ought to be for western scholarship. A reconciliation of the two can be found in the classics of Islamic historiography. Long before the urban *ulema* sought to solidify their power by affirming the absolute priority of the written word, pious Muslim scholars and proto-ethnographers seeking clues about Muhammad and his life had gone into the Bedouin hinterlands in order to collect genealogies and customs, as well as oral tales of battles and poetic recitations, from the tribesmen. These accounts were placed side by side with documentary sources to produce what remain the greatest histories of early Islam, as written by al-Tabari (d. 923 AD) and al-Baladhuri (d. 892 AD). These compendiums, along with the vast collections of *hadith* covering every conceivable aspect of daily life, continue to provide the irreplaceable basis for an ethno-historical understanding of the nature of Islam, which is, as I have already indicated, an annunciation placing the knowledge of history at its very core. Yet anthropologists, though uniquely qualified to interpret the hortatory narratives, recitations of custom and genealogical trees inscribed at length in these ancient texts, have generally continued to be loyal to their traditions of illiteracy and ahistoricism, and to the standard forms of symbolic analysis, and have left the study of these crucial writings to Orientalist scholars with little, if any, knowledge of social theory or tribal life.[15]

New directions in the anthropology of Islam

Through the seventies and even into the eighties, the majority of Middle Eastern anthropologists remained primarily concerned with the study of peripheral societies, and concentrated their research on warrior issues of honour and power or, among peasant groups, on the ways in which state domination was resisted or suborned. For them, as noted above, Islam was of interest mostly as a legitimizing ideology justifying the interventions of saintly mediators in tribal disputes, and arguments were primarily over the exact causal relationship between social structure, mode of production and the political function of Sufi orders.

At the same time, some fieldworkers – ever seeking new locations for study – had begun to wonder what actually went on within the brotherhoods. Jamil Abun-Nasr's account of the Tijaniya order (1965) was primarily historical, but it broke a pathway for later researchers. More explicitly anthropological was Gilsenan's pioneering account of the evolution and workings of the Shadiliya order of Cairo (1973). This study placed the Shadiliya within a comparative context, analysed its central rituals, correlated its structure with the social organization of premodern Egypt, and showed that modern changes in the state had undermined the *raison d'être* of the Shadiliya and other Sufi orders. Set within the heart of the great city, Gilsenan's book focused on the spiritual and material concerns of the urban poor, and therefore stood very much at right angles to the predominant anthropological research of the period. Yet at the same time, it shared with more standard ethnography an emphasis on social action; Gilsenan also conventionally presented religion as a dependent variable, reflecting its social context and the secular struggle for power.

Important as these works were in giving a more detailed social and historical understanding of Sufism,[16] they still did not enter into the sacrosanct textualist world of the Orientalist. This was left to two of the scholars who accompanied Clifford Geertz during his fieldwork in Sefrou, Morocco. Geertz self-consciously wished to break away from the tribal preoccupations and functionalist theorizing of earlier ethnographers. But to accomplish this end he turned his attention to the merchant in the bazaar, not to the cleric in the mosque. In his accounts of Morroco,

Islam is a side issue at best, as he studied instead the way dyadic relationships were negotiated between maximizing entrepreneurs in a teeming and confusing marketplace.

Geertz did succeed, for better or worse, in moving the anthropology of the Middle East away from the study of tribal structure and toward the study of individual manipulation.[17] However, since his work in the market led him to emphasize contingency and self-interest, he portrayed Middle Eastern society as a completely fluid world, without any stable base upon which prediction or comparison could rest. Tribal structures, now debunked, could not provide any grounding for action, and ethnographers were left with the task of finding some basis for order in a universe animated solely by a mixture of 'restlessness, practicality, contentiousness, eloquence, inclemency and moralism' (Geertz 1979: 235). Only personal character and persuasiveness, Geertz seemed to say, had any import in this flexible and competitive universe.

In reaction against this chaotic picture, Lawrence Rosen and Dale Eickelman introduced, each in a different manner, new pathways for the anthropological study of Muslim life.[18] Rosen, a legal anthropologist, began his research in the Geertzian mode by studying the manner in which individuals bargained with one another in the Middle Eastern context (Rosen 1984). But instead of focusing on the marketplace, he was interested in the application of law. And because law in Islamic society is derived from a close study of the Qur'an and *hadith*, Rosen moved away from a Geertzian emphasis on personality and toward the study of texts and on the way Muslim jurisconsults use texts to come to decisions. In so doing, Rosen became the equivalent of a Muslim *faqih*, a legal scholar, preoccupied with the problems of understanding and implementing law within the framework of sacred knowledge. Questions he and his students addressed shifted radically away from the genealogies of tribesmen and the bargains of merchants and toward juridical debates over verifiability of evidence and the range of interpretation and legal authority possible within the range of Islamic discourse. (See Rosen 1989 for a synopsis of his views.)

Meanwhile, Rosen's colleague, Dale Eickelman, was one of the first ethnographers of the Middle East to turn his attention to the study of classical Arabic texts, and decisively breached the wall between Orientalist and anthropological knowledge with his seminal article on the so-called 'false Prophets' who were rivals with Mohammed (1967). Besides devoting himself to the Orientalist (and Muslim) study of sacred history, and besides writing an important book on a rural Sufi order (1976), Eickelman also wrote historical-ethnographic accounts of the methods and means of traditional Islamic education (1978, 1985). This too marked a real shift in the anthropological study of Islam; one characterized more and more by a focus on textual knowledge, and on the manner in which that knowledge is attained and used by a scholarly elite.

Rosen and Eickelman thus began to follow the route recommended by Asad at the beginning of this article: learning about Islam as Muslims themselves would, from the discursive study of sacred tradition.[19] Henceforth, the line between historian, anthropologist and *ulema* would be blurred, though anthropologists would continue to focus on the actual implementation and interpretation of sacred knowledge, while Orientalist historians and theologians, like the *ulema* themselves, would continue to regard any study of the present of interest primarily as an avenue to understanding of the sacred past.

This new area of study has proven itself to be extremely fruitful, both in terms of the anthropology of law and education, and for the broader project of the study of the actual practice and morality of Islam itself, as understood not from the traditional anthropological point of view of tribesmen and their Sufi complements, but from the perspective of the urban guardians of sacred law, the *ulema*. Central texts in this new approach include: Michael Fischer's (1980) important study of the debating Muslim scholars of Qom, which gave new insight into the logic and discursive techniques of Islamic clerics; Richard Antoun's (1989) unique ethnographic account of the life and sermons of a Jordanian mullah; and Shahla Haeri's (1989) study of the institution of 'temporary marriage' among Shi'ites, which blends textual knowledge with ethnographic cases to provide a missing female perspective. Elsewhere, and in a less academic vein, Akbar Ahmed (1988, 1993) has used both historical and ethnographic material in his popular books on Islam (see also Bowen, 1993).

But perhaps the best example of the application, the potential and the limitations of this new approach is to be found in the recent work of Brinkley Messick (1993), who has written brilliantly on the history and political implications of traditional Islamic law in Yemen. Like the Islamic judges who are the heroes of his book, Messick privileges textual knowledge above all, though that knowledge must be acquired through study with moral exemplars, and is best transmitted orally, as a personal gift from teacher to student. As against anthropologists who – because of their work in the hinterlands with rebellious Sufis – have emphasized the oppositional nature of Islam, Messick argued strongly that the legitimacy of the Yemeni state rested in the first instance on the capacity of scholars associated with the government to gain 'control of the cultural capital acquired in advanced instruction' and thereby establish cultural hegemony, and 'appropriate' resistance and silence protest against the government (Messick 1993: 166).[20]

Much of this is very convincing indeed, and Messick's book seems destined for status as a classic. But here I wish to draw attention to some of the deficits of his approach, since these deficits are also likely to mark other books written from within this new textualist orientation. Most importantly, Messick's efforts to demonstrate the hegemonic authority of scholar-jurists as vehicles of state domination lead him to short-change what older anthropologists were most interested in: the local negotiations undertaken by ordinary people who wished above all to avoid interference from the state, and who saw the claims of the educated *ulema* to power and prestige as morally suspect. Furthermore, in his post-Saidian refusal to 'essentialize' his subject matter, Messick tends to undercut the larger theoretical or comparative argument of his own work, concluding that 'the "calligraphic state" is itself a construct, referring neither to a specific polity and its dissolution nor to a particular discursive moment and its transformation. It is instead a composite of historical materials and must finally give way to the phenomenon out of which it was built' (Messick 1993: 255) – a process left to the reader's imagination. He also ignores, as I noted above, the potential oppositional role of Islam, so much stressed by earlier anthropological studies. And finally, by being state-centred, and by accepting the professional *ulema*'s own view of their predominance, Messick's textualist and juridical anthropology of Islam is in danger of swinging the pendulum too far away from what anthropologists have always done best; that is, provide descriptions of the strategies and constraints of average individuals for whom religion is only one aspect of their existence.

None of this vitiates Messick's fine work; my comments are only intended to temper a too fervent embrace of the new textualism in the anthropology of Islam and to draw attention to the fact that anthropological studies of the traditional sort, which ignored or backgrounded Islamic texts and practice, are an important balance to the present-day emphasis on Islamic learning and Islamic law. It is too easy to imagine, given the present-day hysteria about fundamentalist revivalism, that ordinary Muslims are consumed by a dogmatic faith, immersed in slavish devotion to their religious leaders and convulsed with savage hatred of all unbelievers. For some few zealots, that may indeed be the case, and their noise and influence is likely to continue to be great beyond all proportion to their numbers. But it is also well to recall that most Muslims, like most Christians and Jews, must spend their time simply getting on with their daily tasks. Ethnographies of the old style help to remind us of this uncomplicated but important reality.

At the same time, the contemporary anthropological focus on Islamic learning and discourse is to be commended for demonstrating that most Muslim scholars, like most scholars in the West, are hardly rigid extremists, but rather are engaged in an endless round of interpretation and reinterpretation. By detailing the debates among the *ulema*, modern anthropological scholarship offers us a far more nuanced picture of Islamic knowledge than we had previously. The danger is that such studies may tend toward mere reportage, and may refuse to make any theoretical or comparative claims whatsoever for fear of being indicted with the much feared label of 'Orientalist'.[21]

This position, while morally understandable, is an abdication of responsibility. As anthropologists, we are not asked to, nor should we wish to, deny our role as outsiders and our commitment to furthering our disciplinary knowledge. Muslim scholars in the classical tradition, it is clear, did not have any qualms about making strong cases for their own philosophical positions, marshalling all the evidence they could muster to bolster their arguments, and leaving it to the consensus of their own scholarly community to decide right and wrong. Anthropologists are well advised to emulate this aspect of Islamic scholarship, and, while respecting the opinions and sensibilities of our Muslim colleagues, we should not be ashamed to make our analyses from within our own intellectual tradition, regardless of where the chips may fall.

In any case, whatever the future of the anthropological study of Islam, one thing is certain: it will no longer be possible for naïve researchers to venture into any Muslim society without being far more knowledgeable about Islam than were most of their predecessors. This is certainly all to the good. But the question still remains as to how that knowledge will be put to use. It is evident that the study of the actual practice of Muslim education and the study of Islamic law and its applications, as pioneered by Eickelman and Rosen, will remain important topics. Also critical, though difficult, will be following the example set by Burkhardt, Gilsenan and others and venturing the in-depth ethnographic study of contemporary Islamic social movements. Literate anthropologists also ought now dare to use our discipline's hard-won knowledge of contemporary tribal social structure and behaviour to re-examine and reanalyse the central Muslim texts that detail the life and times of Muhammad. This research could add a new voice to scholarly debates both within Islam and among western textualist scholars about the Muslim past, and also serve to give some much-needed historical base to present-day anthropological research on the region. Finally, as I have argued at length elsewhere (Lindholm 1996), we should not forget the inevitable conflict between ideal and real (see Ba-Yunus, Chapter 6, this volume), and should continue to try to understand how ordinary Muslim people throughout history and today have sought to reconcile the ethical ideals of their deeply egalitarian religion with the invidious distinctions that actually divide human beings. This existential tension remains, it seems to me, at the heart of Islamic society – and our own.

Notes

I would like to thank Hastings Donnan for his editorial comments and Michael Feener for his perceptive critique of an earlier draft of this paper. The perspective on the anthropology of the Middle East offered in this chapter is very much my own, and reflects my American anthropological background.

1. For more on the responses of anthropologists to Said, see Lindholm (1995).

2. For a critical view of Geertz's understanding of Islam, see Munson (1993).

3. I wish to be very clear here that the Muslim concern with textual exegesis and historical study does not mean that Islamic scholarship banishes reason or interpretation in its approach to scripture – far from it, as any review of the long record of heated intellectual debates among Islamic scholars would soon amply reveal (for an example, see Wheeler 1996). The point is that within orthodox Muslim scholarship explication is in principle confined to the legal implications of the sacred word and the historical validity of a particular tradition; it cannot be extended to put limits on God or to make speculations about symbolic meaning (though the latter is practised by the more esoteric branches of Islam). Working within these restrictions, mainstream Muslim scholarship has evolved a dynamic and complex tradition of religious dispute, one that anthropologists have been professionally disinclined to study, though, as we shall see, this has changed of late.

4. Although out of fashion today, the study of segmentary genealogies and the political organization they express still remains crucial for understanding Middle Eastern peoples, particularly those of the periphery. For a recent study demonstrating this fact, see Shryock (1997).

5. Middle Easterners generally have a low opinion of peasants, who are seen as close to slaves, while tribesmen, though feared and denigrated as savages by urbanites, are recognized also as pure, independent and honourable. They also gain status as the earliest supporters of the Prophet (see Ibn Khaldun 1967). The preference of ethnographers for tribal studies partially reflects this indigenous attitude, which resonates with the western ethnographer's own romantic preference for the 'freedom' of tribal life.

6. The attitude of the tribesmen toward Islamic scholarship is satirized in a story heard everywhere in the Middle East. A learned *faqih* arrives in a tribal area. He is asked his occupation, and tells the tribesmen that he is an educated and holy man. They immediately kill him so as to worship at his tomb.

7. See Ahmed (1976), Asad (1972), Lindholm (1982) and Meeker (1980) for other perspectives on Swati saints and politics.

8. See Hart (1970, 1972) and Montagne (1973) for parallel accounts. Attacks on Gellner's model have mostly come from the 'tribal' side of his equation (cf. Hammoudi 1997; Munson 1997). For a more 'urban' critique, see Lindholm (1997).

9. See El-Zein (1977) for another anthropological effort to conceptualize urban and rural Islam, emphasizing the different notions of time and order characteristic of town and country.

10. See Rosenfeld (1965) for one of the rare ethno-historical accounts of religious social movements and state formation among Middle Eastern tribes.

11. See Asad (1973) for a discussion of Hurgronje's imperialist assumptions; and Eickelman (1981: 39–42) for a defence of Hurgronje's ethnographic work.

12. Nor is this the end of Robertson-Smith's influence. His claim that sacrifice was at the centre of ancient Semitic religion also inspired Freud's imaginative reconstruction of human history in *Totem and Taboo* (1950 [1913]). For a discussion of Robertson-Smith's work see Beidelman (1974).

13. Robertson-Smith claimed Islam originated as a religion of the Bedouin while the more general Orientalist notion is that it resulted from popular resistance to Meccan merchants. This debate continues to rage. See Crone (1987) for the most recent and sophisticated 'tribal' version, Watt (1956) for the more standard 'mercantile' rendition. A few anthropologists have also entered into this fray, notably Wolf (1951), who favours Mecca, and Aswad (1970), favouring tribal influence.

14. See Crone (1987) for arguments against Serjeant's reading back the South Arabian present into the North Arabian past.

15. See Watt (1956, 1988) for two classic Orientalist texts in this genre; Crone (1987) for a modern Orientalist taking a more 'ethnographic' approach.

16. See also the essays in Keddie (1972).

17. Pierre Bourdieu and Fredrik Barth also must be credited with influencing the shift toward the study of individual strategy and away from structural functionalism. For a critical discussion of this shift, see Lindholm (1995).

18. Credit also should be given to Michael Meeker (1979), who put forward a strong, if controversial, claim for a more textual interpretation of Bedouin ethnography. But Meeker did not put his method to use in the study of Islam *per se*.

19. Although he has written important critical work about the way anthropologists should approach Islam, to date Asad has not followed his own advice, but has instead turned his eye toward medieval western monasticism (Asad 1993).

20. See Munson (1993) for a very different and more traditional perspective, which emphasizes the anti-state character of Sufi Islam.

21. For an example, see Fischer and Abedi (1990); a laudible but incoherent attempt to construct a dialogical ethnography.

References

Abun-Nasr, J. 1965. *The Tijaniyya: A Sufi Order in the Modern World.* London: Oxford University Press.

Ahmed, A.S. 1976. *Millennium and Charisma Among Pathans.* London: Routledge and Kegan Paul.

Ahmed, A.S. 1988. *Discovering Islam: Making Sense of Muslim History and Society.* London: Routledge.

Ahmed, A.S. 1993. *Living Islam: From Samarkand to Stornoway.* London: Penguin.

Antoun, R. 1989. *Muslim Preacher in the Modern World: A Jordanian Case Study in Comparative Perspective.* Princeton, NJ: Princeton University Press.

Asad, T. 1972. Market model, class structure and consent: a reconsideration of Swat political organization. *Man* (n.s.) 7: 74–94.

Asad, T. 1973. Two European images of non-European rule. In T. Asad (ed.), *Anthropology and the Colonial Encounter.* Ithaca, NY: Cornell University Press.

Asad, T. 1986. *The Idea of an Anthropology of Islam.* Washington, DC: Georgetown University Press.

Asad, T. 1993. *Genealogies of Religion: Discipline and Reasons of Power in Christianity and Islam.* Baltimore: Johns Hopkins University Press.

Aswad, B. 1970. Social and ecological aspects in the formation of Islam. In L. Sweet (ed.), *Peoples and Cultures of the Middle East.* Vol. I. Garden City, NY: The Natural History Press.

Barth, F. 1965. *Political Leadership Among Swat Pathans.* London: Athlone.

Beidelman, T.O. 1974. *W. Robertson-Smith and the Sociological Study of Religion.* Chicago: University of Chicago Press.

Bowen, J. 1993. *Muslims Through Discourse.* Princeton, NJ: Princeton University Press.

Burckhardt, J. 1831. *Notes on the Bedouins and Wahabys.* London: Henry Colburn and Richard Bentley.

Burton, Sir R. 1964 [1855]. *A Personal Narrative of a Pilgrimage to al-Madinah & Mecca.* New York: Dover.

Crone, P. 1987. *Meccan Trade and the Rise of Islam.* Princeton, NJ: Princeton University Press.

Daniel, N. 1960. *Islam and the West: The Making of an Image.* Edinburgh: University of Edinburgh Press.

Doughty, C. 1888. *Travels in Arabia Deserta.* Cambridge: Cambridge University Press.

Eickelman, D. 1967. Musaylima: an approach to the social anthropology of seventh century Arabia. *Journal of the Economic and Social History of the Orient* 10: 9–20.

Eickelman, D. 1976. *Moroccan Islam: Tradition and Society in a Pilgrimage Center.* Austin: University of Texas Press.

Eickelman, D. 1978. The art of memory: Islamic knowledge and its social reproduction. *Comparative Studies in Society and History* 20: 485–516.

Eickelman, D. 1981. *The Middle East: An Anthropological Approach.* Englewood Cliffs, NJ: Prentice Hall.

Eickelman, D. 1985. *Knowledge and Power in Morocco: The Education of a Twentieth-Century Notable.* Princeton, NJ: Princeton University Press.

El-Zein, A.H. 1977. Beyond ideology and theology: the search for the anthropology of Islam. *Annual Review of Anthropology* 6: 227–54.

Evans-Pritchard, E.E. 1940. *The Nuer.* New York: Oxford University Press.

Evans-Pritchard, E.E. 1949. *The Sanusi of Cyrenaica.* Oxford: Clarendon Press.

Fernea, R. 1970. *Shaiykh and Effendi.* Cambridge, MA: Harvard University Press.

Fischer, M. 1980. *Iran: From Religious Dispute to Revolution.* Cambridge, MA: Harvard University Press.

Fischer, M. and Abedi, M. 1990. *Debating Muslims: Cultural Dialogues in Postmodernity and Tradition.* Madison: University of Wisconsin Press.

Freud, S. 1950 [1913]. *Totem and Taboo* (trans J. Strachey). New York: Norton.

Geertz, C. 1968. *Islam Observed: Religious Development in Morocco and Indonesia.* New Haven, CT: Yale University Press.

Geertz, C. 1979. Suq: the bazaar economy in Sefrou. In C. Geertz, H. Geertz and L. Rosen (eds), *Meaning and Order in Moroccan Society.* Cambridge: Cambridge University Press.

Gellner, E. 1969. *Saints of the Atlas.* London: Weidenfeld and Nicolson.

Gellner, E. 1981. *Muslim Society.* Cambridge: Cambridge University Press.

Gellner, E. 1983. *Nations and Nationalism.* Ithaca, NY: Cornell University Press.

Gellner, E. 1990. Tribalism and the state in the Middle East. In P.S. Khoury and J. Kostiner (eds), *Tribes and State Formation in the Middle East.* Berkeley: University of California Press.

Gilsenan, M. 1973. *Saint and Sufi in Modern Egypt.* Oxford: Clarendon Press.

Haeri, S. 1989. *Law of Desire: Temporary Marriage in Shi'ite Iran.* Syracuse, NY: Syracuse University Press.

Hammoudi, A. 1993. *The Victim and Its Masks: An Essay on Sacrifice and Masquerade in the Maghreb.* Chicago: University of Chicago Press.

Hammoudi, A. 1997. Segmentarity, social stratification, political power and sainthood: reflections on Gellner's thesis. In J. Hall and I. Jarvie (eds), *The Social Philosophy of Ernest Gellner.* Poznań: Poznań Studies in the Philosophy of the Sciences and the Humanities.

Hanoteau, A. and Letourneux, A. 1873. *La Kabylie et les coutumes Kabyles.* Vol. 2. Paris: Imp. National.

Hart, D. 1970. Clan, lineage, local community and the feud in a Riffian tribe. In L. Sweet (ed.), *Peoples and Cultures of the Middle East.* Vol. II. Garden City, NY: Natural History Press.

Hart, D. 1972. The tribe in modern Morocco: two case studies. In E. Gellner and C. Micaud (eds), *Arabs and Berbers: From Tribe to Nation in North Africa.* Lexington, MA: Lexington Books.

Hodgson, M. 1974. *The Venture of Islam: Conscience and History in a World Civilization. Vol. I: The Classical Age of Islam.* Chicago: University of Chicago Press.

Hurgronje, C.S. 1931 [1888–9]. *Mekka in the Later Part of the Nineteenth Century* (trans J.H. Monahan). Leiden: E.J. Brill.

Ibn Khaldun 1967. *The Muqaddimah.* (trans F. Rosenthal). Princeton, NJ: Princeton University Press.

Keddie, N. (ed.) 1972. *Scholars, Saints and Sufis.* Berkeley: University of California Press.

Lane, E.W.1871. *An Account of the Manners and Customs of the Modern Egyptians, Written in Egypt During the Years 1833, –34, and 35 Partly From Notes Made During a Former Visit to that Country in the Years 1825, –26, –27, and –28.* 2 vols. London: John Murray.

Lindholm, C. 1982. *Generosity and Jealousy: The Swat Pukhtun of Northern Pakistan.* New York: Columbia University Press.

Lindholm, C. 1992. Quandaries of command in egalitarian societies: examples from Swat and Morocco. In J. Cole (ed), *Comparing Muslim Societies: Knowledge and the State in a World Civilization.* Ann Arbor: University of Michigan Press.

Lindholm, C. 1995. The New Middle Eastern ethnography. *Journal of the Royal Anthropological Institute* (NS) 1 (4): 805–20.

Lindholm, C. 1996. *The Islamic Middle East: An Historical Anthropology.* Oxford: Blackwell.

Lindholm, C. 1997. Despotism and democracy: state and society in the premodern Middle East. In J. Hall and I. Jarvie (eds), *The Social Philosophy of Ernest Gellner.* Poznań: Poznań Studies in the Philosophy of the Sciences and the Humanities.

Marx, E. 1967. *Bedouin of the Negev.* New York: Praeger.

Meeker, M. 1979. *Literature and Violence in Early Arabia.* London: Cambridge University Press.

Meeker, M. 1980. The twilight of a South Asian heroic age: a rereading of Barth's study of Swat. *Man* (n.s.) 15: 682–701.

Messick, B. 1993. *The Calligraphic State: Textual Domination and History in a Muslim Society.* Berkeley: University of California Press.

Montagne, R. 1973. *The Berbers: Their Social and Political Organization* (trans D. Seddon). London: Frank Cass and Company.

Munson, H. 1993. *Religion and Power in Morocco.* New Haven, CT: Yale University Press.

Munson, H. 1997. Rethinking Gellner's segmentary analysis of Morocco's Ait Atta. In J. Hall and I. Jarvie (eds), *The Social Philosophy of Ernest Gellner.* Poznań: Poznań Studies in the Philosophy of the Sciences and the Humanities.

Musil, A. 1928. *Manners and Customs of the Rwala Bedouins.* New York: American Geographical Society.

Niebuhr, C. 1994 [1792]. *Travels in Arabia and Other Countries of the Middle East* (trans R. Heron). Edinburgh: R. Morison and Son.

Robertson-Smith, W. 1967 [1885]. *Kinship and Marriage in Early Arabia.* Boston: Beacon Press.

Robertson-Smith, W. 1972 [1889]. *Lectures on the Religion of the Semites.* New York: Schocken Books.

Rosen, L. 1984. *Bargaining for Reality: The Construction of Social Relations in a Muslim Community.* Chicago: University of Chicago Press.

Rosen, L. 1989. *The Anthropology of Justice: Law as Culture in Islamic Society.* Cambridge: Cambridge University Press.

Rosenfeld, H. 1965. The role of the military in state formation in Arabia. *Journal of the Royal Anthropological Institute* 95: 75–86, 174–94.

Sahlins, M. 1961. The segmentary lineage system: an organization of predatory expansion. *American Anthropologist* 63: 332–43.

Said, E.W. 1978. *Orientalism.* New York: Pantheon.

Serjeant R.B. 1981. Haram and Hawtah: the sacred enclave in Arabia. In R.B. Serjeant (ed.), *Studies in Arabian History and Civilization.* Aldershot: Variorum.

Shryock, A. 1997. *Nationalism and the Genealogical Imagination: Oral History and Textual Authority in Tribal Jordan.* Berkeley: University of California Press.

Smith, W.C. 1957. *Islam in Modern History.* Princeton, NJ: Princeton University Press.

Watt, W.M. 1956. *Muhammad at Medina.* Oxford: Clarendon Press.

Watt, W.M. 1988. *Muhammad's Mecca: History in the Qur'an.* Edinburgh: Edinburgh University Press.

Westermarck, E. 1926. *Ritual and Belief in Morocco.* 2 vols. London: Macmillan and Company.

Wheeler, B. 1996. *Applying the Canon in Islam: The Authorization and Maintenance of Interpretive Reasoning in Hanafi Scholarship.* Albany: State University of New York Press.

Wolf, E. 1951. The social organization of Mecca and the origins of Islam. *Southwestern Journal of Anthropology* 7: 329–56.

8

ISLAM AND THE SEA

The causes of a failure

Xavier de Planhol

In the conflict that pitted Christianity against Islam on the seas of the Mediterranean for more than a millennium, Islam was twice defeated. Following four centuries of bitter struggle, which was marked from the seventh century by large-scale Arab naval assaults on Constantinople, and then by Arab sojourns in Crete, Malta, Sicily and the Balearics, as well as on the Mediterranean's northern shores in continental Italy and Provence, Islam's spread into Europe was gradually repulsed. From the end of the tenth century, it had been forced to abandon all of its European outposts (Eickhoff 1954; Lewis 1951). Christian maritime supremacy did not emerge for another fifty years or so, but it was to persist throughout the Crusading era, and underpinned the Latin Kingdom of Palestine for almost two centuries. When the Andalusian Ibn Jubair undertook his famous pilgrimage in 1183–5, he borrowed four ships on the Mediterranean, all of them Christian, and encountered ten other Christian ships during his voyage (see Broadhurst 1952). In the modern era, the Ottoman fleet, which had long rivalled the fleets of Christendom, finally disintegrated at Navarin in 1827. At about the same time the Barbary corsairs disappeared, freeing the western Mediterranean and North Atlantic from a reign of terror that had lasted since the sixteenth century (Bono 1964; Coindreau 1948).

In the South Seas the Muslims were never really able to challenge Europe's maritime superiority. The Ottomans took control of the Red Sea after the conquest of Egypt, but they failed to prevent the incursions of the Portuguese into the Persian Gulf, followed by those of the Dutch and the British (Hess 1970; Özbaran 1972). Süleyman Pasha's expedition to Diu in 1538 was inconsequential, and the plan to send a Turkish fleet to the aid of the Sultan of Atjeh in 1567 never materialized (Reid 1969; Saffet Bey 1912). Subsequently, neither the short-lived fleet developed by the great Moghuls with the help of Portuguese sailors in the Gulf of Bengal in the seventeenth century, nor that of the Sultans of Oman in the eighteenth and nineteenth centuries, nor even the pirates of the Persian Gulf and Malaysia, were ever seriously to threaten European maritime traffic, which did not even have to flex its muscles to maintain its position.

Muslim maritime cultures

This primarily military failure had cultural dimensions. Muslim involvement in the exploitation of marine resources and in maritime trade has been limited in both modern and contemporary times. In the Mediterranean all foreign trade with the North African coast was conducted by European ships. Fairly perfunctory explanations have been offered for this state of affairs: the danger of inquisition for renegades, who could not have been employed in Christian ports, and harassment of captains of Moorish origin by the merchants of Marseilles and the French authorities (Emerit 1955). We need only make a comparison with the eastern basin of the Mediterranean during the same modern period to see that neither of these factors could have had any real influence. For here, even though the seas were controlled by the Ottomans (with the exception of the Black Sea, which was closed to outsiders until the late eighteenth century), most trade was conducted in the same way, by 'maritime caravan', a system by which Ottoman traders chartered European, mainly French, ships (Panzac 1982, 1985). In 1785, for example, 40 per cent of intra-Ottoman trade in Alexandria was conducted using European vessels. Moreover, the Ottoman Empire was almost entirely represented by Greek ships. This situation prevailed in Salonika and elsewhere throughout the eighteenth century (Svoronos 1956). In the seventeenth century most trade conducted under the Ottoman flag in the port of Istanbul was carried out by Greek captains, and the few Turks involved rarely ventured beyond the Aegean Sea (Mantran 1962: 120, 184, 352, 421, 450–1, 488, 491).

The same was true of fishing. The Mediterranean coast of Morocco, Algeria and northern Tunisia was colonized by Spanish fishermen. As naturalized Frenchmen, they provided the main body of French fishermen in Algerian waters, underlining the almost total lack of indigenous activity. Indeed, Italian trawlers and Greek fishermen from Rhodes almost entirely dominated the Levantine coast until the Second World War (Weulersse 1940: Vol. I, 168, 170). Even where the Muslim flag was flown, it could be deceptive. The Muslim sailors of Sitia, the eastern peninsula of Crete, who fished for sponges off the Tunisian coast until the beginning of the twentieth century, were Greek (Bérard 1900: 233). Most of the Muslim fishing communities to be found today in the eastern Mediterranean basin are actually very recent developments, and exhibit European acculturation. Likewise with the Berber fishermen of the Faroua Peninsula in Tripolitania, near the Tunisian border, whose activities can be traced to Italian colonization (Paradisi 1962). Again, it is Greek Cretan Muslims who have developed fishing, mostly for sponges, at Bodrum on the Turkish coast, and this only since 1930 (Mansur 1972: 45–52; Nicolas 1971). Egyptian fishing along the Nile Delta did not really take off until the nineteenth century, in the wake of European influence.

Overall, authentic traditional maritime cultures among the Muslims of the Mediterranean are rare indeed, and can be counted on the fingers of one hand. There are a few small islands off the Rifian coast, like Alhucemas, where the tradition seems to be of ancient origin. But even here these fishing communities seem to have sprung from a mixed population that Jean-Léon l'Africain (1956: 274–6) has referred to as 'Brothers of the Coast', Christian and Muslim pirates who lived together on friendly terms (see also Grohmann-Kerrouach 1977: 134–40). In fact, there are only two significant exceptions to this almost universal absence of authentically Muslim maritime cultures. First, there is the very isolated case of the island of Rouad on the Syrian coast (Charles 1973; Weulersse 1940: Vol. I, 173–90). This was an overpopulated island refuge where the maritime calling was virtually a prerequisite for survival. Second, the head of the Gulf of Gabès and the Kerkenna Islands were the source of numerous technical innovations, including flat boats of a uniquely local construction. Here the maritime culture appears to have been a spontaneous development, arising from a specific physical environment with a large number of sandbanks (Louis 1961–3). This is the only originally Muslim maritime domain of real significance in the Mediterranean, and it can certainly be attributed to these natural conditions.

Maritime life was similarly impoverished in the Atlantic prior to French colonization. There were some scattered fishing centres on the Moroccan coast in the estuary ports and on the shores of the High Atlas from the Oued Draa to Cap Cantin (Ras Bedouzza) (Montagne 1923). These scattered communities were recent developments linked to the overpopulation of the mountains in the Chleuh region. Regional navigation, which was still active on the coastal fringes of Muslim Andalusia and from Morocco to the Sous (Picard 1997) in the Middle Ages, had almost completely disappeared by modern times. In Mauritania, before contemporary developments, there were only very primitive groups of Chenagla (north of Cap Blanc) and of Imragen (to the south of Cap Blanc). These were inshore fishermen without boats, who were widely despised by Mauritanian society, and probably belonged to low castes (Anthonioz 1967–8). In Senegal there were only a few groups of Islamized fishermen (Sy 1965; Vanchi-Bonnardel 1967, 1985). Muslim sailors never dared to venture on to the Atlantic Ocean itself. It remained for them 'the sea where no ship sails' (Ibn Rostih 1949: 67), 'the dark sea' (Picard 1997: 31–2), the exclusive realm of fantastic stories (Picard 1995). All regular relations with the Canaries had ceased, and the Guanches of these islands had themselves lost the skills of sailing. Muslims were never involved in the great transoceanic discoveries.[1]

Muslim non-involvement in seafaring was similarly striking in the inland waterways of continental Eurasia where Islam was long dominant. The Turks preserved the Black Sea from European commercial intrusion until the late eighteenth century, but they were nonetheless incapable of organizing maritime activity systematically. Such activity remained a confused swarming of irregular traffic, largely entrusted to indigenous Caucasians, and lacking sufficient nautical equipment. The southern shores of the Caspian Sea had constituted the northern frontier of Muslim civilization from the eighth to the twelfth century, abutting the Khazar steppes where the conversion of the Mongols had created a Muslim zone in the thirteenth century. Christian adventurers (notably the Genoese of Caffa) nevertheless penetrated the area at an early stage and were the most active exploiters of the Caspian until the arrival of the Russians, who, from the sixteenth century onwards, progressively gained exclusive supremacy in commercial navigation, eliminating all Persian competition, even before the treaty of Torkemân Tchay in 1828 awarded them a monopoly on owning warships there. The only Muslim maritime activity that survived in the Caspian was that of the Turkmen, initially pirates (emerging from a population surplus in a saturated nomadic pastoral society), then reverting to coastal navigation on the southern coasts at the end of the nineteenth century (see Planhol 1992).

The South Seas were a more favourable area for peaceful Muslim maritime expansion from early on, although maritime development there was not fundamentally different from that already described for other areas. The great maritime trade routes leading to the Far East, inherited from the Sassanids, which led the Arabs and Persians as far as China at the time of the Abbasid Caliphate (Ferrand 1945; Hourani 1951: 40–1, 46–50, 61–79; Whitehouse 1977; Whitehouse and Williamson 1973: 46–8), declined considerably from the eleventh century, to the point where it is not clear whether there was any continuity at all in these maritime relations (Aubin 1963; Sauvaget 1948). Although a real maritime power still endured in the western part of the Indian Ocean from the end of the fifteenth century, in the form of the kingdom of Hormuz (Aubin 1973), the geographical horizons revealed by the texts of Ibn Madjid hardly extended beyond the western coast of Malaysia (Ferrand 1921–8; Khoury 1971, 1985–6, 1987–8; Tibbetts 1971). The arrival of the Europeans only served to deliver the final blow to what in any case had only ever been ‘a small trade in costly products transported by a multitude of hawkers from Suez to Nagasaki’ (Van Leur 1955: 219). Maritime activity in the whole western sector of the Indian Ocean, in trade as well as in fishing, remains to this day very fragmented and limited, consisting of isolated and distant outposts operating coastal routes using ships that are still very primitive, and that owe most of their profits to smuggling.[2] It is only in Malaysian waters where true ‘people of the sea’ assembled in any significant numbers (and here not exclusively) under the Muslim flag, which most of them adopted while maintaining a way of life whose origins clearly predate the advent of Islam (Lombard 1990: Vol. II, 80ff.; Sopher 1965). More ambitious developments did actually occur among these people, such as the trade of the Bugis of Sulawesi, who began crossing the high seas in the sixteenth century in sailing ships of up to 250 tonnes. This trade, which is documented in precise written legal texts and portrayed in literature (an exceptional phenomenon), is a unique case in traditional Islam, evidently linked to the very particular atmosphere of the society that had emerged in the Strait of Malacca and the Indonesian ‘Mediterranean’, and whose evolution had resisted Islamization.

Yet the general impression of Muslims at sea is of mediocrity, even of deficiency. The most clear-sighted Muslims have always been aware of this. In 1540, at the height of the Turks’ maritime presence in the Mediterranean, when the western basin was wide open to them after their triumphal expedition to Toulon at the time of the alliance with François I,[3] the Grand Vizier Lutfi Pasha wrote that ‘many Sultans of the past dominated on land, but few ruled the seas. In the organization of naval expeditions, the unbeliever is our superior’ (cited in Tschudi 1910: 30–3). Even in 1668, when the Ottoman Empire had just taken possession of Crete thanks to its fleet, an interlocutor for the secretary of the British Embassy in Constantinople declared to him that ‘God has given the sea to the Christians but the land to the Turks’ (Rycaut 1668: 216). The Mamluk Sultan

Baybars I (1260–77) adopted the same tone in a letter addressed to the King of Cyprus in 1270, praising the actions of his cavalry, in which he acknowledged the Frankish superiority at sea: '[As for] you, your horses are [your] ships, whereas [for] us, our ships are [our] horses' (that is, at sea you are strong, but our power lies on land and on horseback; cited in Ayalon 1967: 6). At the end of the seventeenth century, at a time when the power of the Salé corsairs was still at its height, the Moroccan Sultan Moulay Ismaïl wrote to the dispossessed King of England, James II, apologizing for his inability to help him because 'we are Arabs and unversed in maritime matters' (cited in Barbour 1970). One could cite many other examples.

For their part, Christian observers were not to be outdone and were quick to pinpoint the weaknesses of the enemy. As early as 1390, on the subject of the Christian expedition to the coasts of Tunisia, Jean Froissart (1837: Vol. III, 89–90) reported that

> the Saracens have no strength at sea in the form of galleys or vessels, unlike the Genoese and Venetians. And when the Saracens put to sea they do nothing except plundering and thieving, neither can they catch Christians unless they are right on top of them, for an armed Christian galley could defeat four of Saracens.

Texts such as this succeed one another through the generations, and an unsophisticated Christian faith lost no opportunity to boast. A somewhat 'hagiographical' biographer of Christopher Columbus even wrote at the end of the nineteenth century: 'A French philosopher rightly noted that all the great navigators were Christian. The Prince who pioneered the navigation of the Atlantic Ocean was also a true Catholic (Dom Henrique)' (Roselly de Lorgues 1880: 15).

Islam's incompatibility with the sea

The almost total absence of seafaring Muslims has not failed to attract the attention of modern Orientalists. Herbert Jansky (1920), Louis Brunot (1921), Wilhelm Hoernebach (1950–5), Eckehard Eickhoff (1954), David Ayalon (1967) and Nevill Barbour (1970), to name but a few, have written highly pertinently on the subject, and have assembled numerous texts that underline this incompatibility between Islam and the sea. But they have confined themselves almost exclusively to reporting and even explaining the fact without really looking for its causes, which I will attempt to uncover here. Why this inferiority?

Initially one might think of technical deficiency. Certainly, this was strikingly obvious in the modern era in the Indian Ocean. The superiority of the solid European iron-clad sailing ships over the native boats, whose frames were held together by palm thread (Moreland 1939), was never in question. Nor was the fact that all significant maritime innovation in the Mediterranean during that period originated in Europe. However, this is somewhat deceptive. The practical advantages of being the source of maritime innovation at the time were negligible, for the intermixing of people, ideas and things that characterized the Mediterranean in the modern era meant that innovations spread remarkably quickly. The role of pirates in this technology transfer was fundamental. Advances made by Christian navies were rapidly assimilated by those on the North African coast, as well as by the great Ottoman fleet. In the sixteenth century, for example, the Venetians revolutionized the speed and manoeuvrability of galleys by having all oarsmen on the same bench operate a single oar, an innovation that immediately spread to Algiers (Boyer 1985: 97). At the beginning of the seventeenth century, Algiers was equally quick to adopt three-masted sailing ships like those that plied the Atlantic, imitating the pirate vessels by also furnishing these ships with oars (Boyer 1985). This kind of borrowing never ceased. A nineteenth-century signal book of the Algiers navy reveals a close familiarity with the practices of the western navies (Devoulx 1868). The transfer of technical innovations to the Ottomans was also very rapid, down to the smallest detail. There were certainly some discrepancies, but these were short-lived. In 1571 at Lepanto, the Venetians used galeasses, which combined the advantages of galley and galleon by arranging artillery on their flanks that could fire broadsides, whereas traditional galleys still only had cannon in their bows. In the following year the Ottomans introduced such galeasses to their own fleet (Imber 1980: 180). Their role in the battle at Lepanto had not been decisive, but the rapidity of the imitation is clear. In 1650, the first high-sided vessel in the fleet was immediately shipwrecked (Kâtip Çelebi 1329/1911: 13, 128). But two decades later at the siege of Candia, this type of ship was widespread in the Ottoman fleet, and it was their presence that eventually accounted for the successful conquest of the city and the island in 1669. In fact, the Ottoman navy was much quicker to borrow from the West than was the army, which was rather more resistant to change. It was through the navy that Selim III, the 'enlightened' late eighteenth-century Sultan, was to undertake the first serious effort to modernize the country, an effort that was actually to cost him his throne (Shaw 1969).

The facts are naturally less clear concerning the earliest confrontations. The Byzantines were definitely superior in certain areas, such as Greek fire for example, though this was not a specifically maritime technique. But many innovations at this time passed from the Arab world to Christianity. It was from the Arabs that Byzantium introduced types of ships (*saktoura, koumbarion*) previously unknown there. The Arabs can also be credited with the first use of sailing vessels as warships, which was not widespread in Byzantium until the tenth century (Ahrweiler 1966: 414–5, 418). As to the triangular 'lateen' sail, which entered general use in the Mediterranean at this time (the earliest evidence of this innovation was long thought to be a Byzantine manuscript of 880; Brindley 1926), and which was often considered to be of Arab design, originating in the South Seas and transferred to the Mediterranean with the expansion of Islam,[4] we now know this to have been used on large boats from the beginning of the seventh century, and perhaps from even earlier on small boats (Adam 1970; Basch 1989, 1991; Casson 1956; Sottas 1939). But even if it was not specifically an Arab sail, it was certainly the dominant sail of the Arab era, and it was mainly Arabs who popularized its use, if only because its versatility made it particularly well suited to the nature of their maritime enterprises, notably piracy. We also know the intermediary role played by classical Muslim civilization in the introduction of Far Eastern technologies to the West, such as the compass (Klaproth 1834;

Saussure 1925). On the whole, the situation of cultural and technical intermixing does not seem to have been fundamentally different in the medieval Mediterranean than in the modern era (see Christides 1988).

However, the Muslim fleets remained unquestionably second-rate during this period. It has been possible to demonstrate that for the most part their ships were still slow and heavy, much less mobile than those of the Christians, and to estimate their maximum speed at a little over four knots, which was around one knot slower than the Byzantine ships (Eickhoff 1954). This difference in speed had serious consequences in combat, especially at a time when the only known rudder was the very inadequate lateral one. Less manoeuvrable, these ships were also unsuited to navigating dangerous shoal-waters, and this inadequacy had not escaped that shrewd observer Leon VI (*Taktika*, XIX, 69; cf. Eickhoff 1954: 88).

Why this contrast? The same Coptic carpenters from Alexandria had built ships for the Byzantines as well as for the first Muslim fleets launched against Constantinople. They also constructed the ships that the Muslim conquerors of the Maghreb berthed at Tunis when they created their first arsenal there in about 700 (Bekri 1965 [1911–13]: 80). Great store has been set by certain natural constraints that could have impeded the construction of the Muslim fleets, such as the lack of mature timber on the southern shores of the Mediterranean (Lombard 1972: 107–76). On this point we know how the loss of the Maghreb and of Sicily played an important role in the decline of the Fatimid fleet of Egypt in the eleventh century. But this is applicable neither to the preceding centuries, when timber supplies came from the northern Algerian and Tunisian *tell*, or from Cyprus, nor, with greater reason, to the Ottoman era. Besides, prodigious feats were sometimes accomplished to obtain supplies of wood. When Nâder Shah wanted to construct the last great Persian fleet in the 1740s, he brought tree trunks from the Caspian forest to Bouchir on the Gulf, transporting them across the passes of the Alborz and the dreadful roads of the Fars escarpment (Lockhart 1936). This explanation is far too simple.

We must look instead to human and cultural factors. One major initial observation is worth making. None of the three main ethnic groups that embarked on the Mediterranean Sea under the banner of Islam at different moments in history had a continuous maritime tradition. This fact is obvious in the case of the Arabs and the Turks, who came from the interiors of continental landmasses. The former had, at the time of the birth of Islam, almost entirely forfeited the gains of the Himyarite navy, which had ruled the Red Sea several centuries before. Their maritime vocabulary was almost entirely foreign, and indeed borrowed from different languages on the two fronts of their expansion, where the vocabularies differ profoundly: essentially from Persian in the Gulf and in the Indian Ocean, and from Aramaic in the Mediterranean (Ferrand 1924; Fraenkel 1886: 209–32). Even today, despite the subsequent development of a specifically Arabic maritime vocabulary, lexical statistics taken at various points, and particularly on the Syrian and Lebanese coasts (Mutlak 1973), show that the proportion of foreign terms is still considerable. The picture is identical in the case of the Turks, who, on their arrival in the Middle East, even lacked a specific word to designate the sea, and who today still use a term that was initially applied to lakes. Almost all of the seafaring vocabulary used in the Turkish spoken in Turkey is of Italian origin (Kahane and Kahane 1942), whereas that concerning fishing is borrowed largely from the Greeks.

Although the causes of the phenomenon are much more enigmatic in the case of the third ethnic group – the Berbers – we must in any event acknowledge that they had always shown, before their Islamization, a deep reluctance to take to the sea, a reluctance that they largely retained. The very rare cases of specifically Berber maritime activity in antiquity (Strabon III, 4, 2; Pliny VI, 203, 205; cf. Gsell 1913–28: Vol. V, 151–2) do not alter this general fact, which is in large part responsible for the various colonizations (Phoenician, Greek in Cyrenaica, Roman) that succeeded one another on the North African coast. Berber piracy of the Barbary cities is an exception that developed from very particular circumstances only from the thirteenth and fourteenth centuries onwards. It was only the invasion by the great Arab Hilalian nomads, shortly before the time when Ibn Khaldun was writing, that forced these Arabized Berbers to reorientate their activity towards the sea by cutting them off from the cities of the interior (Marçais 1946: 215–28). Ibn Khaldun (1934: III, 777) was the first to record this transformation, some three centuries before a massive influx of renegades triggered the definitive expansion of corsairing, as we will see below. Apart from this special case, neither the Mediterranean, nor, more understandably, the Atlantic Ocean, has ever really witnessed Berber seamen. When the Europeans arrived on the Canary Islands the Guanches no longer had boats, and the different islands no longer communicated with each other. Among the Kabyles, forced back to their coastal massif, and of whom one might have expected a similar evolution to that which pushed the Imragen towards the sea, or the few Chleuh fishermen referred to earlier, no such thing happened. For them the sea remained an unknown, the domain of ogresses and genies, and a place of no return. Even its shores were the object of taboo. Only pious individuals, protected by their virtue, could settle and live there (Lacoste-Dujardin 1982: 118–19). Here again, the maritime vocabulary is revealing. That of the Berbers is almost all borrowed from Arabic and only post-dates their Islamization (Serra 1973).

In these conditions of almost total ignorance of the sea, it is not surprising that when Muslims did venture onto it, they had to draw on the knowledge of others. Even apart from the activities of the Coptic carpenters mentioned earlier, it was entirely Christian crews who sailed the first Egyptian fleets, and this was the case at least until the mid-ninth century. Only the soldiers who sailed with them, and who played the decisive role in the battles, were Muslims (for the sources, see Bell 1910; Kubiak 1970: 46, 49). The omnipresence of the renegades over the centuries is the most striking manifestation of this deficiency. It was almost always they, Venetians or Greeks, or recruits from the *devsirme*, who led the Ottoman fleets (Imber 1980: 255). For example, in Algiers in 1588 a survey covering thirty-four *raïs* (a 'chief captain of the vessel') allows us to identify the presence of at least nineteen renegades (eighteen Christians and one Jew) and two sons of renegades, not to mention those of the second generation who can no longer be distinguished (Boyer 1985: 97; Vovard 1951: 208). At that time the

Pasha of the city and approximately half of its fifty thousand inhabitants were renegades (Boyer 1985: 94). Renegades can also be credited with the great expansion of the corsairing at Salé at the beginning of the seventeenth century (Coindreau 1948: 41, 57, 66ff.). While there are no similar statistical records for the period of the first great confrontation in the Mediterranean, the role of the renegades was also certainly considerable then. Two of their number particularly distinguished themselves at the head of the Abbasid fleets at the beginning of the tenth century. These were Damien of Tarsus,[5] who died in 913, and Leon of Tripoli, director of the expedition that ended in 904 with the sack of Salonika (Fahmy 1966: 109, 161–2). A little later, it was the Slavs who played a decisive role in the development of the Fatimid navy (Dachraoui 1981: 152, 155, 290, 301–3, 384, 393–4; nothing comparable can be reported in the land-based forces). Through Jewish merchant intermediaries, Christians were then selling to Muslims great numbers of Slavs as slaves, who subsequently adopted the faith of their new masters.

Some exceptions

However, by itself the 'ethnic' interpretation of Muslim absence at sea is inadequate. We need only remember that the Persians – who so distanced themselves from the sea that they were almost totally absent from it by the nineteenth century – preserved for several centuries after their Islamization the great maritime tradition they had inherited in the South Seas (Planhol 1996). The lack of seafaring Muslims was far from absolute. There were some remarkable maritime vocations among them. We may consider the exemplary destiny of Bosr ibn Abî Artât, a companion of the Prophet born at Mecca some ten years before the Hijra, who was to be the first admiral of the Arab fleets launched against Constantinople. We might also remember Malikite Kadi Asad ben al-Forât (759–828), a charismatic character, who, when approaching the end of his life in 827, at the 'Council of the Wise', which met at Sousse to examine the possibility of an expedition to Sicily on the occasion of the betrayal of the Byzantine admiral Euphemios, influenced, alone in his opinion, the decision of the reluctant assembly, and placed himself at the head of the fleet that was to initiate the conquest of the island (Talbi 1966: 411–12, 417–18). Or the first Turkish sailor whose memory has been preserved by history, Çaka, Emir of Smyrna, who from the end of the eleventh century was to build a fleet and threaten Constantinople. (It is true that in his youth he had been a prisoner at the Byzantine court and had certainly familiarized himself there with matters of the sea; see Hess 1970: 1896; Sevim and Yücel 1990: 82–4). There was also the creator of the second Turkish fleet, Umũz, Emir of Aydin, in the first half of the fourteenth century,[6] but this was to be more than three centuries later, and the interval is significant in itself. But how many *raïs*, beginning with the most prestigious ones in the final period of corsairing, such as those of Embarak or Hamidou (Devoulx 1872, 1911 [1859]), were pure products of the human environment of Algiers at a time when the renegades had made themselves scarce and when successive injections of 'new blood' had largely ceased? The overall conclusion is clear. There was no intrinsic ineptitude, no individual incompatibility. We must search further.

The problem really remains that of the *rarity* of these maritime vocations. Here we must introduce an element of another order, one more general than personal attitudes. This is what can be regarded as Muslim society's global lack of interest in, even its persistent repugnance towards, the sea.

This was already clearly evident in the orientation of the Caliphate. Despite the construction of great fleets, the sea was never at the heart of the Caliphate's pre-occupations. Its capitals, at Damascus and later at Baghdad, were continental. In Egypt, Cairo was to replace Alexandria as the focal point of the nation. The titles of the Caliph were never to include any reference whatever to sovereignty of the sea, while in contrast Byzantine texts always emphasized the fact that the empire stretched 'over all the Mediterranean and as far as the columns of Hercules' (Hoernebach 1950–5: 391, 395). For one of the two great powers then sharing the eastern Mediterranean, the sea was an essential constituent. This was not the case for the other. The situation was to be no different at the end of the sixteenth century when the Portuguese and the Ottomans clashed on the Red Sea. In 1499, Manuel I proclaimed himself 'Lord of Guinea and of the Conquests, *Seaways and Trade* of Ethiopia, Arabia, Persia and India' (emphasis added). But some years later, at the time of the conquest of the Arabian provinces, Sultan Selim announced that

> now all the *territories* of Egypt, Malatya, Aleppo, Syria, the *city* of Cairo, Upper Egypt, Ethiopia, Yemen, the *lands* up to the Tunisian border, the Hijaz, the *cities* of Mecca, Medina and Jerusalem, may God fully and completely increase their honour and respectability, have been added to the Ottoman Empire. (cited in Hess 1970: 1911 emphases added)

This attitude was widespread. The Muslim states were never really interested in the sea for any length of time. Their great maritime policies, while not entirely lacking, were only episodes, sporadic impulses followed by long periods of neglect and abandonment. Thus it has been possible to calculate that during the period of Mamluk domination in Egypt and Syria (1250–1517) no fewer than six or seven fleets were constructed; that is, one around every forty years on average. Quickly and badly built, the ships soon fell into disuse and disappeared until the next revival.

These fits of interest in the sea were only responses to circumstantial chance (Ayalon 1967: 6). It was ever so. The naval policies of the Omayyads of Cordoba in the mid-ninth century were purely a response to the Norman invasions (Picard 1997: 99). It has been suggested that those of the Aghlabids of Kairouan some years earlier were the product of 'geographical chance', linked to the proximity of Sicily and to the betrayal of Euphemios (Eickhoff 1954: 65–6). These bursts of active naval construction were followed by periods of total inaction. The capriciousness of the leaders could reach such a point that ships were sometimes left half-built. This was the case after the attack on Alexandria by the Franks of Cyprus in 1365. The Mamluks started to construct an enormous fleet in their Egyptian and Syrian ports, then suddenly changed their minds. The ships under construction in the arsenal at Beirut were abandoned and the local inhabitants looted the metal components, while the wooden frameworks were left to rot

(Hamblin 1986: 77). During the era of the great Ottoman fleet, which was a powerful and continuous force for almost three centuries, the lack of maintenance and the widespread slackness in daily practice is evidence of the same deficiency. In 1588, the Venetian ambassador, Antonio Barbarigo, described the ships as 'lasting no more than a year, so that when they come back to be decommissioned, it is pitiful to see their state of decline' (cited in Imber 1980: 225). It is understandable that under these circumstances naval officers always held a relatively inferior rank in the social hierarchy. When the Mamluk fleet was defeated in 1270 in Cypriot waters, the naval command fell almost entirely into the hands of the Franks, including the governors of the three ports of Alexandria, Damietta and Rosetta. A long list of the names of these officers has survived. It does not contain a single Mamluk name. No member of Egypt's ruling caste was among them. What is more, in the thousands of biographies preserved from the historical literature of the Mamluk period, not one concerns a seafarer or a naval commander (Ayalon 1967: 5). Obviously it did not occur to the elite of this military society to take to the sea, and it was certainly not the route to fame and fortune. Ibn Khaldun, during the same period, stated that in Ifrîqya, as in the other eastern Berber states, the commander of the navy held a lower rank than the commander-in-chief of the land army. 'In many cases', he adds, 'he is obliged to obey his orders' (*Prolégomènes* II, 37).

It was to be no different for the Turks at the time of the great Ottoman fleet. The *kapudan pasha*, who commanded it, was a very weak figure in the imperial hierarchy. He was normally a *sancak beyi*, a provincial governor – of whom there were dozens – a rank below a commander of the land forces, who held the title of *beylerbeyi*. Because of his personal merits, Hayreddin (Barbarossa) was to attain the rank of *beylerbeyi*, along with certain of his successors, like Piyale Pasha in 1555, but this was exceptional. In any event, the *kapudan pasha* was never a member of the imperial *divan*, with the unique exception of Barbarossa. This rank was well below that of the viziers. It is also astonishing to see that the *kapudan pasha*, who effectively commanded the fleet (it was by no means an honorific title), was very often someone with no maritime experience, and whose relationship with the naval experts under his command, almost all of them renegades, was always difficult. Throughout the sixteenth century there were only to be two who were men of the sea – Barbarossa again, and Kılıç Ali Pasha, who was appointed after the battle of Lepanto at a moment when there was an obvious need for someone with experience. At Lepanto itself, the *kapudan pasha* was Muezzinzade Ali Pasha, an aga of the Janissaries, and his mistakes were the main cause of the disaster. As for the troops, matters were even worse. There were no specialized naval troops in the Ottoman fleet. The Janissaries served at sea under the command of their regular officers, among them many Kurds who had never even seen the sea before embarking. The galley slaves, mainly Anatolian peasants recruited from the land army, had no maritime experience either (Imber 1980: 247–69). Any comparison with the European navies of the period would be cruel and superfluous. The Muslim navies were remarkably specific with regard to the recruitment of the sailors themselves. Like more or less every navy in the world, they practised forced enlistment, 'the press gang', but whereas in Europe this was carried out exclusively in ports, at the expense of a transient population of vagabonds and sailors in breach of enlistment, but who were nonetheless always familiar with the sea, in Islam it was brought to bear on people who lived far in the Egyptian or Ifrîqyan interior,[7] which gives an idea of the execrable quality of human material it might provide. Baybars, after the disaster of 1270, congratulated himself on having lost only 'peasants and riffraff' (cited in Ayalon 1967: 5). Such views on the part of the rulers were in fact only the expression of attitudes even more widespread in civil society.

Lack of any real interest in the sea manifested itself above all in the rarity of texts concerning it. It has often been noted that Christian sources alone are insufficient to compile the history of the Muslim navies, but that Muslim writings on the subject are extremely scarce (Ayalon 1967: 4; Fahmy 1966: 149; Guichard 1983: 55; Kubiak 1970: 45; Lev 1984: 246). Knowledge of the South Seas, for example, declined when they were under Muslim control. At the time of the great Abbasid voyages of discovery to the Far East, the first texts, like the account of the journey attributed to the merchant Suleiman composed in 851 (Suleiman 1948), bear witness to a good working knowledge of the South Seas. But from the tenth century onwards, in the *Supplément* of Abu Zaid, written around 915 (see Ferrand 1922), and more strikingly in the *Book of Wonders of India*, written around 950 (Devic 1878), the tone changed: the role of myth becomes disproportionately inflated, and precise facts disappear, to be buried for centuries under a jumble of extraordinary tales and stories. Why did all this fantastic material get the better of objective knowledge? The controversy that has arisen on this subject is significant. Jean Sauvaget (1948) suggested that it was because voyages had ceased at the time of the decline of the Abbasid Caliphate from the eleventh to the fourteenth centuries, and it required all the erudition of Jean Aubin (1963) to find evidence, peremptory in tone but actually little in quantity, that this was not the case, and that maritime activity had been continuous until the texts of Ibn Madjid at the end of the fifteenth century. How could that tremendous Arabic scholar Jean Sauvaget have made such an error? The fact is that this great expert on classical Arabic literature found no mention of the sea or any accounts of it. There is here the clear indication of a deep rift, of a chasm, between the culture of the lettered society of Baghdad and matters of the sea. Although now, several centuries later, the stories of Sinbad have been bracketed together with the collection of *A Thousand and One Nights*, it is clear that these sailors' tales held no interest for the pious individuals whose works have mainly survived. Let us remember that the *Haouiya*, Ibn Madjid's most important text, is only known in six manuscripts,[8] while the great religious, philosophical and even historical texts of Muslim culture are known by dozens, even hundreds of copies. Things have hardly changed today. We need only recall the words of a Kuwaiti captain on board whose ship Alan Villiers took passage in 1939 during his voyage along the east coast of Africa. When he learned that his passenger wanted to write a book about the journey, his only reaction was that not a single Arab would read it (Villiers 1940: 13).

We need not dwell on this. The apathy and neglect on the part of Muslim society towards the sea were absolute. Prior to really recent times, nothing can be found in the literature, whereas the sea has profoundly marked the emotions and the imagination of Christianity since the Middle Ages. While in almost all western languages the image of the voyage is maritime, in Muslim countries it is linked to a journey by land (Lewis 1991). Sailors' songs, such a rich genre in the West, are here notably impoverished, confined to invocations of the greatness of God and his mercy.[9] When compared to the flowering of ex-votos and the liturgy of the sea in Catholic Christianity, there is no particular spirituality, but rather, at most, a few superstitions (Brunot 1921: 10–12, 19–23, 54).

There have, of course, been exceptions to this general picture. For example, in Muslim Andalusia the navy rose to prominence in society on at least several occasions: under the Omayyads in the ninth and tenth centuries, under the *Reyes de Taifas*, and again under the Almohads. Under Abd-ur-Rahman III (912–61), the commander of the fleet was one of the three principal figures of state, together with the commanding general at Zaragoza and the Kadi of Cordoba (Eickhoff 1954: 173; Lirola Delgado 1993; Morales Belda 1970; Picard 1997). One text even states that he shared 'power with the Caliph, one governing on land, the other at sea' (*Kitab az-Zahrat*, cited by Lévi-Provençal 1932: 85–86). A number of factors converge to underline the special case of Andalusia, among them the early and important role played by Spanish pirates, who in the ninth century carried out the conquest of Crete at the other end of the Mediterranean before making numerous forays into the Aegean Sea (Brooks 1913; Christides 1981, 1984); and the flourishing of a specialized legal maritime literature that, from the eleventh century onwards, demonstrated the place of commercial maritime activity in civilian society (Picard 1997: 302, 468–72). These factors combine with other characteristics to indicate that Andalusia was a province culturally distinct from the Muslim zone, a 'European' culture before the term existed, where the Christians, whether Islamized or not, constituted an essential substratum and played an active part in maritime life (Picard 1997: 499–501). The same interpretation can be offered for the Malaysian exception already mentioned (see Lombard 1990; Sopher 1965). Such exceptions only confirm the rule.

Why were Muslims indifferent to the sea?

However, by considering these exceptions we only shift the emphasis of the problem, to the core of which we now return. Why this widespread Muslim indifference to the sea? In fact, this indifference expresses an intrinsic incompatibility. 'Islam', as we know, means 'submission'.[10] The Muslim is 'he who has submitted'. The sailor is essentially rebellious, or at least independent. 'Homme libre, toujours tu chériras la mer!', remarks Baudelaire in *Les fleurs du mal* (XV). In the eyes of Muslim society, sailors remain marginal, suspicious characters, even if they are generally good believers. In the South Seas, even today, only a few Omani and Kuwaiti captains enjoy respect, and this merely because of their involvement in trade and their links by origin and alliance to the social aristocracy of merchants. The fishing communities along the Indian coast, in contrast, were originally peopled by low castes or by former slaves (Siddiqi 1956: 33–5).

Sailors were a bunch of vagabonds and men who had gone down in the world (Villiers 1940: 142, 347). Their conduct was far removed from conventional morality. They provoked unanimous retribution. 'Any country bordering the sea … abounds in fornicators and paederasts,' wrote Moqaddasî at the end of the tenth century (Moqaddasî 1963: 80–1). When his contemporary, the pious Ibn Hauqal, discussed the *ribât* of Palermo, a coastal fortress where seafarers assembled, charged with being the privileged defenders of the faith, he deplored the disorderly behaviour and debauchery of its occupants (Ibn Hauqal 1964: Vol. I, 120). Is this the overreaction of men of letters and religion? In fact, it expresses the scorn that an entire society had always felt about sailors. A famous and frequently cited text by Maqrîsî (*Kithath*, II, 194, 17–22; cf. Ehrenkreutz 1955; Levi della Vida 1944–5: 218) informs us that service at sea, after Saladin's death and the end of his naval policies, 'had become a shameful thing which was grounds for insult. When one addressed a man in Egypt with the words: "Hey, sailor!", he would become very angry.' This text (from the late fifteenth century) was clearly intended as a counterpoint to the highpoints of Muslim maritime history, first under the Caliph Mutawakkil, who developed the fleet after the Byzantine raid on Damietta in 853, and then under Saladin at the end of the twelfth century. The text clearly incorporates a constant in the attitude of the Egyptian population that was already evident by the eleventh century in relations between Cairo and Alexandria, as illustrated by the subordinate role and low esteem in which the maritime inhabitants of the latter were held (Udovitch 1978). This perception of sailors and boatmen has not changed to this day, and many pejorative proverbs in contemporary Egyptian still target them. All this can be explained, and here we come to the heart of the problem, by the fact that the culture of seafarers is quite unlike normal Muslim culture (cf. Prins 1965: 263–75). Seafaring culture is fragmented and schizophrenic, in perpetual conflict between the pragmatic values of adaptability and flexibility necessitated by life at sea, and the normative values of Islam, to which one was forced to return on land. It is a culture veering between excitement and inaction, based on discontinuity, while the life of the Muslim is fundamentally ordered, rejecting excess and over-indulgence, the expression of the urban bourgeois ideal of the cities of the Hijaz. Sailors are really no better integrated into Muslim society than nomads (Planhol 1968: 25–6). Islam has always considered them to be outsiders.

But if sailors are undesirable, the sea itself also invites condemnation. Such condemnation has often been repeated, showing the reluctance of the true believer to venture on to the water. The first unequivocal expression dates back to Omar himself, when he refused Mu'awiyya, then governor of Syria, authorization to build a fleet to attack Cyprus. 'The Syrian Sea, I am told, is longer and wider than the desert, and threatens the Lord himself, night and day, trying to swallow him up … no, no, my friend, the safety of my people is more precious than all the treasures of Greece.'[11] Such texts were common from this point on. Shortly after the founding of the arsenal at Tunis, at the beginning of the eighth century, when Mousa, the governor of the city, wanted to develop its shipbuilding, the Kadi told him clearly that no man of normal behaviour would even think of going to sea. One was even justified in withdrawing the civic rights of a man who entrusted himself to a ship (Al-Maqqarî 1840: Vol. I, lxvi; Eickhoff 1954: 16, 246–7). There had to be a supreme sanction for all this: that of the Prophet himself. This was provided in numerous *hadiths.* We will simply note one, vouched for by Ibn Hanbal, one of the four great doctors of Islam. It is of very doubtful attribution, but even more significant if it is apocryphal in that it clearly indicates the general attitude of Muslim society during the first centuries of the Hijra. 'The sea', the Prophet is supposed to have said, 'is Hell, and Satan reigns over the waters' (Ibn Hanbal 1313/1895: Vol. III, 66, 333; see also Hoernebach 1950–5: 385).

So the believers turned their backs on this infernal element. As we have seen, there were certainly transgressions into the forbidden; remarkable individual enterprises since that of Mu'awiyya, who, some years after Omar's refusal, obtained from his successor Othman, in 648–9, the authorization to equip a fleet for an attack on Cyprus. Many farsighted minds in Islam perceived the need to 'break the taboo', whose disastrous effects they witnessed. In order to attract believers to service at sea, certain individuals had recourse to expedients like favourable pay, endeavouring at least to align it with that of the land army (compared to which it was much lower). Such individuals include Saladin in 1172 (Ehrenkreutz 1955: 105), and Al-Mu'izz, the fifth Fatimid Caliph (953–975) and conqueror of Egypt (Eickhoff 1954: 167; Hamblin 1986: 78). When the lure of worldly goods was not enough, there was always the promise of the hereafter. Contact with such an odious element must be possible and even desirable if in pursuit of a good cause. Thus exceptional merits were attributed to seafaring warriors, and corresponding rewards announced, the promise of which was even put in the mouth of the Prophet. Those who suffered from sea-sickness, as well as those who drowned, were credited with martyrdom. One seaborne expedition in a holy war was worth ten on land. A simple look towards the sea was serving God (Hoernebach 1950–5: 384–5). With a surprising pragmatism, the *hadiths* associate with the unequivocal condemnation of the sea the compensation essential for the righteous pursuit of *jihad.* Thus the Fatimids accorded believers who ventured on to the water the prestigious title of *Ghazi al-Bahr*, 'warrior for the faith at sea'. Even earlier, in the Omayyad period, many of the Qureish (the tribe of the Prophet) and the *Ançar* (his first companions and their descendants) had insisted on participating in the first maritime expeditions to show their ardour in overcoming their disgust (Eickhoff 1954: 167). We find movements of this kind periodically across the centuries. They never lasted long. Faith could sometimes triumph over the waters, but social pressure always remained the strongest force.

Conclusion

The consequences of all this are worth considering, even briefly. Much has been written about the decline, or relative decline, of Islam. The causes, which are certainly many and various, have been sought. We must acknowledge that this incompatibility of Islam and Muslim society with life at sea is one of them, if not the principal one. Two points in particular must be mentioned. First, the almost total absence of Muslims among the great maritime traders at the end of the Middle Ages and in modern and contemporary times, and their consequent failure to benefit from increasing prosperity in a period when the so-called 'global economy' was emerging. And, second, their non-participation in the great transoceanic discoveries of the fifteenth century, at a time when Muslim power was still more or less equal to that of Europe. Had they been resolute and ventured to sea, the fate of the world could well have been different.

Notes

This chapter presents the principal conclusions of a book published by Éditions Plon-Perrin (Paris: 2000) entitled *L'Islam et la mer: La mosquée et le matelot*, to which the reader should refer for further elaboration of the argument and for additional references. The chapter was translated from French by Lucy Baxandall.

1. The only possible contribution would be that of the 'Adventurers of Lisbon' (prior to 1147, at a time when the city was still Muslim). However, there is no evidence to prove that the 'adventurers' were Muslims. Cf. the decisive clarification by Mauny (1960: 86–8, 121). On the phantasmagorical transoceanic Arab voyages of the Middle Ages, and on the supposed Manding maritime expeditions (around 1307), see Mauny (1960: 104–10).
2. The best depiction remains that of Villiers (1940). For the situation in the nineteenth century, see Guillain (1856); for ships, see Hawkins (1981).
3. On the naval atmosphere of this period, see the memoirs of Hayreddin (Barbarossa), the *Gazevat-i Hayreddin Pasa*, attributed to his secretary, Sinan Cavus, of which a translation has been provided by Deny and Laroche (1969).
4. Presented as a hypothesis by Brindley (1926: 14), and clearly formulated by Laird-Cloves (1931: 12–13), who sought its distant origin in Micronesia-Polynesia, this theory was adopted by many authors between 1930 and 1950, notably Bornelle (1933) and Poujade (1946: 140–1, *passim*), and circulated in many works of synthesis. However, Paris (1949) considered the theory as unproven.
5. The most comprehensive collection of sources on the subject of Damien was compiled by Fahmy (1966: 126–7).
6. His exploits have survived in the form of a learned versification, the *Düstür nâme* of Enveri, edited and translated by Mélikoff-Sayar (1954).
7. For Egypt in the ninth century, see Levi della Vida (1944–5: 215) and Kubiak (1970: 56–57). For Ifrîqya, see Idris (1935: 169–70) and Ibn Idhârî (1901: Vol. I, 334–7) (cf. Eickhoff 1954: 220; Lev 1984: 250; Marçais 1946: 217).
8. Khoury (1971: 270) still only knew of three at this date. Three others were mentioned, but not described by him in Khoury (1985–6: 163).
9. There are several examples in Villiers (1940: 201–3, 223, 225, 231). It also seems that the offshore mariners had no original poetic development, but that their material came from the culture of pearl fishers in the Gulf (Villiers 1940: 396).
10. The fact is undeniable, despite the recent, and improper, attempts by Muslim authors, who want to refute an idea that is pejorative in their view, to broaden the semantic field. See, for example, Abdoljavad Falaturi cited in Ehlers (n.d.: 73–4).
11. This text has been passed on by Tabari (Part I, Vol. 5, pp. 2819–22), with variants, which have been happily combined in the piece by Muir (1924). It has been commented on by, for example, Hourani (1951: 54–5), Eickhoff (1954: 211) and Fahmy (1966: 73–4).

References

Adam, P. 1970. À propos des origines de la voile latine. In M. Cortelazzo, *Mediterraneo e Oceano Indiano: Atti del Sesto Coloquio Internazionale di Storia Maritima, tenuto a Venezia dal 20 al 29 settembre 1962, a cura di. ...* Florence: Civiltà Veneziana, Studi 23.

Ahrweiler, H. 1966. *Byzance et la mer.* Paris: Bibliothèque byzantine, Études 5.

Al-Maqqarî, 1840. *The History of the Mohammedan Dynasties in Spain* (trans P. de Gayangos). London.

Anthonioz, R. 1967–8. Les Imragen, pêcheurs nomades de Mauritanie (El Memghar). *Bulletin de l'Institut Fondamental d'Afrique Noire*, Série B, XXIX–XXX: 695–738, 751–68.

Aubin, J. 1963. Y a-t-il eu interruption du commerce par mer entre le golfe Persique et l'Inde du XIe au XIVe siècle? *Studia* (Lisbon) II: 165–71.

Aubin, J. 1973. Le royaume d'Ormuz au début du XVIe siècle. *Mare Luso-Indicum* II: 77–179.

Ayalon, D. 1967. The Mamluks and naval power: a phase of the struggle between Islam and Christian Europe. *Proceedings of the Israel Academy of Sciences and Humanities* I (8).

Barbour, N. 1970. L'influence de la géographie et de la puissance navale sur le destin de l'Éspagne musulmane et du Maroc. *Revue de l'Occident Musulman et de la Méditerranée*, No. spécial: 45–54.

Basch, L. 1989. The way to the lateen sail. *The Mariner's Mirror* LXXV: 328–32.

Basch, L. 1991. La felouque des Kellia: un navire de mer à voile latine en Egypte au VIIe siècle de notre ère. *Neptunia* 183: 2–10.

Bekri, Abou-Obeïd-el 1965 [1911–13]. *Description de l'Afrique septentrionale* (trans Mac Guckin de Slane). Paris.

Bell, H.I. 1910. The naval organisation of the Kaliphate. In *Greek Papyri in the British Museum* IV: Xxxii–Xxxv, The Aphrodito Papyri.

Bérard, V. 1900. *Les affaires de Crète.* Paris.

Bono, S. 1964. *I corsari barbareschi.* Turin.

Bornelle, F. 1933. Origine et histoire de la voile latine. *Provincia* XIII: 186–92.

Boyer, P. 1985. Les renégats et la marine de la Régence d'Alger. *Revue de l'Occident Musulman et de la Méditerranée* 39: 93–106.

Brindley, H.H. 1926. Early pictures of a lateen sail. *The Mariner's Mirror* XII: 9–22.

Broadhurst, R.J.C. (trans) 1952. *The Travels of Ibn-Jubayr.* London.

Brooks, E.W. 1913. The Arab occupation of Crete. *The English Historical Review* XXVIII: 431–43.

Brunot, L. 1921. *La mer dans les traditions et les industries indigènes à Rabat et Salé.* Paris.

Casson, L. 1956. Fore- and aft-sails in the Ancient World. *The Mariner's Mirror* XLII: 3–5

Charles, H. 1973. L'organisation de la vie maritime à l'île d'Arwâd (Syrie). *Revue de l'Occident Musulman et de la Méditerranée* 13–14: 231–8.

Christides, V. 1981. The raids of the Moslems of Crete in the Aegean Sea: piracy and conquest. *Byzantion* LI: 76–111.

Christides, V. 1984. *The Conquest of Crete by the Arabs (ca 824): A Turning Point in the Struggle between Byzantium and Islam.* Athens.

Christides, V. 1988. Naval history and naval technology in medieval times: the need for interdisciplinary studies. *Byzantion* 58: 309–32.

Coindreau, R. 1948. *Les Corsaires de Salé.* Paris: Publications de l'Institut des Hautes Études Marocaines, XLVII.

Dachraoui, F. 1981. *Le califat fatimide au Maghreb, 296–362/909–973: histoire politique et institutions.* Tunis.

Deny, J. and Laroche, J. 1969. L'expédition en Provence de l'armée de mer du sultan Suleyman sous le commandement de l'amiral Hayreddin Pacha dit Barberousse. *Turcica* I: 161–211.

Devic, L.M. 1878. *Les merveilles de l'Inde: En premier lieu.* Paris.

Devoulx, A. 1868. *Le livre des signaux de la flotte de l'ancienne Régence d'Alger ... traduit et publié par ...* Algiers, lithograph.

Devoulx, A. 1872. Le raïs El-Hadj Embarek. *Revue Africaine* XVI: 35–45.

Devoulx, A. 1911 [1859]. *Le raïs Hamidou.* Algiers.

Ehlers, E. 1990 (ed.) n.d. *Der islamische Orient* I. Cologne (Kóln).

Ehrenkreutz, A. 1955. The place of Saladin in the naval history of the Mediterranean Sea in the Middle Ages. *Journal of the American Oriental Society* 75: 100–18.

Eickhoff, E. 1954. *Seekrieg und Seepolitik zwischen Islam und Abendland bis zum Aufstiege Pisas und Genuas (650–1040)*. Schriften der Universität des Saarlandes.

Emerit, M. 1955. L'essai d'une marine marchande barbaresque au XVIIIe siècle. *Cahiers de Tunisie* IV: 363–70.

Fahmy, A.M. 1966. *Muslim Sea Power in the Eastern Mediterranean, from the Seventh to the Tenth Century A.D.* Cairo.

Ferrand, G. (trans) 1921–8. *Instructions nautiques et routiers arabes et portugais des XVe et XVIe siècles*. 3 vols. Paris.

Ferrand, G. 1922. *Voyage du Marchand Sulayman en Inde et en Chine*. Paris.

Ferrand, G. 1924. L'élément persan dans les textes nautiques arabes. *Journal Asiatique* CCIV: 193–257.

Ferrand, G. 1945. Les relations de la Chine avec le golfe Persique avant l'Hégire. In *Mélanges Gaudefroy-Demombynes*. Paris.

Fraenkel, S. 1886. *Die Aramäischen Fremdwörter im Arabischen*. Leiden.

Froissart, J. 1837. *Les chroniques de Sire* (ed. J.A.C. Buchon). 3 vols. Paris.

Grohmann-Kerouach, B. 1971. *Der Siedlungsraum der Ait Ouriaghel im östlichen Rif: Kulturgeographie eines Rückzugrgebietes*. Heidelberg: Heidelberger Geographische Arbeiten, 35.

Gsell, S. 1913–28. *Histoire ancienne de l'Afrique du Nord*. 8 vols. Paris.

Guichard, P. 1983. Les débuts de la piraterie andalouse en Méditerranée occidentale (798–813). *Revue de l'Occident Musulman et de la Méditerranée* 35: 55–73.

Guillain, M. 1856. *Documents sur l'histoire, la géographie et le commerce de l'Afrique orientale*. 3 vols. Paris.

Hamblin, W. 1986. The Fatimid navy during the early Crusades 1099–1124. *The American Neptune* 46: 77–80.

Hawkins, C.R. J. 1981. *Les boutres, derniers voiliers de l'Océan Indien*. Lausanne.

Hess, A.C. 1970. The evolution of the Ottoman seaborne empire in the Age of the Oceanic Discoveries, 1453–1525. *The American Historical Review* LXXV: 1892–1919.

Hoernebach, W. 1950–5. Araber und Mittelmeer: Anfänge und Probleme arabischer Seegeschichte. In *Zeki Velidi Togan'a Armağan/Symbolae in honorem Z.V. Togan* Istanbul.

Hourani, G. 1951. *Arab Seafaring in the Indian Ocean in Ancient and Early Medieval Times*. Princeton, NJ.

Ibn Hanbal 1313/1895. *Mosnad* (6 volumes). Cairo.

Ibn Hauqal 1964. *Configuration de la terre* (trans G. Wiet). Paris and Beirut.

Ibn Idhârî 1901. *Al-Bayân al-Moghrib fi Akhbar al-Maghrib* (trans E. Fagnan) vols. Algiers.

Ibn Khaldun 1934. *Histoire des Berbères*. Paris.

Ibn Rostih 1949. *Kitâb al-a'lâq al-nafîsa*. Partial edn. and trans M. Hadj Sadok, *Descriptions du Maghreb et de l'Europe au IIIe/Ie siècle*. Algiers.

Idris, H.R. 1935. Contribution à l'histoire de l'Ifrikya d'après le Riyad en-Nufus d'Abu Bakr El-Maliki. *Revue des Études Islamiques* 105–78.

Imber, C.H. 1980. The navy of Süleyman the Magnificent. *Archivum Ottomanicum* VI: 211–82.

Jansky, H. 1920. Das Meer in Geschichte und Kultur des Islams. In H. Mžik (ed.), *Beiträge zur historische Geographie, Kulturgeographie, Ethnographie und Kartographie, vornehmlich des Orients* (Festschrift E. Oberhummer). Leipzig and Vienna.

Jean-Léon l'Africain 1956. *Description de l'Afrique* (ed. and trans A. Epaulard). Paris.

Kahane, H. and Kahane, R. 1942. Turkish nautical terms of Italian origin. *Journal of the American Oriental Society* 62: 238–61.

Kâtip Çelebi 1329/1911. *Tuhfet-ül-kibar fi esfar-il-bihar*. Istanbul.

Khoury, I. 1971. La Hâwiya: Abrégé versifié des principes de nautique, par Ahmad bin Mâgid. *Bulletin d'Études Orientales* XXIX: 250–384.

Khoury, I. 1985–6. Les poèmes nautiques d'Ahmad ibn Mâgid, 2ème partie. *Bulletin d'Études Orientales* XXXVII–XXXVIII: 163–276.

Khoury, I. 1987–8. Les poèmes nautiques d'Ahmad ibn Mâgid, 3ème partie. *Bulletin d'Etudes Orientales* XXXIX–XL: 191–422.

Klaproth, J. von 1834. *Lettre à M. Le Baron de Humboldt sur l'invention de la boussole.* Paris.

Kubiak, W.B. 1970. The Byzantine attack on Damietta in 853 and the Egyptian navy in the 9th century. *Byzantion* XL: 45–66.

Lacoste-Dujardin, C. 1982. *Le conte kabyle, étude ethnologique.* Paris.

Laird-Cloves, G.S. 1931. *Sailing Ships: Their history and Development.* London.

Lev, Y. 1984. The Fatimid navy, Byzantium and the Mediterranean Sea 909–1036/297–427 A.H. *Byzantion* 54: 220–52.

Levi della Vida, G. 1944–5. A papyrus reference to the Damietta Raid of 853 A.D. *Byzantion* 17: 212–21.

Lévi-Provençal, E. 1932. *L'Espagne musulmane au Xe siècle.* Paris.

Lewis, A.R. 1951. *Naval Power and Trade in the Mediterranean A.D. 500–1100.* Princeton, NJ.

Lewis, B. 1991. *The Political Language of Islam.* Chicago: University of Chicago Press.

Lirola Delgado, J. 1993. *El poder naval de al-Andalus en la epoca del califato Omeya.* Granada.

Lockhart, L. 1936. The navy of Nadir Shah. *Proceedings of the Iran Society* I: 3–18.

Lombard, M. 1972. *Espaces et réseaux du haut Moyen-Âge.* Paris.

Lombard, D. 1990. *Le carrefour javanais: Essai d'histoire globale.* 3 vols. Paris: Civilisations et sociétés 79.

Louis, A. 1961–3. *Les îles Kerkena (Tunisie): Étude d'ethnographie tunisienne et de géographie humaine.* 3 vols. Tunis: Publications de l'Institut de Belles-Lettres Arabes – Tunis, 26–7 bis.

Mansur, F. 1972. *Bodrum, a Town in the Aegean.* Leiden: Social, Economic and Political Studies of the Middle East, III.

Mantran, R. 1962. *Istanbul dans la seconde moitié du XVIIe siècle.* Paris: Bibliothèque Archéologique et Historique de l'Institut Français d'Archéologie d'Istanbul XII.

Marçais, G. 1946. *La Berbérie musulmane et l'Orient au Moyen-Âge.* Paris.

Mauny, R. 1960. *Les navigations médiévales sur les côtes sahariennes antérieures à la découverte portuguaise (1434).* Lisbon.

Mélikoff-Sayar, I. 1954. *Le destan d'Umūr pacha.* Paris: Bibliothèque Byzantine (Documents 2).

Montagne, R. 1923. Les marins indigènes de la zone française du Maroc. *Hespéris* III: 175–215.

Moqaddasî 1963. *Ahsan at-tâqasîm fi ma'rifat al-aqâlîm* (trans A. Miquel). Damascus.

Morales Belda, F. 1970. *La marina de al-Andalus.* Barcelona.

Moreland, W.H. 1939. The ships of the Arabian sea about A.D. 1500. *Journal of the Royal Asian Society*: 63–74, 173–92.

Muir, W. 1924. *The Caliphate, its Rise, Decline and Fall* (revised T.H. Wei). Edinburgh.

Mutlak, A.H. 1973. *Dictionary of Fishing Terms on the Lebanese Coast: A Philological and Historical Study.* Beirut.

Nicolas, M. 1971. La pêche à Bodrum. *Turcica* III: 160–80.

Özbaran, S. 1972. The Ottoman Turks and the Portuguese in the Persian Gulf, 1534–1581. *Journal of Asian History* VI: 45–87.

Panzac, D. 1982. Afréteurs ottomans et capitaines français à Alexandrie. *Revue de l'Occident Musulman et de la Méditerranée* 34: 23–38.

Panzac, D. 1985. Les échanges maritimes dans l'Empire Ottoman au XVIIIe siècle. *Revue de l'Occident Musulman et de la Méditerranée* 39: 177–88.

Paradisi, U. 1962. I pescatori berberi della penisola di Fàrwa (Tripolitania). *L'Universo* XLII: 295–300.

Paris, P. 1949. Voile latine? Voile arabe? Voile mystérieuse. *Hespéris* XXXVI: 69–96.

Picard, C. 1995. Récits merveilleux et réalités d'une navigation en Océan Atlantique chez les auteurs musulmans. In *Miracles, prodiges et merveilles du Moyen-Âge* (Société des Historiens Médiévalistes de l'Enseignemant Supérieur Public, Orléans, 1994). Paris: Publications de la Sorbonne.

Picard, C. 1997. *L'Océan Atlantique musulman de la conquête arabe à l'époque almohade: Navigation et mise en valeur des côtes d'al-Andalus et du Maghreb occidental (Portugal–Éspagne–Maroc).* Paris.

Planhol, X. de 1968. *Les fondements géographiques de l'histoire de l'Islam.* Paris.

Planhol, X. de 1992. The Caspian. *Encyclopaedia Iranica* V: 51–7.

Planhol, X. de 1996. Darya. *Encyclopaedia Iranica* VII: 79–81.

Poujade, J. 1946. *La route des Indes et ses navires.* Paris.

Prins, A.H.J. 1965. *Sailing from Lamu: A Study of Maritime Culture in Islamic East Africa.* Assen.

Reid, A.J.S. 1969. Sixteenth century Turkish influence in Western Indonesia. *Journal of Southeast Asian History* X: 395–414.

Roselly de Lorgues, Comte, 1880. *Christophe Colombe.* 2nd edn. Paris.

Rycaut, P. 1668. *The Present State of the Ottoman Empire.* London.

Saffet Bey, Bir Osmanli Filosunun Sumatra Seferi 1912. *Tarihi Osmanlı Encümenı Mecmuası* X–XI: 604–14, 678–83.

Saussure, L. de 1925. L'origine de la rose des vents et l'invention de la boussole. *Archives des Sciences physiques et naturelles*, Ve période, 5 (reprinted in G. Ferrand, *Introduction à l'astronomie nautique arabe.* Paris, 1928).

Sauvaget, J. 1948. Sur d'anciennes instructions nautiques arabes pour les mers de l'Inde. *Journal Asiatique* 236: 11–20.

Serra, L. 1973. Le vocabulaire berbère de la mer. *Actes du Ier Congrès d'études des cultures méditerranéennes d'influence arabo-berbère.* Algiers.

Sevim, A. and Yücel, Y. 1990. *Türkiye Tarihi 1: Fetihten Osmanlılara kadar (1018–1300).* Ankara.

Shaw, S.J. 1969. Selim III and the Ottoman navy. *Turcica* I: 212–41.

Siddiqi, M.I. 1956. The fishermen's settlements on the coast of West Pakistan. *Schriften des Geographischen Instituts der Universität Kiel* XVI (2): 33–5.

Sopher, D.E. 1965. *The Sea Nomads.* Singapore: Memoirs of the National Museum 5.

Sottas, J. 1939. An early lateen sail in the Mediterranean. *The Mariner's Mirror* XXV: 229–230.

Suleiman 1948. *'Ahbar as-Sin wa llHind/Relation de la Chine et de l'Inde* (trans and commentary J. Sauvaget). Paris.

Svoronos, N.G. 1956. *Le commerce de Salonique au XVIIIe siècle.* Paris.

Sy, E. 1965. Cayar, village de pêcheurs-cultivateurs du Sénégal. *Cahiers d'Outre-Mer*: XVIII: 342–368, 342–68.

Talbi, M. 1966. *L'Emirat aghlabide 184-296/800-909: Histoire politique.* Paris.

Tibbetts, G.R. 1971. *Arab Navigation in the Indian Ocean before the Coming of the Portuguese: Being a Translation of ... Ahmad b. Majid ... with an introduction ... Notes ...* Leiden.

Tschudi, R. 1910. *Das Asafname des Lutfi Pascha.* Berlin.

Udovitch, A.L. 1978. A tale of two cities: commercial relations between Cairo and Alexandria during the second half of the eleventh century. In H.A. Miskimin, D. Herlihy and A.L. Udovitch (eds), *The Medieval City.* New Haven, CT and London: Yale University Press.

Vanchi-Bonnardel, Nguyen, R. 1967. *L'économie maritime et rurale de Kayar, village sénégalais.* Dakar.

Vanchi-Bonnardel, Nguyen, R. 1985. *Vitalité de la petite pêche tropicale: Pêcheurs de Saint-Louis de Sénégal.* Paris.

Van Leur, J.C. 1955. *Indonesian Trade and Society.* The Hague.

Villiers, A. 1940. *Sons of Sinbad.* New York.

Vovard, A. 1951. La marine des puissances barbaresques: Les renégats en Barbarie. *Comité des Travaux Historiques et Scientifiques, Bulletin de la Section de Géographie* LXIV: 203–10.

Weulersse, J. 1940. *Le pays des Alaouites.* Tours.

Whitehouse, D. 1977. Maritime trade in the Arabian Sea: the 9th and 10th centuries A.D. *South Asian Archaeology* 1977: 865–85.

Whitehouse, D. and Williamson, A. 1973. Sasanian maritime trade. *Iran* XI: 29–49.

9

ORGANIZED CHARITY IN THE ARAB–ISLAMIC WORLD

A view from the NGOs

Jonathan Benthall

'Nobody's ever come to ask about *zakat* before' (the Islamic doctrine of obligatory alms), said the public relations officer in the Ministry of Religious Affairs in Amman when I was beginning my research. And there was practically nothing published anywhere about any of the twenty-eight Red Crescent national societies. Organized charity in general – so it seems to have been taken for granted except by a few punctilious anthropologists – was a speciality of the Judaeo-Christian West: with the corollary that the non-West was one of charity's objects.

This chapter is written from the perspective of 'NGO studies', which is not an academic discipline in itself, but a problem area to which a number of disciplines have contributed insights. Though non-governmental organizations (NGOs) are far from constituting a homogeneous category, the frequency of use of this term today reflects an increasing attention to the significance of the non-profit sector – sometimes known as the 'third sector' – which itself is part of a wider and indeed somewhat ill-defined field known as 'civil society'. My own interest has developed partly from efforts on behalf of the Royal Anthropological Institute to promote social anthropology in its more applied modes; partly from practical participation in the management of a large international NGO, Save the Children (UK), and more recently the NGO support organization INTRAC (International NGO Training and Research Centre); and partly from studying the interactions between the international humanitarian NGOs and the mass media (Benthall 1993).

Self-criticism within the aid profession has followed a trajectory that parallels post-colonial self-criticism within academic anthropology – where the challenges advanced in the 1970s by Talal Asad, Dell Hymes and Edward Said appeared subversive to the establishment of the day but have now been absorbed as part of received wisdom. I remember a conversation in about 1972 with one of the founders of the London Technical Group, then an influential ginger group in the world of aid agencies. He criticized aid agencies for having so many retired military officers in management posts. At that time, Save the Children's overseas committee was chaired by the redoubtable daughter of a Viceroy of India, whose connections used to enable her to have a problem solved by getting straight through on the telephone to a government minister in Whitehall. In the aid agencies as in the academic world, work was done, however effectively, with less reflection and soul-searching than today. One of the achievements of the last quarter-century, in both the aid agencies and anthropology, has been to disturb the self-satisfaction of the expeditionary from a white metropolis confronting a feminized and unsophisticated Third World, assisted by unobtrusive local ancillary workers.

One major change in the NGOs has been to appreciate and examine the role of non-western or local voluntary organizations in providing welfare and other services to vulnerable populations. It is clear that all societies, rich and poor, have developed systems of mutual aid to mitigate social suffering. These can of course be eroded, whether as an incidental result of prolonged conflict, or by the intentional policies of governments whose ideologies seek either to stamp out spontaneous grass-roots activities, or to discourage what they see as passive dependency on welfare provision. However, voluntary associations can show surprising resilience. The most thoughtful western relief and development agencies now seek to encourage and support local-level organizations in the non-West with judicious subsidy and also by providing such services as training. Religious organizations are often among the most effective in mitigating social suffering. This has enabled the London-based Christian Aid to become one of the most effective in its campaigning – with its emphasis on troubling the conscience of the affluent West – while becoming entirely 'non-operational', that is, confining its field activities to selecting locally inspired projects for grant-aid and then monitoring and auditing them. Many of these local initiatives are run by church organizations, especially in highly Christianized regions such as Latin America and sub-Saharan Africa. Western agencies are now developing similar links with Christian associations in the former Eastern Bloc. An important current trend is for western governments to give serious consideration to direct funding of local initiatives in developing countries, thus making less pivotal the traditional intermediary function of the metropolitan relief and development agency, though also introducing a number of new problems such as the rise of a new class of local NGO organizers more or less dependent on foreign aid (INTRAC 1998).

Many countries that have only small Christian minorities, such as India and Indonesia, are nonetheless richer than is usually recognized in voluntary associations of every kind, including ones with religious affiliations other than Christian. An injunction to help the socially disadvantaged is one of the hallmarks of all the world religions. Up-to-date research on this topic is sparse, but Roger A. Lohmann (1994) has attempted to assemble evidence from Buddhist traditions in China, Japan and Korea in order to refute the hypothesis that a 'third sector' did not exist in Asia before the introduction of western-style not-for-profit organizations after the Second World War.

My own interest in Islamic organized charity arose from researching the International Red Cross and Red Crescent movement, a structurally complex organization much of whose work is tightly controlled from Geneva but which also seeks to foster grass-roots efforts through the Red Cross and Red Crescent national societies. I was interested in exploring how it came to be that some twenty-eight national societies in Muslim countries use the red crescent rather than the red cross as their emblem, and this led me to explore how organized charity in some of these countries, principally in the Middle East, relates to its western equivalents (Benthall 1997).[1] To understand this I had to investigate Islamic doctrine and law: especially the Qur'an's extensive teaching on alms (Benthall 1999) and the history of Islamic charitable trusts.

*Waqf*s

Waqf in Arabic means 'standing' or 'stopping', hence 'perpetuity'. Property is passed under Islamic law by gift or will to the state for pious works, such as the building of mosques and schools, providing the public with drinking water, facilitating pilgrimages to Mecca, or the relief of poverty and other needs. *Waqf*s (Arabic plural: *awqaf*) have their historical origins in the earliest days of Islam, perhaps deriving from the 'pious causes' of the Byzantine church (Schacht 1964: 19). It would be naïve to assume that the economic function of the *waqf*s has ever been purely altruistic. As far back as the tenth and eleventh centuries, *waqf*s were beginning to be used in the Arab–Muslim world to build up the *ulema* or religious leaders as a hereditary rentier class (Lapidus 1988: 165, 360), and the institution has also been used by large landholders to prevent the division of family property (Ruthven 1991: 171–2).

Islamic law does not recognize juristic persons. *Waqf* (or *habs* in North Africa) is seen as the withdrawal from circulation of the substance of a property owned by the founder and the spending of the proceeds for a charitable purpose. There is no unanimous doctrine as to who becomes the owner of the substance. The beneficiaries may be descendants of the donor, but the poor or some other permanent purpose must be appointed as subsidiary beneficiaries in case the original beneficiaries die out. The private or family *waqf* is distinguished from the so-called 'public' or charitable *waqf*, which is immediately destined for some public or charitable purpose. But in strict Islamic law, the private *waqf* is a charity too (Schacht 1964: 125–6).

The survival of *waqf* varies from one Muslim country to another with the wide variety of legal traditions. In the Sultanate of Oman, for example, which has only been a modern state for some thirty years, hundreds of *waqf*s are administered by the Ministry of Awqaf. As well as the purposes outlined above, *waqf*s exist for such purposes as funerals for poor people and washing of the deceased. People give property such as farms as well as money, and some *waqf* holdings have been converted into prime commercial property in order to improve the income. The Ministry owns two buildings in Mecca, one for the accommodation of pilgrims and the other rented to bring in money.

So many citizens in Oman wish to fund the building of mosques that (when I visited in 1996) the Ministry was trying to make a law that there must be a distance of one kilometre between each mosque, or two kilometres between big mosques. The religious authorities believe that regular meetings of Muslims in a vicinity for prayers enable them to know one another and so facilitate the solving of problems and the reduction of potential conflict. However, there is no voluntary sector whatsoever in Oman, though during my visit, some notables were asking the Sultan's permission for a charitable society to be formed for the relief of poverty.

Owing to the absence of written records until recently in Oman, almost all *waqf* property is held on trust by word-of-mouth tradition. According to my informants (who admittedly I must assume were intent on conveying a favourable impression to the visiting researcher), the whole society is based on trust, and this tradition continues even in the modern state, though gradually the legal status of *waqf* property is being formalized. Disputes over such matters are apparently very rare.

By contrast, extensive written archives on *waqfs* survive in some countries that were formerly part of the Ottoman Empire. In the Old City of Jerusalem, the Tikiyat Khaski Sultan is a 550-year-old *waqf* soup-kitchen that still serves vegetables to about a hundred people a day, and meat to about a thousand people a day during Ramadan. According to my Arab informants, some 70 per cent of the Old City is *waqf* – including many of the Christian monasteries and churches – and this will clearly be a bargaining point during any final status negotiations with Israel (for a scholarly analysis see Dumper 1994).

The voluntary sector in Jordan

The above examples from Oman and east Jerusalem have an 'Orientalist' appeal deriving from their historical depth, which gives the western observer the impression of walking into the premodern past. We must here leave on one side the question of whether this appeal is spurious or an essential component of anthropology. In any case, *waqfs* are on the whole marginal to contemporary Middle Eastern states, some of which, such as Egypt, have absorbed them completely into government ministries as nationalized assets.

Though given little publicity in the West, humanitarian agencies in the Islamic world are many and various. As many as 168 organizations are members of the Islamic Council for Da'wa (call to Islam) and Relief, which was founded in Cairo in 1988 (Bellion-Jourdan 1997: 73; 2000).

Jordan, which I will take as a case study, is the site of a rich variety of voluntary agencies, new and old, indigenous and international. Over 650 voluntary societies are registered there, serving a population of about 4.5 million. (In Egypt, with a population of some 60 million, the number of voluntary societies is between 12,000 and 14,000.) Islam is enshrined in Article 2 of the Hashemite Kingdom of Jordan's Constitution ('Islam is the religion of the State and Arabic is its official language') and some 90 to 95 per cent of the population are Sunni Muslim. Whereas in some other Muslim states the Islamist revivalists have been excluded from legal recognition, the Muslim Brothers have for political reasons been accepted for many years as part of the social fabric, albeit with a perhaps increasing reserve on the part of the government authorities. This 'policy of inclusion', as it is called, has resulted in the Muslim Brothers adopting pragmatic and moderate policies in Jordan. Charitable work plays an important part in their blend of social, religious and political activity.

Jordan is a kind of seismograph of the political convulsions of the Middle East. Its prominence in regional politics has given it a salience exceeding its economic power, through a deliberate strategy adopted by the Hashemite leadership. Also, Amman has become a centre for numerous regional offices of international agencies. Some of these moved from Beirut during the Lebanese civil war, and have stayed.

The country has considerable domestic and humanitarian needs. Some 37 per cent of the population is estimated to live below the accepted poverty line, and public health is declining in the poorer areas, especially in the southern governorates. Jordan is a host to a number of so-called 'camps' for Palestinian refugees that are still in part the responsibility of the UN Relief and Works Agency (UNRWA). In fact, these are strictly regulated townships that only in theory are regarded as temporary. The country is poor in natural resources, except for phosphate and potash, and in rainfall and water supplies. Its economy was severely hurt by the outcome of the 1991 Gulf War, since it had become dependent both on trade with Iraq and on aid from Saudi Arabia and Kuwait, aid that was to be withdrawn for some years as a punishment for its non-alignment during the Gulf War. Jordan succeeded in absorbing some 300,000 Palestinian 'returnees' from Kuwait (or nearly 10 per cent of the previous population of Jordan) after the Gulf War, but at considerable economic cost. In common with many other Arab countries, the birth-rate is high: some 41 per cent of the population are under the age of fifteen. It imports 70 per cent of its food, some of this from the World Food Programme under an aid scheme whereby the country pays only 10 to 15 per cent of the market price for grain. Urbanization is taking place rapidly, with only 6 per cent of the working population still employed in the agricultural sector; but political tribalism is only slowly declining in importance (Freij and Robinson 1996: 14, 29).

Just how important a part does Islam play in the life of contemporary Jordan, and specifically in its voluntary sector? The answer must depend to some extent on the observer's own biases. Some researchers tend to see religion as a hazy background presence or as an ideological screen, in either case a by-product of the real tensions in a society, which are political and economic. Ernest Gellner's masterly interpretations of the functioning of Islamic societies acknowledged no interest in the content of their belief systems. One variant of this point of view, deriving from the influential work of Gilsenan (e.g. 1982) among others, is that there is no such thing as 'Islam' – the famous *umma* (community) of Muslims being exposed as a myth – only innumerable Islams. Hence the entry for Islam in the Routledge *Encyclopedia of Social and Cultural Anthropology* (1996) fails to mention Muhammad, Mecca or Medina. The view has even been advanced by one prominent Jordanian anthropologist that militant Islamism is being sustained to some extent by western scholarly interest in Islam as an entity.

It is possible and reasonable, without becoming an apologist for any religion, to ascribe more autonomy to religious determinants. The similarity of mosques and other Islamic institutions from Morocco to Malaysia is perhaps more remarkable – given the lack of any overarching bureaucracy – than the differences. Again, consider the way many western intellectuals can claim 'I am not a Christian, but a humanist' (the latter term being replaceable by synonyms according to current fashion). The equivalent statement is not normally made by Jews, because Jewishness is an ascribed ethnic identity that seems to survive the loss of religious conviction. In the eyes of many Muslims, Christianity permeates western culture much more extensively than we are aware, especially if a ritual institution such as the family Christmas, when kinship as an inclusive and exclusive force comes into its own once a year, is seen (*pace* most Christian theologians) as an integral part of the religion. A session at the American Anthropological Association's annual meeting a few years ago broke new ground in examining Protestantism as a major unexamined element in western worldviews.[2] To look no farther afield than the voluntary sector, the Red Cross and Red Crescent movement, though entirely non-confessional in intention and policy, is pervaded by an unintended semiotics with resonances of the Crusades; Britain's leading relief and development agency, Oxfam, was founded by a group of Quakers and other Christians; the principle of universal human rights, as formulated in the eighteenth century and developed in the twentieth, may be interpreted as a codification of Judaeo-Christian convictions about the sanctity of the individual human soul.

There can be no simple answer to the question I have posed. If one were asked to point to the dominant tensions in Jordanian society today, one would mention first the acute divisions between rich and poor (with the relative lack of a middle class); the uneasy balance of power between the Palestinian majority and the Transjordanians; not forgetting gender inequality and population pressures. Yet to spend Ramadan in Amman is to become aware of the strength of religious observance. Every afternoon, the traffic becomes frantic as drivers hasten home for *iftar* (breaking of the fast), many of them irritable after fasting, and at six o'clock a great roar of relief goes up all over the city, then for an hour the streets are almost empty. It is more likely than not that this strength of Islamic culture has a bearing on the way the society addresses problems of welfare.

Many elements in the voluntary sector in Jordan today would appear, admittedly, to have little if anything to do with Islam. The national lottery is a clear example. In the early 1970s, leaders of the voluntary movement in Jordan looked around for alternative sources of revenue to government funding, on which they were at that time dependent. Some 80,000 tickets at JD 2 (£1 = 1 JD approx.) are now sold twice a month. Of these proceeds, 40 per cent goes to the General Union of Voluntary Societies (GUVS),[3] 20 per cent in commission to the sellers, and 40 per cent to the winners – the maximum prize being about JD 100,000. With the proceeds inflated by periodic special lotteries with higher ticket prices, the gross proceeds are JD 5 million per year, yielding JD 2 million for GUVS to distribute. The government takes nothing of this, aware that GUVS is satisfying needs that would otherwise fall on the public exchequer. Only rarely is there an article in the press attacking the lottery on the grounds that it is forbidden by Islamic law (*harâm*). However, as many as 85 per cent of the tickets at present are sold in Amman, which has about 33 per cent of the population; one reason being that in some governorates, such as Ma'an in the south, the selling of lottery tickets is looked down on as an undignified occupation, and a second being that people in rural areas are more prone to consider the lottery *harâm*.

GUVS is an entirely secular organization. Voluntary associations began in Jordan (then Transjordan) in the 1930s, when immigrant groups such as the Syrians set up societies to help their own members in need. The Christian churches were also active. The Circassian Charitable Association has the distinction of being the oldest association (it was founded in 1932) that is still active. It has eight branches with some 3,000 volunteer members, and runs a kindergarten and youth centres as well as helping poor families. Its policy is to try to breed new leaders for this influential Muslim minority.

Government institutions began to grow during the 1930s, and by 1948, with the influx of refugees from Israel, new concepts of social work, and a minimum standard of subsistence for all refugees irrespective of ethnic origin, began to be introduced. The government introduced laws on voluntary associations in the 1950s, and in 1958 GUVS was set up as an umbrella organization to coordinate and control the voluntary movement. It is an elected body, but the Ministry of Social Development ultimately controls the whole voluntary movement through its right (subject to judicial appeal) to veto appointments to the governing committees of all voluntary societies.

Government subsidies began in the 1960s. In 1970, the country was deeply shaken by what was in effect a civil war, settled in 'Black September', when some 7,000 Palestinians were killed by King Hussain's troops. This disaster resulted indirectly in expansion of the voluntary sector as the government tried to heal the country's wounds. Expansion has also followed on from economic belt-tightening in the early 1990s and from the influx of returnees after the Gulf War.

A report by the President of GUVS (Khatib 1994) claimed credit for the voluntary sector's effective management of resources, but also underlined Jordan's pressing social needs and the limited funds available to meet them. The most favoured forms of activity for NGOs within the framework of GUVS are kindergartens, vocational training, health centres and clinics, scholarships and loans for students, care for the handicapped, and care of orphans. Recent work has focused also on the role of women in development, income-generating projects and child care. With regard to women, it is recognized that though traditional training in sewing and knitting gives women a potential source of income that can be combined with domestic duties, this does nothing to challenge gender stereotypes and can actually widen the gap between educated and 'traditional' Jordanian women.

GUVS' biggest contribution to Jordan is a much-needed cancer treatment centre in Amman. Substantial funds (I was told the equivalent of US$10 million) have been raised for this through a telethon. This, like the lottery, is an example of western fund-raising techniques successfully transplanted.

All but a handful of privileged associations are legally required to be members of GUVS. Two of these are characteristic of Jordan in that they are patronized by prominent women members of the Royal Family: the Queen Alia Fund for Social Development, founded in 1977, named after one of the late King Hussain's earlier wives who was killed in a helicopter accident in 1977 while travelling home from a visit to a hospital, and now presided over by Princess Basma, the late King's only sister; and the Noor al Hussain Foundation, founded in 1985 and named after the late King's last wife. These are sophisticated operations, attracting extensive sponsorship from governments and international agencies. The former is perhaps best known for its network of community centres, the latter for its projects to encourage and develop traditional crafts in rural areas of Jordan.

Though no doubt modelled on the practices of contemporary British royalty, the involvement of the Royal Palace in charitable works is far more active than one would find in a western monarchy. An Arab monarchy does not stand back from the political fray, but is typically engaged in face-to-face interaction with the various interest-groups on whose support it depends. Critics of the status quo maintain that the Palace's participation in charity goes further than energetic benevolence and is actually a means of controlling and limiting the growth of grass-roots organizations, and this argument has been voiced especially on behalf of the women's movement, for Princess Basma chairs the Jordanian National Committee for Women and makes frequent speeches in support of women's groups. Certainly the fact that royal activities are immune from public criticism means that there is little unfettered debate about the effectiveness of the leading charitable organizations in Jordan. Unflattering critics call these royal foundations 'parallel organizations' rather than voluntary organizations in the proper sense. It is an open question whether they contribute more in professionalism, influence and éclat than they take away by smothering grass-roots initiatives with official control.

By comparison with other countries in the region, and given the harsh political and economic shocks it has had to endure, it is remarkable that Jordan enjoys reasonable internal stability, and in particular that Transjordanian ethno-nationalism has not already taken a more virulent form. Much of the credit is generally given to the political charisma of the late King[4] and the preaching of humanistic tolerance and inclusiveness – for instance, with regard to the small Christian minority. But it should be noted that the Palace has also taken every opportunity to support a humane and tolerant interpretation of Islam. Islam frequently becomes co-opted by patriotic states, of which Jordan is one, and in this case fused with a concept of enlightened monarchy borrowed from the West. But its universalistic message – within the confines of fellow-Muslims and 'people of the Book' – is a powerful counterbalance against ethno-nationalism, when skilfully adapted. The Hashemite leadership even speaks of the possibility one day of a federation of Abrahamic states that would include Israel.

I have heard it argued that the whole of Jordan's voluntary sector is informed by Arab–Islamic values of social solidarity. This claim must obviously be qualified, given that the society is deeply stratified, but a niggling element of truth seems to remain in such an assertion – to do with the strength of face-to-face relationships, family ties and other bonds of reciprocal obligation that anthropologists generally regard as analytically prior to indicators based on money. It is related to the fact that the idea of communism, which depends on the workers subsuming their personal identities in a common solidarity of economic class, has never found favour in Arab states. Rather than try to resolve these difficult interpretative issues, we will consider Jordan's explicitly Islamic voluntary associations, and the special characteristics that seem to distinguish these.

Special characteristics of Islamic voluntary associations

One of the most favoured objects for Muslim charitable works is the care of orphans. Perhaps the most important reason is that the Prophet Muhammad himself was an orphan: his father died either just before or just after he was born, and his mother died when he was only six and he was taken into the family of his paternal uncle. If one speaks of orphans to a pious Muslim, he or she is likely to make a gesture of crossing two fingers, which alludes to a saying of the Prophet that whoever looks after an orphan will be 'like this' with him in Paradise. The Prophet also said, 'I am he who takes care of the orphan.' Several passages in the Qur'an condemn those who misappropriate the property of orphans (e.g. 93:9, 107:2). The result is that there can be few Islamic welfare organizations that do not include orphans among their beneficiaries, and emotive appeals on orphans are distributed to the public. For instance, the British-based charity Islamic Relief supports 4,000 orphans in over ten countries. 'Orphan' is generally defined as a child who has lost his or her father, that is, the family breadwinner; the loss of a mother is not seen as so disastrous. The term 'orphan' also sometimes appears to be used as a euphemism for any child born out of wedlock who is rejected by a family.

I visited a small residential girls' orphanage in Salt, 30 kilometres north-west of Amman, one of the oldest towns in Jordan. It was administered by the local branch of the Red Crescent society, which is secular and non-denominational, though its day-to-day operation was overseen by a devout Muslim, Hajja N., a full-time volunteer, an affectionate and cordial lady in late middle age. It has space for twenty girls, whose ages range from eighteen months to seventeen years. The original aim when the orphanage was started in 1965 was to accept children from four years up, but they cannot refuse younger children. I had coffee in the Hajja's office, and she led in a little girl called Sana, only eighteen months old and clinging to her. An even younger boy was brought in, but he had been accepted just for a short time and would soon go to an orphanage in Amman. The older girls help to look after the younger ones, and some of them go on to higher education. The small size of the orphanage made it relatively easy to take care of, I was told, especially because the Hajja and her husband have no children themselves and treat the orphanage like a large family. Though most of the bigger children were out at school during my visit, I could see that the living spaces were rigorously ordered: the children sitting in bare side-rooms with all the toys in a cupboard in the Hajja's office (possibly tidied up for my visit); a communal cupboard of children's clothes in the dormitory.

I also visited an orphans' day centre in Amman, run by the Saudi-based International Islamic Relief Organization (IIRO). This is just outside the Jabal Al Husayn refugee camp, the oldest of the Palestinian refugee camps. Two hundred children up to the age of fifteen are looked after here, just over half of them boys.

Most of them come from the refugee camp, but some from up to 5 kilometres away. The primary aim of the centre is to enable the families to become economically self-sufficient, and there are courses for the mothers in straw handcrafts, ceramics, knitting and other productive activities that can be carried on in the home.

Boys and girls, on alternate days, attend Qur'anic instruction and extra classes. On the morning when I visited, it was the girls' day. The women teachers were all wearing the veil like a European nun's, the girls had their heads veiled. On request, one of the girls recited some verses from the Qur'an, with only a little prompting from a teacher. The class then rose to their feet, I was invited to sit down together with the Saudi manager, and the girls chanted some verses in Arabic, accompanied by one of the teachers with a tambourine. The meaning of the two rhymes was 'Welcome to guests of the IIRO' and 'Don't forget the rules for reciting the Holy Qur'an.'

I was then invited to the office of the head of the day centre, Basma Sharif, and asked her some questions. She graduated from Jordan University in 1985 after studying Shari'a, then did a postgraduate course in school administration. She had worked with UNRWA as a teacher, the UN body with responsibility for Palestinian refugees, and subsequently as a supervisor in an orphan centre like this one. She is in favour of non-residential orphan centres, and of the sponsorship of orphans within their extended families rather than building up institutions; and she contends that this tendency is envisaged by Islamic principles. She plays an active role in community work outside her paid employment, and is clearly a strong personality of some influence. Basma Sharif is strongly in favour of local initiatives rather than big international agencies, and stresses the importance of Islamic volunteering without reward. She stressed the principle in Islam that poor people have the *right* to assistance, quoting a well-known Qur'anic passage: '[They will be blessed] in whose wealth is a recognized right for the [needy] who asks and him who is prevented [for some reason from asking]' (70: 24–5). Therefore, there should be no loss of dignity in receiving assistance.

According to traditional Islamic education, children would memorize the Qur'an before going on to formal schooling. The emphasis is still on memory, until the children start reading at the age of eight or nine. A few children of this age in Amman, as in many other places in the Muslim world, are still trained to memorize the whole of the Qur'an.

The Jabal Al-Husayn orphan centre represents an approach to the care of children that accords with current expert western thinking in seeking to strengthen family bonds through day centres, rather than board children in institutions. The apparent imposition of rigid gender roles by means of dress is harder to reconcile with the policies of progressive NGOs, though the issue is more subtle than is often realized, and women's clothing is not necessarily a reliable indicator of psychological or economic independence. Many western educators deprecate rote-learning of the Qur'an, but within Islamic cultural terms we must respect the effort made to educate these children in a knowledge of what is for them their priceless religious heritage: a guarantee of human dignity for the child victims of a grim power-game that has left the Palestinian refugee community disinherited and unassimilated for fifty years in 'temporary' housing.

After my discussion with Basma Sharif, it was a little dispiriting a few months later to find that the active and energetic *zakat* committee in Nablus, the historic town in the West Bank – which has built up an effective complex of medical services, income-generating projects and the like, nearly all from Muslims' contributions – had set its heart on building a huge residential orphanage in a walled compound, an architect's vision of which appears as the frontispiece of the committee's glossy annual report. As in the West, large-scale prestige projects have a great appeal for many heads of charities.

Another feature of traditional Islamic organized charity seems to have been a strong emphasis on giving preference to Muslims rather than non-Muslims. This has been challenged in recent years by the more liberal theologians' interpretations of Islamic doctrine (cf. Benthall 1999), and also no doubt by the desire of the more internationally minded voluntary agencies to harmonize with the worldwide humanitarian network with its manifold opportunities for funding. Hence the IIRO has provided relief aid to non-Muslims in, for instance, Rwanda. The issue has not arisen as a critical one in a country like Jordan with a very large Muslim majority and minorities such as Orthodox, Catholic and Protestant Christians who each have that strong sense of group identity that is characteristic of the history of the whole region. There is no shortage of urgent humanitarian needs among Muslims in many countries to be attended to, so the issue is rather a theoretical one except as it relates to countries with non-Abrahamic indigenous minorities such as the Nilotic peoples of the Sudan or the inhabitants of outlying Indonesian islands who do not even adhere to Hinduism or Buddhism. In such contexts, it would seem that even the most tolerant interpretations of Islam cannot easily overcome the traditional, almost visceral dread of paganism and polytheism that is deeply rooted in the Qur'an. This may be a principal reason why charitable and humanitarian institutions in Sudan have been so ruthlessly manipulated by the Islamist government in Khartoum in the context of civil war (Bellion-Jourdan 1997; de Waal 1997a).

Many Islamic charities are concerned with furthering the Muslim cause as well as benefiting already committed Muslims. This is consistent with a major element in much traditional Islamic doctrine: the refusal to acknowledge a distinction between aspects of life that other religions tend to separate; the contention that Islam is a seamless whole in which religion, politics, economics and morality are interfused. To what extent this corresponds to lived reality is debatable.

The Christian churches often adopted a similar position before the Enlightenment, but since then the principles of separation of church and state, and of freedom of conscience, have gradually won wide, if still not complete, acceptance within the Christian world. One outcome is that the mainstream Christian philanthropic agencies are today strongly opposed to the combining of humanitarian aims with proselytizing. It is now condemned as unethical – by churches that belong to the World Council of Churches – to try to effect religious conversion of someone who is hungry, sick or otherwise disadvantaged. This was not always so, from the early centuries of Christianity up to the colonial period when many

Christian organizations, such as the Mission to Lepers and the Salvation Army, sought to combine evangelical and humanitarian aims, and some such as World Vision still do. There are signs that some Islamic charities are moving towards a similar approach to that of the modern Christian agencies, but the doctrine of what I have called Islamic 'seamlessness' still provides resistance.

A related characteristic of the Middle Eastern voluntary sector is that conventional western distinctions between charitable or humanitarian operations and politics do not fit easily into everyday life, notwithstanding what the law may say. The reluctance of the Sultan of Oman, noted above, to permit charities to be set up is understandable in the Middle Eastern context. We need only look at the history of the Society of Muslim Brothers in Egypt. This is now denied registration either as a political party or as an NGO, but continues to enjoy success, popularity and leadership, pursuing its dual goal of socio-economic development and political influence. Founded in 1928, the organization was concerned among other things with public health. In 1945 it was required by the government to split into two: a section concerned with politics and a section concerned with welfare. The latter had 500 branches all over Egypt by 1948 (Mitchell 1969: 36, 289–91). Similarly, both Hamas in Palestine and the Shi'ite Hizbollah (Party of God) in Lebanon are composed of a militant faction prepared to use violence and a broadly based faction that prefers negotiation. Each has built up a formidable network of welfare services to support their respective causes. Documentation of Hamas shows that these networks are not merely devices to gain political support, but also the result of a conscious policy to build up Islam as the basis for a sense of community to replace the sense of nation shattered by the occupation, which is seen as a new Crusade against the *umma* or community of Muslims (Legrain 1991, 1996; see also Milton-Edwards, Chapter 3, this volume).[5] Thus the religious rhetoric of political Zionism is turned against the Israelis. Palestine is conceived by Hamas as a religious foundation or *waqf* until the end of days. Jewish zealots in Israel have achieved their present position of political influence by means of strategies analogous to those of Islamists elsewhere in the Middle East.

So the Islamic voluntary sector covers a wide political spectrum, from official quasi-governmental bodies, pejoratively described as 'parallel organizations', to popular movements of a radical and even politically violent tinge. The privileges of charities are manipulated on all sides. For instance, a Jordanian *zakat* committee for Palestinian relief that I visited seems on all the evidence to raise funds successfully for a variety of projects in the West Bank for sponsorship of orphans, income generation, medical care and the like. They use a picture of the Dome of the Rock – that potent symbol of Islamic claims to Jerusalem – superimposed on a map of the whole of Israel/Palestine, as a logo, and a plastic model of it as a collecting-box. Thus they adapt western fund-raising techniques to the local context. However, when their fund-raising leaflets routinely savage the 'Satanic' Israelis – at a time when the Jordanian government is trying to support the Peace Process – it becomes clear that charitable operations just will not fit into a segregated, politics-proof container. Rather than merely note the permeability of charity and politics in the Middle East, we should also ask how intellectually sustainable is the sharp distinction between the two that the Euro-American law of charities strives so hard to enforce.

The voluntary sector in Algeria

Algeria is exceptional among Islamic countries in the savagery of the 'black years' of civil war since the 1990s (or in Arabic *sinawât ul-fitna*, years of discord) and in the extremism of its armed Islamist movement, which has had less in common with traditional Islam than with millenarian cults, the Cultural Revolution in China or European fascism. The current Bouteflika government may, however, be leading the way among its neighbours in its active encouragement of the country's 'associative movement' or voluntary sector, which the government sees as a major ingredient in relieving poverty and social exclusion and reinforcing the policy of *concorde civile*. Admittedly, actual achievements do not yet measure up to government rhetoric, and it has been argued by critics of Bouteflika that the apparent freedom of the press and civil pluralism are illusions fabricated by the army to disguise its dominance over the civilian authorities (Addi 2001).

Well before the colonial period, the region that was to become Algeria was marked by immemorial Arab–Islamic traditions of mutual aid, in particular by *touiza*, the rural practice of local cooperation. Shortly after the Second World War, Algerians created new forms of association directed towards cultural, associational and sporting objectives, under the French law of 1 July 1901. These were few in number and largely urban, but they played their part in safeguarding the sense of national identity.

Two very different associations that were both influential in the national movement were the Association des Oulémas (religious scholars), founded by Sheikh den Badis in the 1920s, and the Scouts Musulmans Algériens, founded in 1936 by another national hero, Mohamed Bouras. However, according to new research (Arous 2000) there were about a hundred other active associations. The first Islamic charity was the Jam'îyat al-iqbâl ('society for concern'), founded in 1940.

Algerian associations crumbled during the war of independence against the French, but shortly after the Algerian victory in 1962 they revived in the fields of culture, sport, youth and social action, in a very brief flowering for one year only, comparable to the rather longer period at the beginning of Soviet rule in Russia. The ruling FLN (Front de Libération Nationale) policy of 'unity of action and thought' led to their replacement by 'mass organizations' following the Eastern European model. The Islamic movement went underground, making use of the national associations set up by the government and also using mosques to pursue their aims, in a way comparable to the Catholic church in Communist Poland. According to Arous, Muslims drew on the Shi'ite tradition of *taqîya*, that is, dissimulation of one's religion under duress. This situation prevailed until new legislation in 1987 and 1990, which encouraged a rapid growth in the foundation of associations. The number of national non-profit associations, which have to be approved by the Ministry of the Interior, now stands at 823 in a population of some 30 million, and there are said to be as many as 53,000 local associations, regulated at the level of the forty-eight provinces.

The large quantity of associations registered in Algeria is by no means yet matched by a proportionate contribution to national life. Despite its keenness to encourage the voluntary sector, the government is also keen to control it both from unwelcome international infiltration and from the militant Islamist factions. Zoubir Arous's sociological research on Islamic voluntary associations concludes, from his participant observation, that some of them are performing good work with deep roots in the communities they serve. His view contrasts with the establishment position in Algeria that all the Islamic voluntary associations are highly politicized, and in some cases morally compromised, so that they should be approached, if at all, only with great caution. During a visit to Algiers in April 2000 I met with Mr Aissa Benlakhdar, head of the *Jami'a al-Irshâd wal-Salâh* (Society for Guidance and Reconstruction), founded in 1989, now a large association with branches in all forty-eight provinces. Its programmes include social development, education and health. It plans to start a new centre for helping children who have suffered psychologically from the 'years of discord', and Mr Benlakhdar is critical of projects to impose European models of psychotherapy on Algerian patients. He holds that a society in transition needs to build on its own associative traditions. His view is persuasive for, though many mainstream Algerians have drifted away from religious institutions, disgusted by the excesses of the armed Islamist factions, the population remains almost 100 per cent Muslim. My own conclusion is that the country will eventually benefit from the efforts of religious leaders such as Abdelmadjid Mesiane (President of the Haut Conseil Islamique) or Soheib Bencheikh (the Algerian mufti of Marseilles) to formulate interpretations of Islam more consistent with modern life than those currently dominant, yet still offering an alternative to collective self-abasement before the economic victories of the West and the Far East. However, these leaders seem to be underappreciated and they are rather isolated voices. A more widely held view among the francophone intellectual elite, that Islamism is an indivisible movement and even its moderate adherents are not to be trusted, was expressed in the editorial in the Algiers newspaper, *La Liberté*, on 27 April 2000: 'Current developments give one the impression that Algeria is in the same situation as a person who is not quite convinced that AIDS is lethal, and who in order to be convinced asks to be injected with the virus.'

One of the positive factors in Algeria is that, though television is totally government controlled, the press is probably the freest in the Arab world and there is a tradition of outspoken criticism and polemic (albeit with limits set by the military authorities). However, the liberalizing tendency in the government seems unable at present to follow through its declared intentions of allowing more freedom to voluntary associations, and their development is likely to be slow.

Conclusion

It would be a mistake to idealize the voluntary sector in the Islamic world, for a serious lack of accountability is widespread. It would seem that in some cases Islamic charities in Arab countries have been used simply as fronts for organizing political violence. Another extreme example is the huge charitable foundations set up in Iran under the direction of religious leaders after the revolution, on the orders of Khomeini. The biggest is the Foundation for the Oppressed and the Disabled, which was created in March 1979 with a view to taking over the wealth of the Shah and those connected with the court. It is private but exempted from both taxes and reporting requirements. By 1992, it had become a huge conglomerate employing more than 65,000 people and running an annual budget of $10 billion, nearly 10 per cent of the government's own budget, with interests in manufacturing, importing, hotels and even real estate in Manhattan (Waldman 1992). Some published reports concerning these foundations are extremely damning, likening them to the Philippines under Marcos or to the Communist Party under Soviet apparatchiks. Moreover, between two and four million refugees (Afghans, Iraqi Shi'ites and Kurds) are looked after in Iran, for which the country receives little recognition from the outside world. But with no public accountability, it is impossible to know the truth. Genuine accountability in the Middle East voluntary sector is aimed at by some of the more progressive established organizations in their published annual reports, but the kind that is accepted by the general population is more likely to be the personal trust built up by small face-to-face groups.

Some political theorists in the Middle East and North Africa still look forward to a future where the region's economic potential will be realized at nation-state level and there will be social justice for all; and it is a corollary of this point of view that private charity is no more than a palliative that may actually impede or retard progress towards radical political change. This used to be the classic socialist or Marxist perspective on private charity. Faced with objective political realities and the growing power of globalizing capitalism, many nowadays take a more positive view of the voluntary sector. Anthropologists are well placed to extend their discipline's already valuable contribution to NGO studies,[6] towards a cross-cultural comparison of different traditions of almsgiving and organized charity.[7] One particularly promising approach is suggested by the American anthropologist James Ferguson, who argues that the lately fashionable school of 'critical' anthropology, which characteristically seeks to demystify religious and moralistic ideological discourse, is ultimately unsatisfying in that it is driven by a desire to distinguish goodies from baddies. He suggests instead a more modest approach, which he calls 'political analysis', modelled on Anglo-Saxon linguistic philosophy and starting from the proposition that even institutions that appear to be morally impeccable have a 'dangerous' aspect.[8]

In a more practical mode, western NGOs have an important role to play in supporting sustainable local-level initiatives, injecting their own technical skills and accumulated experience of managing projects, and disseminating the important principle of public accountability.

Notes

I am grateful to the Royal Anthropological Institute for giving me six months' sabbatical leave in 1996; to the Nuffield Foundation for a research grant; to the Department of Anthropology, University

College London, for appointing me an Honorary Research Fellow; to the Royal Institute for Inter-Faith Studies (Deputy Director: Randa Mukhar) and El-Quds University, East Jerusalem (President: Sari Nusseibeh) for practical assistance; and to the Centre de Recherche sur le Moyen-Orient Contemporain (Director: Riccardo Bocco) for cooperation and hospitality, including access to research on the Jordanian voluntary sector by Abla Amawi and Brigitte Curmi. During a short visit to Oman, I was given useful information by the Grand Mufti and the Ministry of Awqaf. Thanks also to Akbar Ahmed and Hastings Donnan for consistent encouragement, and to Khaldoon Ahmed, Jean-Nicolas Bitter, Hana Jaber, Mondher Kilani, Yann Le Troquer, Riyadh Mustafa, Jamal Nusseibeh, William C. Young and Ameur Zemmali.

1. As explained in the cited article, there is no 'International Red Crescent'. Some countries have Red Crescent rather than Red Cross National Societies, and the movement as a whole combines the names of the two emblems. The problem of the rejection by Muslims of the red cross as the Movement's main emblem, and other problems arising therefrom, have beset it since almost its earliest years.

2. 'The futures of the anthropology of Protestantism in theory and practice', session organized by Brian M. Howell and James Peacock, 19 November 1997, American Anthropological Association Annual Meeting, Washington DC.

3. Al-ittiHâdu 'l-'âmmu 'l-jam'îyât il-khairîyah.

4. This chapter was prepared in draft before the death of King Hussain. His son, King Abdullah, has emulated his father's prominent commitment to inclusiveness and charitable causes, in a context of ominous political turbulence in the region. The name of the Queen Alice Fund was changed to the Jordanian Hashemite Fund for Human Development in 1999.

5. Cf. also François Burgat (1995: 108) on the Middle East and North Africa more generally:

> If, for some decades, the mosques have had such a success, it is certainly because people speak of God there, but also because the vocabulary used to do so derives from the only domain that has resisted the cultural pressure of the North. In this case, the apparent return of the religious should be seen less as the resurgence of the sacred in a secular universe, than as the rehabilitation of the referents, especially political ones, of the local culture, which are invited to rediscover – at the conclusion of the colonial parenthesis – their lost ambition to universality.

6. See especially de Waal (1997b) and Malkki (1997), which both include useful bibliographies.

7. An article by Bowie (1998) on a non-western (Thai Buddhist) tradition of charitable giving provides a well-documented class analysis influenced by Gramsci and Bourdieu, seeking to lift the veil of hypocrisy and sanctimony from the face of charity with more sophistication than classical Marxism was capable of. See also Ilchman et al. 1998.

8. Summing up paper in session on 'Dreams, desires, hopes: the politics of empowerment and development', 6 December 1998, American Anthropological Association Annual Meeting, Philadelphia.

References

Addi, L. 2001. La Guerre continue en Algérie. *Le Monde Diplomatique* 565: 1, 12.

Arous, Z. 2000. *Al-Harakât ul-majmu'îat ul-islâmîyah bil-jazâ'ir: al-awSûlu, al-wâqi'u wal-âfâq* [The Islamic associative movement in Algeria: roots, reality and perspectives]. Cairo: Medbouli.

Bellion-Jourdan, J. 1997. L'humanitaire et l'islamisme soudanais: les organisations Da'wa Islamiya et Islamic African Relief Agency. *Politique Africaine* 66: 61–73.

Bellion-Jourdan, J. 2000. Islamic relief organizations: between 'Islamism' and 'humanitarianism'. *ISIM Newsletter* 5: 15.

Benthall, J. 1993. *Disasters, Relief and the Media*. London: I.B. Tauris.

Benthall, J. 1997. The Red Cross and Red Cross movement and Islamic societies, with special reference to Jordan. *British Journal of Middle East Studies* November: 153–73.

Benthall, J. 1999. Financial worship: the Quranic injunction to almsgiving. *Journal of the Royal Anthropological Institute* 5 (1): 27–42.

Bowie, K.A. 1998. The alchemy of charity: of class and Buddhism in Northern Thailand. *American Anthropologist* 100 (2): 469–81.

Burgat, F. 1995. *L'Islamisme en face*. Paris: Éditions de la Découverte.

Dumper, M. 1994. *Islam and Israel: Muslim Religious Endowments and the Jewish State*. Washington, DC: Institute of Palestine Studies.

Freij, H.Y. and Robinson, L.C. 1996. Liberalization, the Islamists, and the stability of the Arab state: Jordan as a case study. *The Muslim World* 86 (1): 1–32.

Gilsenan, M. 1982. *Recognizing Islam*. London: Croom Helm.

Ilchman, W., Katz, F.S.N. and Queen II, E.L. 1998. *Philanthropy in the World's Traditions*. Bloomington: Indiana University Press.

INTRAC 1998. *Direct Funding from a Southern Perspective: Strengthening Civil Society*? Oxford: INTRAC NGO Management and Policy series no. 8.

Khatib, A. 1994. *The experience of NGOs in Jordan: a brief description*. Amman: GUVS.

Lapidus, I.M. 1988. *A History of Islamic Societies*. Cambridge: Cambridge University Press.

Legrain, J.-F. 1991. *La voix du soulèvement palestinien*. Cairo: CEDEJ.

Legrain, J.-F. 1996. Les Palestiniens, l'adversité et Allah. *Le Monde*, 13 March.

Lohmann, R.A. 1994. Buddhist commons and the question of a third sector in Asia. *Voluntas* 6 (2): 140–58.

Malkki, L. 1997. Speechless emissaries: refugees, humanitarianism, and dehistoricization. In K.F. Olwig and K. Hastrup (eds), *Siting Culture: The Shifting Anthropological Object*. London: Routledge.

Mitchell, R.P. 1969. *The Society of the Muslim Brothers*. London: Oxford University Press.

Ruthven, M. 1991. *Islam in the World*. Harmondsworth: Penguin.

Schacht, J. 1964. *An Introduction to Islamic Law*. Oxford: Clarendon Press.

Waldman, P. 1992. Clergy capitalism: mullahs keep control of Iranian economy with an iron hand. *Wall Street Journal*, 5 May.

de Waal, A. 1997a. *Food and Power in Sudan: A Critique of Humanitarianism*. London: African Rights.

de Waal, A. 1997b. *Famine Crimes: Politics and the Disaster Relief Industry in Africa*. London: James Currey.

10

SILVER SOUNDS IN THE INNER CITADEL?

Reflections on musicology and Islam

Martin Stokes

Until relatively recently, the 'Music of the Middle East' and the 'Music of the Islamic World' were entirely interchangeable categories in the kinds of reference works to which a non-specialist might turn in search of information about either. Characteristically inserted as an 'Interlude' between the French Ars Nova and the Italian Renaissance, one would encounter it as a sideline in the grand narrative of Western Europe's 'ascent'.[1] More localized ethnomusicological studies often begin with the assertion that it is impossible to proceed without understanding Islam,[2] and an Islamic ethnomusicology (analogous to the idea of an Islamic anthropology) has followed. But is there such a thing as 'Islamic music'? Do specifically 'Islamic' principles underpin music played by Muslims? In the most general terms, is an understanding of Islam a necessary precondition for understanding the cultural worlds that Muslims actually inhabit?

The moment one begins to consider the range of music that might, at a stretch, be classified as 'Islamic', from black nationalist rap to Javanese gamelan, the weakness of the idea readily becomes apparent. But the idea of a monolithic 'Music of the Muslim World', embedded in the wider history of Orientalist scholarship, continues to carry a great deal of weight. The central arguments of Said's *Orientalism* (1978) are now well known. For Said, eighteenth- and nineteenth-century European scholarship fashioned a unitary Orient dominated by a timeless and deeply irrational Islam as a means of highlighting Western Europe's cultural distinction and portraying colonialism as a benign historical inevitability. Islam was the central figure in Orientalist scholarship; in its purest and most essential terms, it was to be understood, by experts, through historical texts, and philology. Orientalism portrayed Islam as the principal motor force in Middle Eastern history, acting on an inert social formation, consisting characteristically of tyrannical Sunni regimes, rebellious tribesmen and unruly Shi'ite urban masses; it led to stagnation, decline or, as Gellner (1981) proposes, an ahistorical, pendular swing between structurally opposed sociological principles. The force of Orientalist discourse was such that the colonized were obliged to draw on these colonial representations to substantiate their own existence. Post-colonial politics, whether Islamist or nationalist, were condemned to a continual replay of a game that had been decisively and brutally rigged approximately two centuries ago. 'Our' continued efforts to understand 'them' were not exempt.

Said's *Orientalism* appeared whilst I was at school, preparing for an undergraduate degree in music at Oxford as an organ scholar, and an eventual career in the service of the Anglican church. I began to read it a year after I graduated in 1984, and had begun to study social anthropology at Oxford with a view to doing research on music in Turkey. I struggled with it briefly, and then gave up. The book, a now battered Penguin paperback, sat on my shelf in the meantime, leaving me feeling guilty and depressed. In retrospect, it is not difficult to see why; whilst I was aware that the book cut to the heart of my own apprehension of the Muslim Middle East, it did not provide me with any practical sense of how the tendrils of Orientalist thought operated in relation to my own peculiar institutional academic upbringing. It seemed to suggest that even if I was to attain this sense of Olympian self-awareness, there was ultimately no escape from the claustrophobic circuitry of the Western European episteme. 'Our' knowledge of 'others' was condemned to repeat the same old story of 'our' cultural distinctiveness, but at the same time I felt it provided no clue as to how (like Said himself) one could rise above the fray.[3]

My initial research plans were framed in terms of a general interest in Islam, and its primary terms of reference were Orientalist. They were deeply entrenched in my own academic background, but also in accidents of personal and family history. High Church Anglicanism and Orientalism were inextricably and coincidentally connected; my musical training began at a small choir school in Herefordshire. Its founder, Sir Frederick Ouseley, was a Tractarian cleric, later the first Professor of Music at Oxford. His father was the first British Ambassador to Persia and a noted Orientalist. The library in which we met for daily choir practices was not only a major repository of early Tudor manuscripts, but was also packed full of Ottoman, Syriac, Persian and Arabic texts; my eyes wandered over the Arabic script on their spines and covers in idle and inattentive moments, of which there were many. It is, in retrospect, not surprising that I should have chosen to defy the world of church music in terms that were already, as it were, institutionally provided. My first unofficial steps away from western musicology took place in Oxford's Oriental Institute, where I took classes in modern Turkish language and literature to escape (what I regarded as) the claustrophobic drudgery of exercises in counterpoint, fugue and Lieder in the Music Faculty, and Victorian psalm chants, hymns, anthems and organ voluntaries in the college chapel. The Oriental Institute operated with a view of Middle Eastern culture to which I was already highly predisposed: texts and language (ultimately the Qur'an and Qur'anic Arabic) were central, history was somewhat peripheral, and sociology and social history were acknowledged, but, simply, done elsewhere.

In many ways, the Oriental Institute enabled me to transfer to new surroundings, more or less intact, an idea of culture that I had formed as a musicologist and church musician. Nineteenth-century Austro-German musicology provided the foundations of the academic musicology in which I had been brought up. Its guiding principles were Hegelian and transcendental, elevating a particular local musical culture (that of eighteenth- and nineteenth-century Vienna) to the status of a universal and autonomous aesthetic code. This musicology worked around a canon of exemplary works and composers, whose core axis stretched from Haydn and Mozart to Brahms and Wagner. Its secular and modernist version stressed the continuities between Wagner and Schoenberg and his post-war disciples; this was the guiding ethos of those whose musical skills, in Britain, took them via the music conservatory to a world of professional and largely secular instrumental music-making. Church musicians such as myself, destined for an Oxbridge organ or choral scholarship and then a cathedral posting, inherited a canon that worked backwards via Bach to the Renaissance; Palestrina constituted the guiding light, and the Tudor composers a vibrant local variant. Like all canons, this was supported by forms of historical research that ultimately denied its history; these composers simply stood outside time, and the particularities of the societies in which they were rooted. Their transcendent aesthetic qualities were to be studied and imitated textually, and the task of a positivistic musicology was to make the texts available in their purest and most original form.[4] Orientalism's textual Orient easily slid into a space vacated by the Anglican canon. Although I believed I was heading off in a radically new direction (and as far as parents and friends were concerned, I was already well off the map), nothing had really changed.

Social anthropology began to provide me with the intellectual means and the institutional base from which I could challenge the twin canons of Orientalism and Anglican music, which were so tightly intertwined in my own experience. But Said's *Orientalism* was peripheral to the dominant concerns of Oxford anthropology in 1985, in which I was immersed in a one-year Diploma course. Evans-Pritchard's *Witchcraft, Oracles and Magic Among the Azande* (1937) provided the cornerstone; questions of logic, rationality and interpretation the dominant slant on a self-conscious structuralist tradition. Citations of Wittgenstein's *Philosophical Investigations* (1953) were *de rigeur*. The canonical texts were Africanist, although the Amazon, South East Asia, the British Isles (particularly the Celtic Fringe) and the Mediterranean were well represented. I was familiar with Davis's critique of the early Oxford Mediterraneanist paradigm (Davis 1977); I was aware that Mediterranean societies had been overdetermined in terms of the honour and shame complex and an exclusive focus on remote and small village societies, but not really sure of what the consequences of this should be. The Middle East was conspicuous by its absence, as was political-economy; the ways in which colonialism impinged upon and constructed the objects of anthropological research figured as a somewhat peripheral issue (which I encountered mainly through Talal Asad's work in the context of a regional course on the Nile Basin). Though a year's anthropology initiated a process of thinking of a worldly, material 'culture', as opposed to the transcendental 'Culture' of high ideas, and the certainties of my earlier interests began to crumble as a consequence, the concerns represented by Said's *Orientalism* were still remote, to say the least.

Finally, *Orientalism* seemed distant from my particular experience of Turkey. This dated back to my pre-university break, most of which I spent as an organ student in preparation for the coming year. Turkey was, in 1981, attractive and sufficiently exotic (having just suffered a military coup). It could be reached after a gruelling but relatively inexpensive rail journey, and, once there, life was cheap. The idea of a backward although aesthetically pleasing Islam giving way to the forces of western modernity fascinated me: a place that contained both, I felt, would show both in their truest, starkest and most dramatic colour. I devoured the neo-Orientalist academic and travel literature in which Turkey was represented less as a place than a set of movements: from East to West, from Islam to Modernity, and from Rural to Urban. This was clearly seen as one-way, albeit slowly moving, traffic, which consequently required the paternalistic hand of an avant-gardist bureaucracy, and the tolerant encouragement of the western democracies. Before I had spent much time there, I had little reason to doubt this picture. Turkey seemed to be the perfect place to study a decaying, but splendid, Islam, and its music provided compelling evidence of some aspect of the Oriental Psyche that had not yet given in to the forces of western modernity.

It was not, in fact, Said, but other authors who undermined this grand Orientalist project. Gilsenan's *Recognizing Islam* (1983) had an incalculable impact, as did his arrival in the Oxford's Middle East Centre during my Diploma year. Where Said seemed to suggest that there was no escape from the Orientalist episteme, and provided no real clues about how one could attain his own particular Olympian vision, Gilsenan described a more variegated, nuanced and open-ended world. Here, western mercantile and military power framed the basic conditions of people's daily lives, but these were lives that responded in complex and creative ways to historical circumstances over which they had little or no direct control. Gilsenan's book described the fabric of urban and small town life with attention to details (decor, ways of walking) that I could relate to my own experience of urban Turkey. It described awkward and intense encounters, in which the observer was a crucial player, and which were often mundane, but full of drama and humour, liable to sudden table-turning, and reversals of fortune; far from the worlds of consensual moral imperatives that I had encountered in the Mediterraneanist literature. It was also a book that seemed to describe a personal struggle with the Orientalist canon, and propose a concrete alternative; something, that is to say, that an anthropologist could actually do. More importantly, it introduced me to work that had been tacitly but quite decisively excluded from the Diploma course at the time, notably that of Weber, Bourdieu, Geertz, and a rich and interdisciplinary literature on the Middle East, which discussed a world shaped not by a timeless Islam, but by nation-states, industrialization and urbanization, colonialism and a global political economy. Matters of culture did not admittedly receive much attention in much of this literature,[5] but where Islam figured, it did so with attention to localized configurations of power and historical circumstance; it suggested islams in place of Islam, and histories in place of a metaphysical History of decline.

If *Recognizing Islam* impelled me towards some kind of critical self-awareness, my dealings with the Turkish government threw them into a sharper perspective. When I applied for a Turkish government grant to study Turkish at Istanbul University's summer school, I was swiftly turned down after the briefest of interviews with the Turkish Cultural Attaché in London. This was a devastating blow. My application indicated my intention to learn the language in order to be able to study 'Islamic' musical practice, and what was happening to it in the secular republic. This was my first, and by no means my last, experience of an official knee-jerk reaction to my no doubt half-baked, but genuinely innocent research proposals. But it sowed a crucial seed of doubt in my own mind: the bureaucratic structures that represented the Turkish state's supposedly inexorable march to 'the West' seemed anxious and defensive, somehow nonplussed by the puzzling persistence of an internal Orient. I began to sense that the West–East binarisms underpinning both the Orientalist and the bureaucratic conception of Turkish society had a prescriptive rather than descriptive function. The apparatus of 'western' bureaucratic order in Turkey (with all that this implied in terms of Enlightenment transparency) began to take on a localized, obscure and somewhat authoritarian cast, and I began to see that the rhetoric of 'Islamic reaction' mobilized by the bureaucracy was a useful means of controlling a rather more complex and turbulent civil domain, fractured along class and ethnic lines. This response forced me to confront the fictions that lay at the heart of official Turkish political culture, and some of the uncomfortable implications of my own participation in them.

Finally, a slow, and very partial introduction to ethnomusicological work on the Middle East in my last year of undergraduate and first year of postgraduate studies began to make me consider localized musical worlds according to their own cultural and historical dynamics. As a consequence, I began to develop suspicions about the use of music to substantiate grand historical or philosophical schemes if they did not take into account the ways in which local musicians and audiences themselves understood their own music. The arrogant suppositions of neo-Orientalist scholarship became particularly clear to me in Bernard Lewis's (1968) study of modern Turkey precisely as a result of his pronouncements on the subject of music. Lewis's book is effectively an endorsement of westernizing bureaucratic reformism in Ottoman and modern Turkey. Attentive to the historical and cultural dead weight that the reformers have to contend with, Lewis candidly sets out the areas in which he feels Turkey has a real opportunity to become 'truly European', and the areas in which the reformers have got something of a job on their hands in shedding their 'Islamic' past. He confidently turns to the subject of music. Having earlier declared that the casual visitor could not help noticing 'the Balkan, almost European tonalities of Turkish music of the kind called popular, as against the "classical" music in the Perso-Arabic manner' (Lewis 1968: 4), he later claims that the Turkish intelligentsia have always had a problem with western music, 'for music, like science, is part of the inner citadel of Western Culture, one of the final secrets to which the aspiring newcomer must penetrate' (Lewis 1968: 441).

This one sentence irritated me beyond measure, and more or less instantaneously constructed a research project that occupied me for over ten years. I could see no reason why an 'almost European' Turkish popular music, which I had experienced and developed something of an affection for, should be dismissed in such a peremptory fashion, despite being evoked earlier in such privileged terms. I could not understand why 'Oriental' Turkish musics should have been good enough for the likes of Béla Bartók (a deity in my own 'inner citadel'), but not for Lewis. I could not understand why the Turks constitute 'aspiring newcomers' to Western civilization, given that the book indicates that many have been 'aspiring' for centuries, and that a great many more among their number seemed less than happy with this role. Was it in fact the case, as endlessly and tediously argued by some Orientalists, that Turkish high culture was nothing more than a poor imitation of something inspired elsewhere? And I could not understand why aspiring to 'penetrate a citadel' that, personally, I badly wanted to get out of should constitute the be all and end all of Turkish historical experience. The musicians whom I had already got to know seemed to me to have a much more interesting, more messy and less conclusive story to tell about Turkish modernity; there was just too much music going on to be shoehorned into a simplistic and arrogant analysis of the shortcomings of 'Oriental civilization' and the undoubted benefits of our own.

My personal experience of seeing the world through music has thus been a contradictory affair. On the one hand, I was drawn to the idea of studying music in the Middle East as a result of my connections with a number of Orientalist institutions; as I have explained, this did little initially to shake the basic tenets and unspoken assumptions of nineteenth-century musicology, with which I had been brought up. On the other hand, the process of absorbing anthropological lessons about culture introduced a new dynamic, opposed to grand history (especially where that was primarily concerned with illuminating Europe's distinctiveness), experiential and empirical, committed to letting others speak and to destabilizing metropolitan theoretical discourse. Owing to the lack of ethnomusicological resources at Oxford, I did not begin to read the regional ethnomusicological literature systematically until I arrived at the Queen's University of Belfast. By this time, I believe, the last vestiges of my original project had been swept away. Islam had figured heavily in my final dissertation,[6] but as a rhetorical trope mobilized by a state that habitually constructed the civil domain as 'Islamic' and was accustomed to interpreting practices that were deemed unacceptable (or worth co-opting) in these terms. I could no longer take the idea of 'secular' state versus 'Islamic' civil society at face value. The ethnomusicological literature on the Middle East has borne out this view in a variety of ways, many useful, and others less so. The remainder of this chapter presents (an inevitably partial) review.

Orientalism and musicology

Orientalism as an intellectual technique was thoroughly concerned with the written word, and early musicological forays into the musics of the Middle East were indeed concerned first and foremost with the translation of Arabic texts, most notably in the work of Kiesewetter, Fonton, D'Erlanger, Rouanet, Chottin and Farmer.[7] Observations on practical music-making by non-specialist observers tended to stress exotic aspects of performance; evidence of barbarism for some, and an erotic, picturesque otherness for others.[8] The Enlightenment was obsessed with documentation (to be seen in Villoteau's superb 1809 lithographs of the instruments he studied in the course of Napoleon's Egyptian expedition), but its apparent clarity of vision obscured deeper contradictions concerning the nature of the Orient, manifestations of which can be identified from the early seventeenth century through to today. On the one hand, the musical practices of Europe's others could provide a source of cultural renewal, often expressed in terms of a quest for the lost art of the Ancient Greeks or the Old Testament,[9] whilst, on the other hand, they provided evidence for decline, a squandered patrimony, requiring resuscitation and a return to the original sources.[10]

The work of Owen Wright, Walter Feldman, George Sawa, Amnon Shiloah, Josef Pacholzyck[11] and others may usefully be considered as a continuation of the scholarly traditions of Kiesewetter, Chottin, D'Erlanger, Rouanet and Farmer, in which Orientalist philology and the textual positivism of nineteenth-century academic musicology converge. The critiques initiated by Said of the textualist traditions of Orientalist philology are well known: it monumentalizes a unitary canon of dead scripts to the exclusion of living and varied oral cultures; it flattens out history except to represent the passage of time as one of decline; and it has invented specialist intellectual techniques concerned exclusively with etymologies and origins, as though original meanings define all subsequent usage, and as though all culture is, at root, verbal.

Can this critique be usefully applied to the work of Wright and others? Some aspects of it certainly can. All apply philological methods to the study of texts. These writers do not venture far into more recent history, and contemporary observations of practical music-making tend to generalize about music from the Maghreb to Central Asia, juxtaposing indigenous and travellers' commentaries, widely separated in place and time (note, for example, the final chapters of Shiloah 1995); words and their etymologies characteristically anchor the argument. Whilst many of these authors have substantial first-hand experience of Middle Eastern music, this is very rarely represented in their published work. One struggles to get a sense of living, breathing musical worlds.

The work of Owen Wright dominates this field, and throws its characteristic preoccupations and techniques into a sharp light. His early work provided detailed analyses of the modal theory of the philosophers of the Ummayad and Abbasid courts, notably that of al-Kindi (d. *c.* 873), al-Farabi (d. 950), Ibn Sina (d. 1037) and Safi al-Din al-Urmawi (d. 1294). His more recent work has examined manuscripts associated with the Ottoman classical tradition, focusing in particular on early Ottoman song collections and instrumental notations from the mid-sixteenth to the early seventeenth century. Speculation is kept on a tight rein, and restricted to what can be inferred from other musicological texts. Wright documents, for example, a rupture between the cosmopolitan musical world represented by sixteenth-century Ottoman texts (which refer to musicians and repertoire items of wide geographic dispersal) and the more self-contained musical-theoretical world represented by Ottoman texts from the mid-seventeenth century, without permitting himself to pursue the question as to why this should have happened. Much of this bears out al-Azmeh's dictum of Orientalism as 'the seizure of the Real without the intervention of Passion' (al-Azmeh 1993: 135). But if Orientalist scholarship is to be taken, *in toto*, as constructing a monolithic 'East', knowable through the antiseptic practices of textual scholarship, and evoking in the process a world that is essentially timeless and ultimately definable in terms of the dead weight of Islam, the work of Wright, Sawa, Feldman and Shiloah cannot be dismissed simply in these terms.

Wright's earlier work on the Systematist philosophers of the Abbasid and Ummayad courts is thoroughly critical of the more sweeping forms of Orientalist generalization concerning 'the Arab contribution to Western culture'. Does this body of theory represent intellectual stagnation and decline, typically associated with Islamic culture in Orientalist writings? Wright (1974: 491) sees the Systematist texts as possessing 'considerable originality and critical acumen'. In the best empirical tradition, Wright (1974: 491) stresses, 'definitions are tested, and often found wanting'. He emphasizes the commerce in musical practices, technologies and ideas between the medieval Muslim and Christian worlds, evidenced particularly by the names of musical instruments and musical genres. If Arab musical theory was not so consequential, this should not, he argues, be attributed to its lack of intellectual vitality, but rather to the fact that it was concerned with radically different musical principles (concerning the 'horizontal' elaboration of modes, rather than their simultaneous and 'vertical' combination, as in the early modern West). And if Orientalist scholarship portrays Islamic history as a kind of global crawler lane, either stagnant, or moving at glacial pace, Wright's work has contributed to exactly the opposite picture. The developments in musical theory and practice that he documents in his studies of the early Ottoman texts suggest a lively intellectual environment in which each generation of court musicians participated in dramatic theoretical and practical innovations, which were no different in magnitude and wider cultural significance to those experienced by their Renaissance Italian contemporaries.

Finally, and perhaps most significantly, Wright's early work demonstrates conclusively just how difficult it is to talk about 'Islamic music'; early medieval Arab theory was an inventive effort to reconcile Pythagorean theory with a variety of indigenous practices, which were themselves being radically transformed by innovations coming from the Persian and, later, Byzantine world. Texts, it would seem, lead one inexorably to a highly cosmopolitan view of Middle Eastern music history, and one that can hardly be reduced to a monolithic and static Islam; this fact is substantiated most notably in Shiloah's work on the traffic in ideas and techniques between Jewish and Muslim scholars in the supposedly 'Muslim' musical tradition of the Middle East. This form of scholarship typifies many of the methodological problems of Orientalist scholarship mentioned earlier, but it has contributed significantly to an understanding of 'the actual course, outcome, institutions and processes of Islamic history and culture' (al-Azmeh 1993: 137). Bitter critics of Orientalism, such as al-Azmeh, claim that this kind of scholarship will inevitably fail to reveal the historical and cultural processes at work, and this charge, surely, cannot be sustained.

Orientalism persists in much more negative and pernicious forms elsewhere. Rock music and the recent fashion for 'world music' provide ample evidence for the continued power of media constructions of a unitary and Islamic 'East', under the deceptive aegis of musical multiculturalism. The music of the Muslim world does not have the appeal of that of Africa, Australia or Latin America for western rock listeners, and is conspicuous mainly by its absence. One could argue that the exceptions, notably Qawwali and Algerian Rai, prove the rule, appealing to western listeners precisely because they are considered heterodox and oppositional.[12] Middle Eastern musics do however have some cachet as a signifier of rock seriousness. Brian Eno and David Byrne's 1981 *My Life in the Bush of Ghosts*, an early venture in the use of sampling, uses recordings of popular Lebanese and Egyptian singers and Algerian Qur'anic recitation as figures in an austere and experimental rock landscape, which they share with recordings of Christian fundamentalist ministers and American politicians. Beyond signifying a dark totalitarianism, these 'Islamic' samples also have an erotic function in the semiotic universe of experimental rock and pop. Samples of anything vaguely Middle Eastern, ranging from the highly secular, westernized Lebanese singer Fairuz (in Madonna's *Erotica*) to the call to prayer (by bands such as Rip, Rig and Panic and Enigma), are juxtaposed with puffing, panting and orgasmic sighs signifying an Islamic world characterized by a repressed but all-consuming sexuality in which 'wailing' is simultaneously its sign and its stigma. It is not difficult to illustrate the ways in which a supposedly multicultural project perpetuates an enduring stereotype of a monolithic Islam. As Ashwani Sharma (1996) puts it, in a volume assessing the radical possibilities of contemporary Asian dance music genres in Britain, the process of reduction to aesthetic form can only take place if one ignores the 'crucial religious and socio-critical elements of the music'. The simultaneous 'elevation and erasure' of Qawwali musicians such as Nusrat Fateh Ali Khan by the recording industry (as in, for example, Real World's 1990 recording of *Mustt Mustt*) and the film industry (a Qawwali track was used, for example, on the 1994 Oliver Stone film *Natural Born Killers*) says much about the new forms of ordering and control that have been accompanied by a distinct rhetoric of hybridity and liberal multiculturalism in conditions of global commodity production (Sharma 1996: 29).[13]

Scholarship, as always, is implicated. The American folklorist and ethnomusicologist Alan Lomax, set out to establish the study of world music and dance forms on a scientific basis in the late 1950s. His cantometrics project used computers to correlate ethnographic information concerning some 233 cultures (characterized by information taken mainly from Murdock's 1962–7 *Ethnographic Atlas*) with detailed and systematic profiles of song and dance styles, covering what he considered to be some thirty-seven objective, cross-cultural parameters. The results were published in *Folksong Style and Culture* in 1968, and the project continues today. Sharing much of the language of contemporary multiculturalism, the project was benign, humanitarian and liberal in conception: musical cultures were all to be given a place on an equal footing and revealed in their glorious diversity. However, major value judgements underpin the entire project, which emerge, unsurprisingly, as conclusions backed up by endless graphs and information technology jargon. The 'Orient' (comprising Mediterranean Europe, the Middle East, North Africa, the Near East, the Sahara, village India, tribal

South East Asia, Malaysia, urban Indonesia, urban South East Asia, East Asia and Central Asia) emerges as a kind of foil to the sub-Saharan African societies, which Lomax views in glowing terms. Within the 'Orient', the Middle East is represented as a domain of particularly high 'complexity', low 'groupiness' and authoritarianism, in which the control of sexuality and restrictions on the movement of women emerge as the defining features. This is manifested in distinct musical features: a prevalence of solo singing, textual complexity, an attention to enunciation, metrical and melodic complexity, with narrow intervals and attention paid to embellishment and vocal 'rasp'. Islam, or the historical presence of Muslim culture (in Spain and southern Italy), is finally invoked (or, rather, evoked) as explanation: 'We hear, in the wail of the muezzin, appealing for mercy from Allah, and in the piercing silver tones of the cafe singers, a restatement of … pain, fear and erotic hysteria' (1968: 197). In various ways, a variety of popular cultural texts represent Middle Eastern musical style as both the sign and the very practice of a sado-masochistic sexual politics in which pain, fear and erotic hysteria become the source of aesthetic pleasure; the ultimate explanation, a repressive Islam. If contemporary textual scholarship actually undermines the Orientalism thesis (see Lindholm, Chapter 7, this volume), another domain of popular representational practice confirms it. The entanglement of ethnomusicology with these practices is worth considering, particularly when it connects, however tangentially, with an Afrocentrism at work in the popular cultural avant-garde.[14]

An Islamic musicology?

The idea that Islam is hostile to music circulates alongside other well-known but misleading commonplaces (including Islamic hostility to visual representation). The legal situation is complex. The Greek term for music was not known in seventh-century Arabia, making an appearance in theoretical texts some two centuries later. The indigenous term for sung poetry, *ghina*, does not figure heavily in the Qur'an itself, and was clearly not a matter of overriding moral concern for the Prophet. But the later hadithic literature, particularly associated with the scholarly 'chains' of al-Muslim and al-Buhari, is more explicit on the matter. In keeping with the Aristotelian, as opposed to Platonic, bent of early Islamic thinking, Muslim scholarship was, and to a certain extent remains, concerned with a careful analysis of its observable social and psychic effects.[15] The Platonic cosmology that dominated early medieval Christian theology, in which the Music of the Spheres plays a central symbolic role, is quite absent in the dominant Muslim scholarly tradition during this period. Qur'anic evidence revolves around a small number of often cited verses discussing errant poets (26:224–6), the sound of an ass (31:19), idle pastimes (31:6), the whistling and clapping of idolaters (8:35) and the voice of Satan (53:59–61 and 17:64).

It is debatable, to say the least, whether these verses can be held to refer to music in any meaningful way, and since Qur'anic evidence is inconclusive, the major schools of jurisprudence have no firm means of categorizing music either as obligatory according to the Qur'an (*farz*) or the hadith (*sünnet*), or as canonically forbidden (*haram*). Debate revolving around the later hadithic literature provides more explicit material, notably concerning the Prophet's disapproval of the selling of musical slave girls and attendance at weddings at which music was being played. In both cases, other material can be found mitigating some of the Prophet's harsher pronouncements, and, according to the weight attributed to these, Muslim scholars are able to consider music 'permissible' (*mubah*) or, more commonly, as 'disagreeable', whilst not specifically forbidden (*mekruh*). According to this, as has been extensively documented (see al-Faruqi 1987; Nelson 1982; Wegner 1986), all forms of public recitation of an unambiguously legitimate nature, including the call to prayer (*ezan*), the recitation of the Qur'an (*kiraat*), hymns for battle (*medh*), the ecstatic 'remembrance' of the names of God (*zikr*) and the performance of other legitimate sacred narratives (notably the *Mevlid*, a narrative on the birth of the Prophet), are terminologically distinguished in ways that minimize any possible overlap with the entirely profane notion of '*musiqi*'.

Many groups in the Middle East have, however, often put ecstatic music and dance at the centre of their communal lives. Those (usually urban) communities that have enjoyed close relations with the dominant political power have devoted substantial scholarly resources to challenging the pervasive (although, as we have seen, far from conclusive) Qur'anic and hadithic commentary. Textual evidence and the authenticated example of spiritual forebears predominate. This literature puts a negative case, refuting critics with arguments based on the lack of firm Qur'anic evidence, the ambiguity of the hadithic literature, and the fact that 'Islamic' objections to music are more usefully considered as matters of local culture in Islamic dress. A more positive case for the legitimacy of music draws on the authority of early classical Islamic thinkers (notably Majd al-Din al-Ghazali) and on the hagiographic traditions of mystics such as Jalaleddin Rumi and Haci Bektas Veli. All of these elaborate in some form al-Ghazali's concept of *sema*,[16] divine 'audition', nuanced by local intellectual and ritual traditions. *Sema* involves the act of perceiving the unity that transcends the dualism of God's Creation, in which we are separated from and normally incapable of perceiving Him. As all of these (from a later and Sunni perspective) 'heterodox' traditions stress, this is a task that can only be accomplished in a carefully controlled ritual situation. The Balkan and Turkish Bektasi-Alevi have the opportunity of completely ignoring the hadithic literature, but the central arguments are substantially similar, characteristically authenticated by communal tradition and fundamental truths of the 'heart' (see Birge 1937).

To a certain extent this literature draws on what might be called indigenous scholarly traditions. To take a specific instance, contemporary Mevlevi writers in Turkey such as Suleyman Uludağ argue from Qur'anic and hadithic texts and saintly examples; the manner of writing owes much to the Ottoman historical tradition of marginal commentary (*şerh*), most of Uludağ's *Islam Acisindan Muriki ve Sema* (1976), for example, consequently consists of footnotes. However, heterodox groups such as the Alevi, who have not enjoyed such a privileged relationship with the dominant powers in later Ottoman or modern Turkey, often adopt a more modern and highly secular language of legitimation, in which Alevi practice is represented as 'folklore', or, in contemporary Turkey's more liberal ideological climate, as an indigenous politics of resistance (for a general discussion, see Stokes 1996). The *sema* polemic works through a large variety of academic styles and languages; despite many points of convergence, it can hardly be taken to represent an indigenous 'Islamic musicology'.

Non-mainstream[17] Sunni Islamic ritual has attracted a great deal of attention from non-Muslim western observers; this attention has also had its effect on indigenous representation. Islamic ecstatic dance and music has long been of great appeal to European travellers in search of the exotic: the Mevlevi ceremony in Galata in Istanbul was for centuries an unmissable item on the western traveller's itinerary. Key texts were translated as part of a wider and rather monolithic interest categorized as 'Sufi' (the term is not, for example, much used or known in Turkey).[18] Other manifestations of non-mainstream Sunni practice and belief attracted the interest of colonial ethnographers (on which Rouget largely relies for his account of music and trance in the Arab world), novelists (such as John Buchan) and travel writers alike.

The musical legacy of Sufi brotherhoods remains an object of interest to ethnomusicologists in view of the somewhat ambiguous opposition of many modernizing states in the Middle East. With their suppression or co-option by state modernizers, institutions that had played vital roles in the transmission of major repertories disappeared more or less overnight (on the Sufi lodges in Tunisia, see Davis 1996), or found themselves driven underground or absorbed by the state and serving quite different purposes (on the Alevi in Turkey, see Markoff 1986). European scholarly methods, texts, translations, to say nothing of the long-standing presence of European observers as tourists or otherwise, all have had a distinct impact on the ways in which non-Sunni groups have written about their own musical practices, making it hard to consider these representations of music as an 'Islamic musicology'; these can be better characterized as a variety of Islamist arguments for the validity of music, sharing a great deal of discursive ground, but reflecting quite localized and specific concerns, articulated with an eye on outside observers associated with the colonial powers or the state.

The idea of an Islamic musicology has, however, been specifically promoted by the American ethnomusicologist Lois Ibsen al-Faruqi. A number of articles reproduce the more generalized *sema* polemic outlined above, discussing the limitations of the Qur'anic material as a means of coming to a sound judgement on the matter, the ambiguous hadithic evidence, and the opinion of recognized contemporary legal authorities, such as the Sheikh al-Saltut at Cairo's al-Azhar (al-Faruqi 1980, 1985). Her conclusions conform in most respects to those of many Middle Eastern authors on the subject: music is permissible as long as it is controlled, and as long as distinctions are made (expressed by al-Faruqi as a hierarchy) between what is acceptable and what is not. Al-Faruqi goes much further, however, in setting out in programmatic form an Islamic ethnomusicology. This outlines the ways in which the predominant cultural and aesthetic concerns of Islamic civilization, stretching from Spain to the Philippines, and incorporating the lives of some 700 million people (whether they are Muslims or not), determine the underlying principles of musical expression (see in particular al-Faruqi 1975, 1983, 1984). In accordance with the transcendentalist philosophy of a revealed and perfect Islam, al-Faruqi allows for no historical movement or cultural variation. Islam thus exerts a consistent and determinable force on musical production; Islam is the ultimate explanation for 'Islamic music', as, indeed, it must be for everything else.

The principal aesthetic disposition derives from the notion of unity and transcendence (*tawhid*); the consequences of this, al-Faruqi argues, are evident in all, but particularly the visual, Islamic arts. The musical form of the *muwashshah* (a musico-poetic form specifically associated with classical North African Islam, but widely distributed around the Middle East) is cited in an early article (al-Faruqi 1975) as an exemplary Islamic form. Analysis reveals a number of structural techniques, including a lack of development (along the 'organic'/climactic lines of nineteenth-century romantic symphonicism) and consequently an emphasis on repetition and the accumulation of 'divisions' in a manner devoid of narrative or representative *telos* (that is to say, the music and poetry does not, and cannot, represent a particular story, a particular psychic or emotional state, and so forth). These in turn are taken to reveal a principle of abstraction analogous to the arabesques of Middle Eastern art, or the self-sufficient episodes in the *One Thousand and One Nights* and Hariri's *Maqamat*, always structurally incomplete, and hence alluding to the greater completion and perfection of God himself.

The ironies that al-Azmeh (1993) identifies in his scathing critiques of Islamist thinking are to be found in abundance in al-Faruqi's work. The attempt to outline the content of an authentically Islamic culture draws heavily on Orientalist intellectual techniques. Orientalists portrayed an Islam that was historically inert. Al-Faruqi defines an Islamic musical culture that is devoid of any historical dynamism or regional variation, despite the fact that *muwashshahat* in contemporary Syria are in structure and performance style part of a very different expressive domain from those currently performed in the North African classical genre, which are largely under state tutelage in Morocco, Algeria and Tunisia.[19] Fairuz turned her back on westernized popular music and embraced the *muwashshahat* repertory (in a heavily orchestrated and arranged manner) as part of her own intervention into the Arab nationalist radicalism of pre-civil war Lebanon. In other words, many different regional histories are at work here that cannot be subsumed by a more generally 'Islamic' principle. Orientalists, just like al-Faruqi, portray an involuted and hermetic Islamic culture. To illustrate this thesis, al-Faruqi chooses the one form whose origins were particularly clearly shaped by a lively and dynamic flow of ideas between Christian, Muslim and Jew in medieval Spain and North Africa.

Finally, the very intellectual techniques that al-Faruqi presses into service in the construction of an authentically 'Islamic' musical culture are themselves the product of Orientalist scholarship. Etymology and the quest for linguistically defined origins predominate, and the structuralist fashions of the mid-1970s social sciences are easily accommodated. Every word of analytical significance is broken down into its Arabic trilateral root, and its meanings are carefully analysed, as though, for example, a Turkish speaker using the word '*misra*' to mean a line of poetry would have any knowledge of (or, probably, interest in) the fact that the word means 'one side of the symmetrical door-flaps of the Arab tent'. As with the Islamist thinking of the nineteenth century, in which al-Azmeh determines the guiding principles of Darwin and Comte, filtered through Arabic/Islamic terminology, the work of al-Faruqi is at root a version of high structuralism common in American ethnomusicology at the time, in which analysis defines underlying structural principles according to a model that is essentially linguistic, whose surface manifestations are traced in a variety of expressive domains (see, for example, Keil's 1979 *Tiv Song*).

It is difficult, in conclusion, to argue that an understanding of music in the Muslim world is served to any useful extent by an 'Islamic ethnomusicology'. The idea that there is such a thing, however, constitutes a social fact that itself cannot be ignored. Moreover, Al-Faruqi's work is widely translated into Middle Eastern languages. I picked up a Turkish translation of her 1985 article in Konya, the home of the Mevlevi order, where, according to the bookshop owner, the book was selling well. Print, and now the web,[20] has done a great deal to construct a transnational Islamist imaginary, and the circulation of the work of progressive western Islamists such as al-Faruqi is clearly an important aspect of this process. This kind of circulation endows the ideas expressed in al-Faruqi's work with a great deal of power, linked, as they are with the author's involvement in the Palestinian struggle and the tragic circumstances of her violent death. But the ideas expressed do little to explain their own conditions of existence, and little to explain the objects that they construct as exemplary items in the repertory of a supposedly 'Islamic' musical culture.

Middle East studies and the anthropology of music

The Middle East has not, perhaps, been a particularly fashionable area for ethnomusicological research. Africa and North India figured heavily in the canonical British ethnomusicological literature, Indonesia for the Dutch, and North American Indians for North Americans. Orientalist scholarship in Britain and France dealt with the Middle East in an antiquarian and textual manner; for the reasons discussed above, this has always been marginal in academic ethnomusicological circles. Academic ethnomusicology received a strong institutional footing in American universities in the 1960s and 1970s; allied with Boasian anthropology (in which fieldwork was a central item of faith), and opposed to folklore and 'armchair' Orientalism, ethnomusicologists built on the canonical literature, and followed the wider geographical movements and theoretical concerns of cultural anthropologists. With the exceptions of Morocco, Iran, Turkey and Afghanistan, Middle Eastern states were not at this time particularly conducive to prolonged fieldwork. The work of Philip Schuyler, Bruno Nettl, Karl Signell and John Baily (in these respective areas) provided me with my first points of reference in the study of contemporary Middle Eastern musics, the work of Ali Jihad Racy, Habib Hassan Touma and Salwa El-Shawan,[21] all, in some sense, 'indigenous' ethnomusicologists, provided virtually the only

English-language accounts of the Arab world available in mainstream ethnomusicological publications when I began my doctoral research. Nettl at Indiana, Racy at UCLA and Schuyler and Signell at Baltimore began to assemble students interested in contemporary Middle Eastern musics, whose work drew heavily on anthropology and the regional studies literature, and whose major work has only relatively recently begun to appear in print.

Islam does not figure particularly heavily in this literature, but there are clear reasons for this. Ethnomusicologists in the Middle East live in a distinctly secular world. The large bulk of the ethnomusicological literature on the Middle East deals with the construction of unitary national cultures by secular states, the parallel effects of urbanization and industrialization, and the processes of theorizing and systematizing oral or improvised (modal) instrumental practices (see Baily 1981, 1994; Baumann 1987; Blum 1978; Davis 1993; El-Shawan 1980, 1984; Farhat 1990; Levin 1981; Marcus 1989; Markoff 1990; Nettl 1978, 1992; Nettl and Riddle 1973; Racy 1978, 1988; Schuyler 1978, 1990; Signell 1977). More recently, the worlds of popular professional music-making that have flourished outside state control have been the object of considerable interest, putting aside a long and largely unspoken tradition of ignoring mass-mediated music. Islam figures in relation to other social, political and ideological issues, which one can break down into three more specific areas.

The first relates to music as a distinctly oppositional force in Muslim communities. The antagonism between indigenous lineage-based notions of community and a superordinate Islam figures heavily in the literature on Berber festivities in highland Morocco. Local Berber tribes meet for festivals in which communal solidarity is represented by large circular dances generically known as *ahwash*. Local clerical lineages see in these dances an assertion of a solidarity that is inimical to their own view of the wider Muslim community, and that challenges their own pretensions to spiritual and political pre-eminence; the *ahwash* are denigrated, and opposed by rival festivities employing professional Berber musicians (*rwayes*), who, for their part, have adopted a partially spiritual repertoire in deference to their new patrons (Schuyler 1985). The *ahwash* takes on a more defiantly anti-clerical cast, lineage-based local solidarities are emphasized, whilst the incursions of outsiders are considered as a breakdown of community mechanisms, and are strongly resisted (Lortat-Jacob 1994).

The strong representation of Berber music in the francophone literature on North Africa requires comment. French observers in North Africa were inclined to replicate a colonial ideology in which mainstream urban Islam was opposed to Berber tribal tradition, an ideology that was politically institutionalized in the colonial division of Morocco into the Maxen (under the sultan) and tribal domains. Berbers reaping the benefits of this situation had much to gain from stressing the local (and non-Islamic) dynamism of Berber cultural life. The ethnographic eye (and ear) entrenched colonial politics, as elsewhere, instituting a tradition of discussing Berber culture with only passing reference to Islam. The French ethnomusicological study of North Africa is well represented by exemplary recordings and analyses of Berber poetics (Rovsing-Olsen 1996) and community (see, for example, Lortat-Jacob 1994). For Lortat-Jacob, the

Berber example provides the first stage in an elegant and Durkheimian tripartite comparative model (also comprising Sardinia and Romania), in which communal solidarities are progressively broken down by the incursion of professional musicians. But the solidarity of the Berber collectivity is not as pristine as it might appear.

It is not only in North Africa that outside observers are inclined to absorb and replicate the politically dominant mode of representation. The secular state tradition in Turkey has put a variety of pressures on outside researchers to endorse its secular view of Turkish national culture: Turkish ideologues from the turn of the twentieth century opposed the culture of the Turkish folk (*halk*) to the Arabized and Islamic 'civilization' (*medeniyet*) of Turkish cities. Involvement with research bodies in Turkey has often demanded accommodation with this essentially ideological distinction. Laurence Picken's monumental study of *Folk Musical Instruments of Turkey* (1975) works with a rather uncritical application of it; rural culture is investigated to the near total exclusion of urban cultures, which, when they are discussed, are represented as points of cultural contact with the Islamic Middle East, and not Western Europe. For Picken, 'Turkish'/Asiatic principles of parallel fourth polyphony gradually give way to the influence of Arabo-Persian monophonic musical forms emanating from the cities. Whilst accounts of Middle Eastern music that do not stress Islam are valuable as a counterweight to the Orientalist idea that all Middle Eastern culture is to some extent 'Islamic', its exclusion from many accounts derives from the wider power of the colonial or secular state, which has defined some objects of research as significant (such as rural hinterlands), and others ('Islamic cities') as areas of dilution and corruption.

Second, ethnomusicologists have gravitated towards professional musicians. Professional musicians are either pariahs in the Middle East, or live lives of moral ambiguity. As a consequence, a large ethnomusicological literature, drawing on gender studies and the more general picture of strategizing introduced into Middle Eastern studies by Bourdieu's Algerian anthropology, has usefully stressed the ways in which professional musicians in the Muslim Middle East construct decent public personae, to compensate for their always potentially poor image in society at large. Professional dancing women in Egypt devote great efforts to constructing a respectable private persona, distinct from their public professional life (Lorius 1996; van Nieuwkerk 1995). Higher status professional performers in Egypt, the paradigmatic example being Umm Kulthum, have a complex job negotiating a public persona that is not only popular and engaging, but also culturally legitimate and sexually demure (Danielson 1997). Women professional musicians in other parts of the Middle East had to observe a number of extremely obtrusive restrictions on their public performances; whilst Umm Kulthum and others were acting in films and singing on stage in Cairo's entertainment districts, female musicians in Turkey and Iran performed to the public on stage, but from behind closed curtains. John Baily's and Veronica Doubleday's extensive work in western Afghanistan illustrates the efforts to which professional musicians go to protect their public reputation, carefully distinguishing the legitimate repertoire of the high-status professional from that of the low-status professional accompanying dancing boys, hashish parties, and so forth (see Baily 1988; Doubleday 1988). Women restrict themselves to 'non-musical' instruments (notably the *daireh* frame-drum and the voice);[22] male musicians assert their cultural distinction through knowledge of the classical Islamic '*ilm-i musiqi*' ('science of music'), although in practice this has more to do with the music-theoretical system of Hindu North India. Turkish transsexual pop star Bulent Ersoy dons the veil, fasts and refuses to perform during the month of Ramadan; Algeria's Cheb Khaled famously performed the pilgrimage to Mecca. As Virolle (1995) illustrates, Rai musicians in Algeria have drawn heavily on local religious expression as a result of a colonial struggle in which Islam and nationalism were often closely elided, and continue to do so today, in deference to Algerian Islamists, who have nonetheless claimed many of their number. In various ways, then, professional musicians can be seen to negotiate a variety of moral imperatives that one can only loosely label 'Islamic'; these are extremely varied, and the responses correspondingly complex.

Finally, Qureshi's *Sufi Music of India and Pakistan* (1986) represents an ingenious attempt to reconcile a musicological interest in the analysis of musical events with an anthropological understanding of their cultural significance. Qureshi's main concern is to demonstrate the logic of a 'context-generated' event: Qawwali musicians respond to complex cues provided by the spiritual leaders and devotees who gather at North Indian and Pakistani shrines. Musicians have to be extremely sensitive to a number of sociological and aesthetic variables: the size and precise composition of the gathering, the varied stages of spiritual arousal expressed by those present, and the choice and maintenance of musical patterns that generate and sustain (through repetition) these states of arousal for specific people. The value of Qureshi's approach lies partly in her determination to demonstrate the context-sensitivity of musicians, but, at the same time, to avoid reducing the music itself to its context. Music is represented not as a particular and derivative manifestation of a generalized Islamic aesthetic system, as for al-Faruqi, but as something that actually establishes the sensory and kinesic framework for a specific event, in which a complex of ideas are literally mobilized and *felt*.

These ideas are complex and contradictory, and not themselves capable of being reduced to some more simple verbal formulation. Qureshi demonstrates the way in which the Qawwali occasion mediates a particularly significant contradiction: an Islam experienced, on the one hand, through direct personal (auditory) revelation, and, on the other, through the institutional framework of the Sufi order. In the first instance, the *sema* is an individual, egalitarian and radical force, potentially seizing anyone, anywhere, leading from cognition (*marifat*) to divine truth (*haq*). In the latter instance, spiritual experience has to be mediated through one's position in a chain of authority. This is expressed in the complex ranking of office and prestige, and in a hierarchically conceived process of arousal, which culminates with a 'gift' of money to the presiding sheikh, expressing and validating the wider spiritual hierarchy of which the particular Qawwali event is only a part. As Qureshi (1986: 90) stresses, Indic Islam is thoroughly informed by the social and cultural forms instituted by a series of dynasties ruling from the eleventh to the eighteenth century, in which 'hierarchical relationships traditionally followed a courtier pattern of submission in return for benefice', a pattern of formalized behaviour known as *adab*, actuated through the giving of gifts (*nazr*). This system regulated the domination of the ruling elite, and their menials, comprising professionals belonging to the Hindu caste system, or their Muslim convert equivalents. Not only does Qureshi show how the Qawwali event negotiates a thorny problem inherent in all revealed religions, but she also demonstrates the ways in which 'classical' Sufism (mediated through 'high' cultural texts and institutions of learning) intersect with the historical peculiarities of Indian social and cultural life.

Conclusion

Orientalism, historical musicology and Islamist scholarship have shaped, and still to a certain extent perpetuate, the idea of an Islamic music, or a music that is organically connected to, and best understood in terms of, 'Islamic civilization'. The more general idea that Muslim cultural worlds are only and ultimately explicable in terms of Islam seems as deeply rooted as ever outside academia, and still has some currency within. Despite this fact, I have tried to indicate some of the ways in which Orientalist musicology might be read more positively, and some of the limitations of the musicology inspired by the regional studies literature. However, a gap remains between the high cultural approach represented by Orientalist scholars such as Wright and Shiloah, and the 'anthropological' gravitation towards the 'low', the ecstatic, the remote and threatened. The inverted commas indicate that this kind of anthropology is now largely defunct. Lindholm (Chapter 7, this volume) and others have stressed the need to incorporate, rather than exclude, the mainstream and the textual in a wider social and cultural perspective; the literature on globalization and modernity provides another avenue, in which 'locality' of the kind that anthropologists and ethnomusicologists used to gravitate towards is itself discussed as a construction, the product of more general forms of power.

Ethnomusicologists should respond to this challenge, and are indeed well situated to do so. Music travels vertically (that is to say, within the social structure) as well as horizontally (across the globe). Though disparaged in some Islamist discourse, the presence of music, at the very least as a form of aesthetically heightened speech, bestows on all gatherings and events significance and emotional power. The usage of music in transnational and 'postmodern' Islam (by which I understand a self-conscious moving away from the spaces allotted to it by modern- ist state traditions in the Middle East and elsewhere) would repay careful and critical consideration.[23] Academics of all backgrounds will no doubt, and rightly, continue to scrutinize the methods and representational forms involved in the discussion of any area of cultural experience in which privileged modes of self-representation are asserted by others. Nonetheless, the secular and experimental traditions of ethnomusicology, rooted in the kind of Enlightenment cultural critique defined and discussed by Bohlman (1991), remain a vital tool in understanding the varied musical cultures of the Middle East and the Muslim world.

Notes

This chapter has benefited greatly from a reading and discussion at the Middle East Center Friday afternoon lecture series at the University of Chicago, and the EthNoise! Workshop at the University of Chicago. Phil Bohlman also gave the chapter a read at a late stage and generously dispensed critique and encouragement.

1. Early editions of *The Grove Dictionary of Music and Musicians*, the first port of call for anglophone readers, discussed the music of the Middle East under the heading of 'Mohammedan Music'; *The New Grove Dictionary of Music and Musicians* of 1980 (ed. S. Sadie) introduces the Middle East under more varied and secular (although mainly national) categories. For a conventional narrative historical treatment of 'Islamic Music', see Abraham (1979).

2. For Sakata (1983: 8), 'it is impossible to understand Afghanistan without understanding Islam'. Conversely, 'the Muslim conceptualization of music is quite different from our own' (Sakata 1983: 38).

3. For a useful overview of critiques of Said in the context of Middle East studies, see Hajjar and Niva (1997).

4. I should quickly point out that critiques of the canon have gathered enormous momentum over the last decade; after decades of disciplinary self-flagellation for lagging behind the intellectual cutting edge, musicologists have caught up with a vengeance. See Bergeron and Bohlman (1992) for example.

5. Antoun and Harik stressed this in their 1972 overview, without providing much in the way of an alternative in which 'culture' could see the light of day. MERIP's special issue on popular culture (ed. T. Mitchell) appeared only in 1989. Stauth and Zubaida's volume appeared in 1987, but I did not manage to get hold of it until many years later.

6. Eventually published as Stokes (1992a). Stokes (1992b) deals with Arabesk's 'Islamic' content more explicitly.

7. Kiesewetter's work is discussed extensively in Bohlman (1986). The work of turn-of-the-twentieth-century French Orientalists can be exemplified by Rouanet's entry in the 1922 *Lavignac Encyclopaedia*, Chottin's publication of the Moroccan classical repertory, the *Corpus de musique marocaine* (1931), and D'Erlanger's monumental *La musique arabe* of 1949. Fonton's work is discussed in Shiloah (1993). Farmer's article on 'Mohammedan Music' in *Grove's Dictionary of Music and Musicians* (1954) was one of the first in this substantial reference work to discuss non-western music.

8. Note the 'ethnographic' postcards of colonial Algeria, in which musical instruments were vital props in erotic *mise-en-scènes*. Some are reproduced in Poché (1995).

9. Charles Perrault, a musician in the court of Louis XIV, understood Turkish music as a survival of the lost art of the Ancient Greeks. This was part of a more general process by which the Bourbon monarchy attempted to establish a French alternative to Italian opera, popular across Europe at the time. Diplomatic flirtations between Bourbons and Ottomans in this period made Ottoman court musical practices a politically convenient point of reference in the French court (see Obelkevitch 1977). Charles Fonton encountered Turkish music, instruments and texts in Istanbul whilst studying at the French Dragoman school in the mid-eighteenth century, providing him with the subject of a lengthy dissertation in which Oriental music was compared favourably for its expressive potential with that of the West (see Shiloah 1993).

10. The Baron Rudolphe D'Erlanger portrayed a lurid picture:

> Bars and nightclubs have displaced the *zawaya*. There are no longer any street processions and fewer people go on pilgrimages. The musicians have forsaken the *cafés*: one hears there only the hoarse coughing of the hashish smokers as their cards slap rhythmically onto the tables. The prince

> has abandoned his private ensemble for a brass band of foreign instruments which vainly blast out notes that grate on the ears. As the palaces crumble, so their music is dying. (Cited in Davis 1993: 84).

He assembled an orchestra to play his own highly idiosyncratic reconstructed version of the classical North African Maluf in his own mock-Oriental palace outside Tunis.

11. See, for example, Feldman (1990, 1993), Pacholczyk (1983), Sawa (1989), Shiloah (1995), Wright (1974, 1988, 1992).

12. In fact, Rai musicians have tended towards caution and deference, and have accommodated popular religiosity in Algeria for some time (see Langlois 1996; Virolle 1995). Nusrat Fateh Ali Khan, one should also note, performed quite different sets in front of Muslim audiences and in front of world music audiences. His world music 'packaging' is extensively discussed in Sharma (1996).

13. But Sharma (1996: 29) cannot help wondering.

> The excess of the film undermines the economy of a misanthropic whiteness – as if the music is 'too Other' for absolute cultural containment. The Qawwali track, with its haunting lyrical harmony and deep violent bass line, has an uncontrollable presence within the anarchic play of the film. Is this 'radical Otherness' of the music, its near-'demonic' presence, one of the ways that the hegemony of the west is being imploded?

The neo-Gramscian critic searches texts anxiously for signs of subcultural subversion. But the point is well made, and might be extended. Does the Rai soundtrack of *The Fifth Element* or the Vangelis soundtrack of Ridley Scott's *Bladerunner* (clearly the prototype of *The Fifth Element*) speak of postmodern 'implosion'? Or do they simply draw new and more insidious lines of exclusion and marginalization?

14. On Afrocentrism, World Beat and popular anthropology and ethnomusicology, see Feld (1996).

15. Characteristically understood in terms of a psychic vocabulary relating to the *nafs* and the *aql*. The meanings attached to these terms vary enormously: at the most general level, however, music's effect on the *nafs* restricts the rational, reflective, essentially masculine and to some extent super-ego, controlling function of the *aql*. Rosen (1978) describes this indigenous psychology in a Moroccan context, arguably in somewhat essentialized terms, but many Muslims would recognize some aspects of his discussion. Sawa's work on al-Farabi is an extremely important resource for considering the medieval context of speculation on music's effects (Sawa 1989).

16. I use, as elsewhere, Turkish transliterations of the Arabic since they are familiar to me. The term is also transcribed elsewhere as *sama'*, and *samah*. For a general discussion see Rouget (1985) and During (1982).

17. I attempt to avoid terms such as 'heterodox' and 'orthodox', since they imply ahistorical norms to which specific historical practices conform, or from which they diverge. The Bektaşi-Alevi only became 'heterodox', for example, much later in the Ottoman period; Bektaşi-Alevi 'heterodoxy' (constructed subsequently, and from the specific position of an anti-Safavid Ottoman state and *ulema*) itself became the means by which Bektaşi-ism could later be secured for a specific role in the (anti-Ottoman) modern state project. On 'orthodoxy', 'heterodoxy' and 'metadoxy', see Kafadar (1995).

18. Majd al-Din al-Ghazali's *Bawaraq al-Ilma* was, for example, translated by James Robson in 1938; Jalaleddin Rumi's *Mathnawi* was translated by Reynold Nicholson in 1934.

19. Note the comparison that Poché (1995) draws between *muwashshahat* in the Maghreb and the Mashriq.

20. See alt.religion.islam for cyberspace *sema* polemic. I am grateful to Dane Kusic and William Beachy for bringing this to my attention.

21. For a sample of their extensive work, see, for example, El-Shawan (1980, 1984), Racy (1981, 1982), Touma (1971).

22. The reversal of this situation amongst the Berber societies on the fringes of the Muslim Arab world seems only to emphasize the rule. The *imzad* a bowed lute, for example, is only played by Tuareg women in southern Algeria (see Brandes 1990).

23. See Ahmed and Donnan (1994) for a notable step in that direction.

References

Abraham, G. 1979. *The Concise Oxford History of Music*. Oxford: Oxford University Press.
Ahmed, A. and Donnan, H. 1994. Introduction. In *Islam, Globalization and Postmodernity*. London: Routledge
al-Azmeh, A.1993. *Islams and Modernities*. London: Verso.
al-Faruqi, L.I. 1975. Muwashshah: a vocal form in Islamic culture. *Ethnomusicology* 19 (1): 1–21.
al-Faruqi, L.I. 1980. The status of music in Muslim nations: evidence from the Arab world. *Asian Music* 12 (1): 56–85.
al-Faruqi, L.I. 1983. The suite in Islamic history and culture. *World of Music* 28 (3): 79–89.
al-Faruqi, L.I. 1984. Structural segments in the Islamic arts: the musical 'translation' of a characteristic of the literary and visual arts. *Asian Music* 16 (1): 59–82.
al-Faruqi, L.I. 1985. Music, musicians and Muslim law. *Asian Music* 17 (1): 13–36.
al-Faruqi, L.I. 1987. The Cantillation of the Qur'an. *Asian Music* 19 (1): 2–25.
Antoun, R. and Harik, I. 1972. Introduction. In *Rural Politics and Social Change in the Middle East*. Indiana: Indiana University Press.
Baily, J. 1981. A system of modes used in the urban music of Afghanistan. *Ethnomusicology* 25 (1): 1–40.
Baily, J. 1988. *Music of Afghanistan: Professional Musicians in the City of Herat*. Cambridge: Cambridge University Press.
Baily, J. 1994. The role of music in the creation of an Afghan national identity. In M. Stokes (ed.), *Ethnicity, Identity and Music: The Musical Construction of Place*. Oxford: Berg.
Baumann, G. 1987. *National Integration and Local Integrity: The Miri of the Nuba Mountains in the Sudan*. Oxford: Clarendon Press.
Bergeron, K. and Bohlman, P.V. (eds) 1992. *Disciplining Music: Musicology and Its Canons*. Chicago: University of Chicago Press.
Birge, J. 1937. *The Bektashi Order of Dervishes*. London: Luzac.
Blum, S. 1978. Changing roles of performers in Meshhed and Bojnurd, Iran. In B. Nettl (ed.), *Eight Urban Musical Cultures: Tradition and Change*. Urbana: University of Illinois Press.
Bohlman, P.V. 1986. R.G. Kiesewetter's 'Die Musik der Araber': a pioneering ethnomusicological study of Arabic writings on music. *Asian Music* 18 (1): 164–96.
Bohlman, P.V. 1991. Representation and cultural critique in the history of ethnomusicology. In S. Blum, P. Bohlman and D. Neuman (eds), *Ethnomusicology and Modern Music History*. Urbana: University of Illinois Press.
Brandes, E. 1990. The relation of women's music to men's music in southern Algeria. In M. Herndon and S. Zeigler (eds), *Music, Gender and Culture*. Floria Noetzel Verlag: Wilhelmshaven.
Danielson, V. 1997. *The Voice of Egypt: Umm Kulthum, Arabic Song, and Egyptian Society in the Twentieth Century*. Chicago: University of Chicago Press.
Davis, J. 1977. *People of the Mediterranean: An Essay in Comparative Social Anthropology*. London: Routledge and Kegan Paul.
Davis, R. 1993. Tunisia and the Cairo Congress of Arab Music. *The Maghreb Review* 18 (1–2): 83–102.
Davis, R. 1996. The art/popular music paradigm and the Tunisian Ma'luf. *Popular Music* 15 (5): 313–23.
Doubleday, V. 1988. *Three Women of Herat*. London: Cape.
During, J. 1982. Revelation and spiritual audition in Islam. *World of Music* 24 (3): 68–84.
El-Shawan, S. (Costello-Branco) 1980. The socio-political context of *al-Musika al-Arabiyyeh* in Cairo, Egypt: policies, patronage, institutions, and musical change. *Asian Music* 12 (1): 86–126.
El-Shawan, S. (Costello-Branco) 1984. Traditional Arab music ensembles in Egypt since 1967. *Ethnomusicology* 28 (1): 144–53.
Evans-Pritchard, E.E. 1937. *Witchcraft, Oracles and Magic among the Azande*. Oxford: Clarendon Press.
Farhat, H. 1990. *The Dastgah Concept in Persian Music*. Cambridge: Cambridge University Press.
Farmer, H.G. 1954. Mohammedan music. In *Grove's Dictionary of Music and Musicians*, Vol. 5 London: Macmillan.

Feld, S. 1996. Pygmy pop: a genealogy of schizophonic mimesis. In *Yearbook for Traditional Music*, Vol. 28, pp. 1–35.

Feldman, W. 1990. Cultural authority and authenticity in the Turkish repertoire. *Asian Music* 22 (1): 129–45.

Feldman, W. 1993. Ottoman sources on the development of the Taksim. In *Yearbook of the International Folk Music Council* Vol. 25, pp. 1-28.

Gellner, E. 1981. *Muslim Society*. Cambridge: Cambridge University Press.

Gilsenan, M. 1983. *Recognizing Islam*. London: Croom Helm.

Hajjar, L. and Niva, S. 1997. (Re)made in the USA: Middle East studies in the global era, *Middle East Report*. 205: 2–9.

Kafadar, C. 1995. *Between Two Worlds: The Construction of the Ottoman State*, Berkeley: University of California Press.

Keil, C. 1979. *Tiv Song: The Sociology of Art in a Classless Society*. Chicago: University of Chicago Press.

Langlois, T. 1996. The local and global in North African popular music. *Popular Music* 15 (3) 259–73.

Levin, T. 1981. Music in modern Uzbekistan: the convergence of Marxist aesthetics and central Asian tradition. *Asian Music* 12 (1): 149–58.

Lewis, B. 1968. *The Emergence of Modern Turkey.* Oxford: Oxford University Press.

Lomax, A. 1968. *Folk Song Style and Culture*. New Brunswick, NJ: Transaction Books.

Lorius, C. 1996. 'Oh boy, you salt of the earth': outwitting patriarchy in Raqs Baladi. *Popular Music* 15 (3): 285–98.

Lortat-Jacob, B. 1994. *Musiques en fête: Maroc, Sardaigne, Roumanie*. Nanterre: Societé d'Ethnologie.

Marcus, S. 1989. The periodization of modern Arab music theory: continuity and change in the definition of *Maqamat*. *Pacific Review of Ethnomusicology* 5: 33–48.

Markoff, I. 1986. The role of expressive culture in the demystification of a secret sect of Islam (Alevi). *World of Music* 28 (3): 42–56.

Markoff, I. 1990. The ideology of musical practice and the professional Turkish folk musician: tempering the creative impulse. *Asian Music* 22 (1): 129–45.

Mitchell, T. (ed.) 1989. *Middle East Report and Information Project*, Special Issue on popular culture in the Middle East 19.

Nelson, K. 1982. Reciter and listener: some factors shaping the *Mujawwad* style of Qur'anic reciting. *Ethnomusicology* 26 (1): 41–8.

Nettl, B. 1978. Persian classical music in Tehran: the processes of change. In B. Nettl (ed.), *Eight Urban Musical Cultures: Tradition and Change*, Urbana: University of Illinois Press.

Nettl, B. 1992. *The Radif of Persian Music: Studies in Structure and Cultural Context*. Champaign, IL: Elephant and Cat.

Nettl, B. and Riddle, R. 1973. Taqsim Nahawand: A Study of Sixteen Performances by Jihad Racy. *Yearbook of the International Folk Music Society* 5: 11–50.

Nieuwkerk, K. van 1995. *A Trade Like Any Other: Female Singers and Dancers in Egypt*. Austin: University of Texas Press.

Obelkevitch, M.R. 1977. Turkish affect in the land of the Sun King. *Musical Quarterly* 63 (3): 367–89.

Pacholczyk, J. 1983. The relationship between the Nawba of Morocco and the music of the Trioubadors and Troveres. *World of Music* 25 (2): 5–16.

Picken, L.E.R. 1975. *Folk Musical Instruments of Turkey*. Oxford: Oxford University Press.

Poché, D. 1995. *La musique arabo-andalouse.* Arles: Cité de la Musique.

Qureshi, R.B. 1986. *Sufi Music of India and Pakistan*. Cambridge: Cambridge University Press.

Racy, A.J. 1978. Arabian music and the effects of commercial recording. *World of Music*, Institute of Ethnomusicology, University of Los Angeles, 20 (1): 47–57.

Racy, A.J. 1981. Music in contemporary Cairo: a comparative overview. *Asian Music* 13 (1): 4–26.

Racy, A.J. 1982. Musical aesthetics in present-day Cairo. *Ethnomusicology* 34 (1): 143–62.

Racy, A.J. 1988. Sound and society: the Takht music of early 20th century Cairo. In J. Porter and A.J. Racy (eds), *Selected Reports in Ethnomusicology Vol. 7: Issues in the Conceptualization of Music*. Berkeley: University of California Press.

Rosen, L. 1978. The negotiation of reality: male–female relations in Sefrou, Morocco. In L. Beck and N. Keddie (eds), *Women in the Muslim World*. Cambridge, MA: Harvard University Press.

Rouget, G. 1985. Music and trance among the Arabs. In *Music and Trance: A Theory of the Relations between Music and Possession*. Chicago: University of Chicago Press.

Rovsing-Olsen, M. 1996. Modalités d'organisation du chant Berbere: paroles et musique. *Journal of Mediterranean Studies*. 6 (1): 88–108.

Sadie, S. (ed.) 1980. *The New Grove Dictionary of Music and Musicians*. London: Macmillan.

Said, E. 1978. *Orientalism*. Harmondsworth: Penguin.

Sakata, H.L. 1983. *Music in the Mind: The Concept of Music and Musicians in Afghanistan*. Kent, NB: Kent State University Press.

Sawa, G. 1989. *Music Performance Practice in the Early Abbasid Era, 132–320 A.H./750–932 A.D.* Toronto: Pontifical Institute of Medieval Studies.

Schuyler, P.D. 1978. Moroccan Andalusian music. *World of Music* 20 (1): 33–44.

Schuyler, P.D. 1985. The Rwais and Zawia: professional musicians and the rural religious elite in southwest Morocco. *Asian Music* 19 (1): 26–45.

Schuyler, P.D. 1990. Hearts and minds: three attitudes towards performance practice in the Yemen Arab Republic. *Ethnomusicology* 34 (1): 1–18.

Sharma, A. 1996. Sounds Oriental: the (im)possibility of theorizing Asian musical cultures. In S. Sharma, J. Hutnyk and A. Sharma (eds), *Disorienting Rhythms: The Politics of the New Asian Dance Music*. London: Zed Books.

Shiloah, A. 1993. An eighteenth century critic of taste and good taste. In S. Blum, P. Bohlman and D. Neuman (eds), *Ethnomusicology and Modern Music History*. Urbana: University of Illinois Press.

Shiloah, A. 1995. *Music in the World of Islam: A Socio-cultural Study*. Aldershot: Scolar Press.

Signell K. 1977. *Makam: Modal Practice in Turkish Art Music*. Washington, DC: Asian Music Publications.

Stauth, G. and Zubaida, S. (eds) 1987. *Mass Culture, Popular Culture and Social Life in the Middle East*. Boulder, CO: Westview Press.

Stokes, M.H. 1992a. *The Arabesk Debate: Music and Musicians in Modern Turkey*. Oxford: Clarendon Press.

Stokes, M.H. 1992b. Islam, the Turkish state and Arabesk. *Popular Music* 11 (2): 213–27.

Stokes, M.H. 1996. Ritual, identity and the state: an Alevi (Shia) *Cem* ceremony. In K. Schulze, M. Stokes and C. Campbell (eds), *Nationalism, Minorities and Diasporas: Identities and Rights in the Middle East*. London: I.B. Tauris.

Touma, H.H. 1971. The *Maqam* phenomenon: an improvisation technique in the Middle East. *Ethnomusicology* 15 (1): 38–48.

Uludag, S. 1976. *Islam Acisindan Musiki ve Sema*. Istanbul: Irfan.

Villoteau, G.A. 1809. *Description de L'Egypte*. Vol. 1. Paris.

Virolle, M. 1995. *La chanson Rai: De l'Algerie profonde à la scène internationale*. Paris: Karthala.

Wegner U. 1986. Transmitting the divine revelation: some aspects of textualism and textual variability in Qur'anic recitation. *World of Music* 26 (3): 57–78.

Wittgenstein, L. 1953. *Philosophical Investigations*. Oxford: Blackwell.

Wright, O. 1974. Music. In J. Schacht (ed.), *The Legacy of Islam*. Oxford: Oxford University Press.

Wright, O. 1988. Aspects of historical change in Turkish classical repertoire. In R. Widdess (ed.), *Musica Asiatica* Vol. 5. Cambridge: Cambridge University Press.

Wright, O. 1992. *Songs Without Words: A Musicological Study of an Early Ottoman Anthology and Its Precursors*. London: SOAS.

INDEX

Index compiled by Indexing Specialists, East Sussex, Great Britain